HIDDEN®

Guatemala

HIDDEN ®
Guatemala

Richard Harris

Ulysses Press ®

BERKELEY, CALIFORNIA

Published by:
ULYSSES PRESS
P.O. Box 3440
Berkeley, CA 94703-3440
www.ulyssespress.com

ISSN 1524-5950
ISBN 1-56975-194-3

Printed in Canada by Transcontinental Printing

10 9 8 7 6 5 4 3 2 1

MANAGING EDITOR: Claire Chun
COPY EDITOR: Steven Zah Schwartz
EDITORIAL ASSOCIATES: Lily Chou, Melissa Millar
TYPESETTER: Jennifer Brontsema
CARTOGRAPHY: Ulysses Press
HIDDEN BOOKS DESIGN: Sarah Levin
COVER DESIGN: Leslie Henriques
INDEXER: Sayre Van Young
COVER PHOTOGRAPHY
   FRONT: Dave Houser (Market day on the plaza in
   Chichicastenango)
   CIRCLE: Steve Cohen (Detail of Maya sculpture at
   Tikal)
   BACK: Dave Houser (Visitors atop the Main Pyramid
   in Tikal National Park)
ILLUSTRATOR: Glenn Kim

Distributed in the United States by Publishers
Group West, in Canada by Raincoast Books,
and in Great Britain and Europe by World
Leisure Marketing

Acknowledgments

Special thanks also to Ellen Kleiner for her encouragement and inspiration, to Carl and Ruth Harris for their support of this project, to Liza Fourre and family at Art Workshops in La Antigua Guatemala for their friendship and hospitality, to the Walker sisters, Neva and Rose, for helping me view Guatemala through fresh eyes, and to Jenny Gagan-Vigil and family for taking care of Oso while I'm in foreign lands.

And as always, my deepest appreciation to Ulysses Press publisher Ray Riegert, whose faith and encouragement have been invaluable throughout this project and many others, and to Leslie Henriques, Claire Chun, Bryce Willett, Steven Schwartz, Lily Chou, Melissa Millar and Jennifer Brontsema for being great at what they do.

✳

What's Hidden?

At different points throughout this book, you'll find special listings marked with a hidden symbol:

◄ HIDDEN

This means that you have come upon a place off the beaten tourist track, a spot that will carry you a step closer to the local people and natural environment of Guatemala.

The goal of this guide is to lead you beyond the realm of everyday tourist facilities. While we include traditional sightseeing listings and popular attractions, we also offer alternative sights and adventure activities. Instead of filling this guide with reviews of standard hotels and chain restaurants, we concentrate on one-of-a-kind places and locally owned establishments.

Our authors seek out locales that are popular with residents but usually overlooked by visitors. Some are more hidden than others (and are marked accordingly), but all the listings in this book are intended to help you discover the true nature of Guatemala and put you on the path of adventure.

Write to us!

If in your travels you discover a spot that captures the spirit of Guatemala, or if you live in the region and have a favorite place to share, or if you just feel like expressing your views, write to us and we'll pass your note along to the author.

We can't guarantee that the author will add your personal find to the next edition, but if the writer does use the suggestion, we'll acknowledge you in the credits and send you a free copy of the new edition.

ULYSSES PRESS
P.O. Box 3440
Berkeley, CA 94703-3440
E-mail: readermail@ulyssespress.com

Contents

Maps

ONE

Exploring Guatemala

 For those of us whose childhood daydreams feature lost jungle cities with monkeys and bright-colored parrots gliding through the canopy of vines and orchid-filled trees with jaguars prowling in the shadows, it comes as a welcome surprise that we can experience that kind of adventure for real just two hours from the United States by passenger jet. Unexplored rainforest, mysterious ruins and colorful indigenous cultures combine to place Guatemala high on any list of the world's most exotic adventure destinations.

On the map, Guatemala appears deceptively small. In fact, it's approximately the same size as Ohio, a moderately small U.S. state that motorists can easily cross via the interstate in less than four hours, and—given that Ohio's population is declining slowly while Guatemala's is growing fast—will have the same number of people living within its borders by the year 2000.

Once you get past these basic numbers, however, the comparison breaks down. You cannot drive across Guatemala in four hours; in this land of "pigs-and-chickens" public transportation and steep, slow roads, you'd be lucky to manage the trip in four days. If, instead, you take four *weeks*, you'd have time to explore the amazingly varied tapestry of Guatemala's terrain—cool, misty cloud forests, deserts of giant cactuses, the highest and most rugged mountain ranges in Central America and the largest undeveloped expanse of tropical rainforest in North America. These environments provide habitat for more animal and plant species than any other region of equal size on the continent. There are more kinds of birds in Guatemala than in the entire continental United States.

Guatemala has about two dozen protected areas—national parks, reserves and archaeological sites—where you can expect to find wildlife. For the traveler looking to fall in love with tropical nature, the sine qua non of any Guatemalan trip has got to be Tikal National Park in the country's northern wilderness. This 222-square-mile expanse of protected rainforest surrounding the ruins of one of the most splendid Maya cities shows us a world where jaguars, tapirs, ocelots, crocodiles, howler monkeys, guacamayas and dozens of other endangered species still live free.

If the magical ruins of Tikal capture your imagination—as they certainly will if you give them half a chance—you'll find another great Maya city far to the south, on the other side of Guatemala's central mountains. Copán, the site of un-equaled Maya stone sculptures and hieroglyph carvings, lies in ruins in a remote corner of Honduras, so close to the border that it fits perfectly into any Guate-malan trip. Then too, real Maya ruins buffs won't want to miss Quiriguá, a pale imitation of Copán surrounded by a vast banana plantation, where you can see the tallest stelae ever erected.

Other extraordinary places that should be part of any Guatemalan trip in-clude Antigua Guatemala, the Spanish colonial capital twice toppled by earth-quakes and now revived as a historic district that brings the 18th century closer than the sprawling metropolis of Guatemala City just over the mountain. From there, a shuttle can take you to Lago de Atitlán, surrounded by volcanoes, Maya villages and the resort town of Panajachel, a low-rent rendezvous for adventur-ous travelers, old-time hippies and footloose expatriates from all over the world. An hour's drive or bus ride away puts you in the middle of the world's largest Indian market, a mind-reeling multilingual spectacle of bright-colored village *traje*, copal incense and bargains, in the old-fashioned Maya mountain town of Chichi-castenango.

Only a few years ago, even the hardiest travelers preferred to stick to Guate-mala's established tourist route. Guerrillas and the national army posed risks to in-ternational visitors in some remote areas. More often, the problem was that once you wandered away from the well-trodden path, there wasn't much lodging or food to be found. And then there was the problem of culture shock. Not long ago the number of international visitors was a fraction of what it is today, and if you went to places other than the major tourist destinations—Antigua, Lago de Atitlán, Chichicastenango, Copán and Tikal—you were always the only foreigner in a town where nobody could speak English—*or* Spanish. In those days, Guatemala enthusiasts were a kind of cult, willing to put up with hassles, inconveniences, dis-comforts and an unspoken edge of genuine danger just to get to Panajachel (known back then by the nickname "Gringotenango") and buy colorful *típica* clothing, which they would sell at flea markets and import stores back in the States for enough profit to pay their way back down south.

Times change. The good old days became numbered in 1991, when the per-ceived threat of communist insurgency throughout Central America ended abruptly with the collapse of the Soviet Union. The low-profile civil war that for decades had hindered travelers with army patrols and dark rumors began to lift. Tourism, already the most important industry in Guatemala's economy almost by default, began to grow, and the number of visitors keeps climbing year by year. At this writing, the number of international travelers arriving in Guatemala averages nearly 1900 per day. Today, travelers find a warm welcome in remote areas where not long ago an army roadblock would have turned them back. At least in the dry season, you will almost never find yourself the only gringo in town.

Far from "ruining" Guatemala with too many visitors—that's still a long way off—the ecotravel boom has opened up many natural areas that used to be risky. Some, like the verdant canyons of the Río Dulce or the tropical evergreen forest that wraps the mountain slopes of the Mario Dary Quetzal Reserve, are easy to

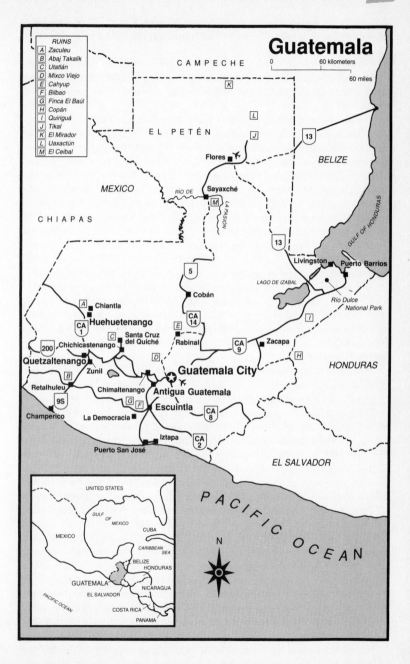

RUINS
A Zaculeu
B Abaj Takalik
C Utatlán
D Mixco Viejo
E Cahyup
F Bilbao
G Finca El Baúl
H Copán
I Quiriguá
J Tikal
K El Mirador
L Uaxactún
M El Ceibal

Guatemala

0   60 kilometers

60 miles

CAMPECHE

EL PETÉN

BELIZE

MEXICO

RÍO DE

Flores

Sayaxché

CHIAPAS

LA PASIÓN

GULF OF HONDURAS

Livingston   Puerto Barrios

LAGO DE IZABAL

Río Dulce
National Park

Cobán

Chiantla

Huehuetenango

Santa Cruz
del Quiché

Rabinal

Zacapa

HONDURAS

Chichicastenango

Quetzaltenango

Zunil

Guatemala City

Retalhuleu

Chimaltenango

Antigua Guatemala

Escuintla

La Democracia

Champerico

Iztapa

Puerto San José

EL SALVADOR

UNITED STATES

GULF OF MEXICO

CUBA

MEXICO

CARIBBEAN
SEA

BELIZE
HONDURAS

GUATEMALA

EL SALVADOR

NICARAGUA

PACIFIC OCEAN

COSTA RICA

PANAMA

PACIFIC OCEAN

N

reach by car or bus. Others, like the waterfalls of Semuc Champey and the underground river route through Grutas de Candelaria, are best visited on guided tours using four-wheel-drive vehicles. Still others, like the untouched cloud forest wilderness of the Sierra de las Minas Biosphere Reserve or the deep roadless rainforest that conceals Mirador–Dos Lagunas–Río Azul National Park at its center, can only be reached on a multiday foot trek, following trails through largely uncharted terrain.

The downside of traveling in Guatemala these days is not violence. Statistics show that tourists are much safer here than in Miami Beach. Instead, the harshest aspect of Guatemalan reality today is plain, old-fashioned poverty. These are the facts. Following centuries of exploitation, dictatorship and internal turmoil, Guatemala has become one of the poorest nations in the Western Hemisphere. The average income of Guatemalans is only about one-third that of Mexicans, or one-sixteenth that of U.S. residents. Maya people earn less than half as much as ladinos (people of mixed Spanish and Indian blood). Poverty is so severe that half of all Guatemalan families cannot get enough food to meet minimum nutritional needs. Compared with Mexico, life expectancy is ten years shorter, infant mortality is 50 percent higher and there are only half as many hospital beds per capita. Forty-five percent of the population, including most Maya people, cannot read. More than one-third cannot speak Spanish. Nor is poverty confined to the countryside and the slums. Even the few richest families in Guatemala boast only a few more assets than a typical American suburban household, and the government is so underfunded that police, army officers and civil servants earn the equivalent of around US$800, making law enforcement less than enthusiastic and public corruption inevitable.

Visitors from the United States and other industrialized nations who are new to Third-World travel may find this kind of poverty disturbing. Their discomfort arises not from any spectacle of human misery or degradation, but rather from the challenge to their own values and beliefs. Visitors realize that, though lacking such conveniences as cars, television, telephone service and indoor plumbing, most rural people in Guatemala are far more cheerful and optimistic than people in a shopping mall back home. After spending a couple of weeks in the country, some people lose rationality completely and start fantasizing about trading in their back-in-the-USA lives for an easygoing, largely cashless existence in a Guatemalan village. In fact, some people actually do it. You'll most likely meet a few in your travels.

Paradoxically, it is poverty more than any other factor that has protected Guatemala's ancient Maya folkways and sensitive natural ecosystems from being engulfed by the modern world. A major obstacle to development throughout most areas of the country has been the government's chronic lack of road-building funds. Most rural people live along steep, narrow, rocky, unpaved mountain roads where a driver in a hurry can average up to 12 miles an hour. In fact, many villages are situated beyond the reach of any road, along public foot trails and steep log stairways that wind their way up mountainsides among homesteads and impossibly sloped cornfields. From this remote, medieval-seeming world, the journey to the capital with its frenetic commerce and industry cannot be made in a day. In the northern wilderness of the Petén, difficult access has so far protected much of the rainforest and its amazing abundance of animal and plant life from the slash-and-burn agricultural destruction that has become the norm just over the border in Mexico.

Much of Guatemala's future is now in the hands of international travelers. Tourism, though still in its infancy, is Guatemala's fastest-growing industry. Revenue from tourism has grown by more than 560 percent since 1986, and it is now seen as the country's best hope for economic recovery. Given the understandable reluctance of international hotel chains to invest in Guatemalan resorts, the government has made a commitment to encourage development of an ecotravel industry patterned after the successful experiences of Belize and Costa Rica. This has brought unprecedented measures to protect Guatemalan wildlife and even, sometimes grudgingly, to improve the situation of the Maya people. It also translates into friendly, hospitable and protective attitudes among the local people toward foreign visitors.

There has never been a better time than now to explore Guatemala's strange magic. Marvel at the abundance of bright color: macaws and parrots in the skies, flowers that bloom all year, native women in lavishly embroidered *huipiles* and men in pink-striped pants. Listen to the music of marimbas, the whispers of waves lapping on lakeshores, the din of jungle birds and beasts. Wander through labyrinthine public markets where incense, spices and a cacophony of strange native languages assail the senses. Scale lofty, smoldering volcanoes and hike trails through cloud forest and deep jungle. Experience the timeless Maya spirit that built a sophisticated and complex civilization in ancient times only to witness its collapse and ruin, and still to endure in a world just beyond time's reach.

Few visitors opt to spend much time in **Guatemala City**, a metropolis the size of Chicago. The fine museums of history, archaeology and folk art are hardly worth braving the capital city's heavy traffic and squalor. Yet travelers have no choice but to go to Guatemala City—at least briefly—when arriving and departing by air or when asking for permission to stay in the country more than 30 days. A little sightseeing can help make these city trips less traumatic.

▼▼▼▼▼▼▼▼▼▼
Where to Go

Base camp for most excursions into the heartland of Guatemala is **La Antigua Guatemala**, the old restored capital from which Spanish colonial governors reigned over Central America in the 16th, 17th and 18th centuries. Although this town is just half an hour's drive over a mountain ridge from Guatemala City, it seems far removed in space and time, setting the stage for even stranger "time travels" to the remote villages of the Altiplano. Besides the best-preserved colonial architecture in Guatemala, Antigua boasts more fine hotels, restaurants and galleries than anyplace else in the country. Caution: La Antigua Guatemala possesses an enchanting quality. Spend a week here, and you may never want to return to the real world. Which explains why so many *norteamericano* expatriates call Antigua home.

Natural beauty and cross-cultural exchange make **Lago de Atitlán** the country's highest-ranking visitor attraction—for international travelers and Guatemalans alike. This "bottomless" lake is ringed by walls of towering volcanos, its shores dotted with large Maya Indian villages, some of which date back to the dawn of human memory. At one end of the lake, the village of Pana-jachel has most of the area's hotels and other visitor accommodations. Ferries run regularly back and forth carrying tourists to explore the Indian villages, and Indian women to Panajachel where they sell their weaving and embroidery work in the narrow streets. For tranquility, plan to visit Lago de Atitlán during the week; on weekends, Panajachel becomes a madhouse of beach partiers from Guatemala City.

The Maya Highlands, known in Guatemala as **El Altiplano**, offer some of the most exotic cultural experiences to be found today. Here you'll be immersed in a way of life that has changed little since medieval times. Although roads in this region have been much improved over the past few years, walking is still the main mode of transportation. The economy revolves around colorful open-air markets held weekly in most towns. Little Spanish is spoken, and the indigenous Maya languages are fractured into so many dialects that people from neighboring valleys often cannot understand one another. Large areas of the Altiplano were off-limits to travelers during Guatemala's civil war and have only recently been reopened, making this a perfect time to experience places such as the Ixil Triangle, where a tourist economy has barely begun to develop.

La Costa del Sur, Guatemala's Pacific coast, with its mosquito-infested swamplands and seedy port towns, is generally lacking in touristic appeal, with a couple of important exceptions. Monterrico, a village adjoining the UNESCO Biosphere Reserve of the same name, has a long, straight black-sand beach that has recently become a low-rent resort area popular among families from Guatemala City; visit on weekdays for peace and quiet. Inland, at several archaeological sites near Santa Lucía, you can see monumental stone sculptures left by the mysterious Cotzumalguapa-Pipil civilization, believed to have been a missing link between the Olmec and Preclassic Maya cultures.

Las Verapaces, a region that separates the Maya Highlands of the west from the lush tropical lowlands and banana plantations of the east, was largely ignored by travelers until the mid-1990s, when tour operators began to recognize its ecotourism potential. North of Cobán, beyond the sprawl of coffee *fincas* and experimental farms, small roads and whitewater rivers lead into a forest wonderland of caves, canyons, hot springs and waterfalls. Guides are eager to show you the way.

Heading east from Guatemala City toward the lowland region known as **El Oriente**, travelers have a chance to visit Quirigua, site of the tallest stone statues found anywhere in the Maya world. The gigantic monuments were apparently the result of an ancient artistic rivalry with the larger city of Copán, which lies just over the border with Honduras and makes for a fascinating side trip. Farther along the route to the Caribbean coast lie Lago Izabal, Guatemala's largest lake, and Río Dulce, the broad, slow jungle river that connects the lake to the sea. At the river's mouth, Livingston, a secluded Belizean-style town that can't be reached by road, beckons visitors who are serious about getting away from it all.

Of all Guatemala's natural and cultural treasures, however, nothing can compare to **El Petén**, the vast rainforest that covers the northern one-third of the country. Rich in its biodiversity, the forest teems with monkeys and other exotic animals as well as an astonishing assortment of colorful birds. The central attraction for most visitors is Tikal, the site of the largest and most important city in the Maya world in ancient times. Although it would be easy to spend several days at Tikal without leaving the park grounds, adventuresome travelers can make their way to any of two dozen other lost cities scattered throughout the Petén.

SAMPLE ITINERARIES

Guatemala is small but complicated, and travel days can be exhausting. Allow at least two days in the same place between trips. Driving a rental car is not really much faster than taking buses, though it is more comfortable and allows the freedom of spontaneous roadside stops. Allow a full week for a cursory "Best of Guatemala" visit. This is insufficient time to adjust to the country's inconveniences enough to appreciate its charms, so keep it simple.

A thorough tour of the country takes a full month. (Thirty days is the usual duration of a tourist card. It's no problem to extend the time limit, but it means a trip to Guatemala City to extend your visa or spending 72 hours in a neighboring country and then reentering Guatemala on a new visa.) As soon as you break away from the Basic Guatemala plan, any semblance of an itinerary is sure to go all to hell. That's okay. Just remind yourself once in a while of when you're scheduled to fly back to the real world.

BASIC GUATEMALA (ONE WEEK)

Day 1 Fly to Guatemala City. Board an airport shuttle to Antigua and check in at the hotel of your choice (or one that your shuttle driver recommends). Enjoy an evening stroll around the Parque Central and a good dinner.

Day 2 See the sights of Antigua. Stroll through the market. Sit on a park bench for hours. Get used to the fact that you're in Guatemala. Book a shuttle to Panajachel for tomorrow.

Day 3 Take the two-hour shuttle trip to Panajachel. Shuttle vans are inexpensive; buses are almost free but take much longer because you have to change to another bus en route. Upon arriving, get oriented by locating Lago de Atitlán. Watch the sunset over the lake.

Day 4 Ride the ferries across the lake to Santiago Atitlán and maybe other villages. Forget about schedules. If you miss the last ferry back to Panajachel, you'll spend the night someplace even more unforgettable.

Day 5 Shop with the *típica* vendors of Panajachel in the morning. Their prices are the best. In the afternoon, take a shuttle van or public bus to Chichicastenango. If you started this trip on a Saturday then this is Wednesday, which means you can watch vendors from all over the highlands set up for tomorrow's huge Indian market.

Day 6 Thursday? (Or Sunday?) If not, rearrange you itinerary so it is. The twice-weekly public market in Chichicastenango is quite simply one of the world's greatest marketplaces. It's non-stop action and your best chance to photograph traditional Maya women in village *traje*.

Day 7 Take a bus or shuttle van back to Antigua. If you really have to fly back today, okay. Otherwise, spend a relaxing last night in Antigua and leave tomorrow. Or, for a longer Guatemala trip, add on your choice of these other one-week trip segments . . .

(If you have only two weeks, jump forward to Week 4, The Petén, for one of the most spectacular wilderness experiences in North America.)

THE MAYA HIGHLANDS (ONE WEEK)

Day 8 Whether from Antigua, Panajachel or Guatemala City, travel to Quetzaltenango, about a two-hour trip. The rest of the day will be sufficient time to appreciate this neo-colonial city, which is graceful though not exciting.

Day 9 Take an excursion to Zunil (or any of several other unique villages around Quetzaltenango). Later in the day, relax at Fuentes Georginas, probably the best geothermal spa in Guatemala.

Day 10 Head north to Huehuetenango. Travel early and you'll have plenty of time to see the town's main attractions—the colorful public market (maybe something of a letdown after Chichicastenango) and the great, concrete-covered ruins of Zaculeu (maybe a letdown if you've seen any other restored Maya ruin).

Day 11 Drive or catch a local bus to the high mountain village of Todos Santos, one of the most dramatically traditional Maya villages in Guatemala—and undoubtedly the coldest. Return to Huehuetenango for a second night.

Day 12 Take the back road from Huehuetenango through the colorful Maya village of Aguacatán to the crossroads town of Sacapulas. From here you can choose to head south and see the ruins of K'umarcaaj, the last Maya capital of Guatemala, just outside dreary Santa Cruz del Quiché. (From there, it's no problem to return to Antigua and prepare to fly back home.) Or you can head east on the bumpy back road to Cobán (jump to next week). Or you can head north to the Ixil Triangle for yet one more experience of a lifetime and check into a hotel in Nebaj.

Day 13   If you opted to head north to Nebaj in the Ixil Triangle, this is your chance to explore the other two points of the triangle—the villages of Chajul and Cotzal—and experience the truth of Guatemala's Maya heartland.

Day 14   Reluctantly head back to Antigua and thence to your Guatemala City shuttle and the plane trip home. Or . . .

EASTERN GUATEMALA (ONE WEEK)

Day 15   Take the spectacular unpaved route eastward through the highlands, through Rigoberta Menchú's hometown, arriving (at last) in Cobán.

Day 16   Explore Cobán, Guatemala's most underrated city. Take a cloud forest hike in Las Victorias National Park. Check out one of the riverside *balnearios* just out of town. Don't miss the orchid rescue center or the Chinese tea plantation.

Day 17   Proceed south, perhaps stopping for a two-hour to half-day hike through the cloud forest of the Mario Dary Quetzal Reserve. Evening will bring you to Chiquimula, the staging area for your expedition to the great Classic Maya city of Copán.

Day 18   Drive (or take the bus) for hours along unpaved roads to the basically comical border between Guatemala and Honduras. Getting to the other side will be the day's big event. Spend tonight and tomorrow night in Copán Ruinas, one of North America's quintessential ecotourist towns.

Day 19   Wonder at the ruins of ancient Copán. One day is hardly enough.

Day 20   It will take most of day to return to Guatemala's Atlantic Highway. If you're running out of vacation time, head back to Guatemala City right now and you'll be back in the United States by Monday. Otherwise, if you choose to continue eastward, you can see the remains of Quiriguá, a second-rate sequel to Copán surrounded by banana orchards, and still reach your next destination—the Río Dulce—by nightfall.

Day 21   Catch a boat down the Río Dulce to Livingston, perhaps the most isolated and idyllic town in all of the Caribbean. Spend a week or a month there if you like, or return to your Río Dulce lodgings and head back to Guatemala City and the airport tomorrow. (Leave in the morning and you'll be back well before nightfall.)

THE PETÉN (ONE WEEK)

Day 22   Head north to Flores in the Petén. You can do this from either Cobán or the Río Dulce. Either way, it's a long trip. If you fly from Guatemala City, it takes just over half an hour. No matter how you get there, it's one of the ultimate pleasure travel destinations in North America—the greatest of all restored Maya ruins, concealed in the depths of the continent's largest surviving rainforest.

Day 23   Take a shuttle van from Flores to Tikal National Park—not just one of the best sights in Guatemala but undoubtedly the most spectacular archaeological site west of the Mediterranean. Hike 'til you can't take another step. Try to figure out Maya hieroglyphs. Sweat a lot. Watch monkeys. Be amazed that you're here. Return to your jungle lodge accommodations.

Day 23   Do it all some more.

Day 24   Once you've thoroughly experienced Tikal, you may want to investigate some other wonders of the Petén rainforest. For instance, you could hire a guide and take a ride to the ruins of ancient Uaxactún, Tikal's neighbor to the north.

Day 25   Take a hike in Cerro Cahui Reserve on the shore of Lago Petén Itzá.

Day 26   Drive or take a bus or tour van to the town of Sayaxché to see the nearby ruins of Ceibal, known for its beautiful sculpture.

Day 27   Motorists and bus travelers can return directly from Sayaxché through Cobán, which lets them spend today visiting a northern Alta Verapaz sight such as Grutas de Lanquín or Semuc Champey. Plane travelers should plan to fly out of Santa Elena by today. That way, if your flight is canceled (as quite often happens), you can relax and try again tomorrow.

Day 28   Motorists and bus travelers should return to the Guatemala City/Antigua area.

FINALLY

Day 29   It's time to do last-minute shopping before flying back to the States (or visit the Guatemala City immigration office and get your visa extended for a longer stay).

Day 30   Unless extended, all Guatemalan visas and tourist cards expire after 30 days. Most low-cost plane fares between the United States and Guatemala also require that travel be completed within 30 days. In short, you'll have to go home.

▼▼▼▼▼▼▼▼▼▼
When to Go

**CLIMATE &
SEASONS**

Like most of the tropics, Guatemala has just two seasons: rainy and dry. Rain falls during summer and autumn months, from mid-May through early October. This is the off-season as far as North American travelers are concerned, not because summer weather is particularly miserable but because there's no cold weather back home to escape from. The dry season in Guatemala lasts from mid-October through mid-May, but the vast majority of international tourists visit between Christmas and

Easter. These two holidays pack the hotels wall-to-wall, with sky-high price tags in some locales, especially Antigua.

Lowland destinations like Quiriguá, Copán, Río Dulce and especially Tikal have the climate you'd expect in a tropical forest. In the rainy season, daily storms can soak jungle roads, creating sludge trails that are impassable without four-wheel-drive. Temperatures tend to run higher in the rainy season, and the humidity makes it feel much hotter. Early fall is an especially good time to visit Tikal and the Petén rainforest, because at the end of the rainy season the vegetation is at its most luxuriant. Early spring, through the end of April, presents the tropical forests at their driest and brownest. At that time, many trees lose their leaves briefly so they can grow a new set as the rains come.

Highland towns like Antigua and Huehuetenango are quite cool most of the time. Although Guatemala lies well north of the equator and theoretically has the same cycle of seasons as the United States, the summer months are so damp and chilly that gringo expatriates often refer to that season as "winter." If you venture higher into the mountains, to Maya villages like Nebaj or Todos Santos, you should buy a warm wool jacket first; these places can be surprisingly cold at any time of year.

CALENDAR OF EVENTS

You may plan your Guatemalan visit around a certain holiday or festival and join in the local spirit. As you may already know, Central Americans need no reason to celebrate, though they certainly have many. Fiestas, which in Guatemala blend solemn religious rituals with family fun and drunken revelry, provide a vital liberation from solitude, stoicism and the restraints of poverty. Remember that because of the festivities, practically everything else shuts down, including government agencies, businesses and professional offices. In other words, if there's a holiday, forget about business and join the party!

Semana Santa, or Holy Week, is by far the most important and spectacular holiday in Guatemala. From the preceding Monday through Easter Sunday, the religious processions and vigils for which Antigua is famous attract more than 100,000 onlookers each day, both Guatemalans and international visitors, to witness the largest Easter celebration held in the Western Hemisphere. Other Holy Week observances reach virtually every town and village in Guatemala and often involve folk traditions such as offerings to Maximón (a.k.a. St. Simon), the unofficial saint of money and self-indulgence, as well as the hanging of effigies representing Judas, reenactments of Christ's crucifixion by *penitentes* and numerous pre-Christian Maya ceremonies, often involving bird sacrifices. Meanwhile, less religious Guatemalans mob waterfront resort areas such as Panajachel and Monterrico in uncontrollable numbers. Banks, government offices and most other businesses throughout the country close down from Wednesday noon through Easter Sunday. More details on Semana Santa observances are included in chapters of this book covering specific destinations.

Here is a calendar of the most important and interesting festivals held throughout Guatemala:

JANUARY

January 1 New Year's Day (Día del Año Nuevo) is celebrated as a national holiday, complete with parades, prayers and fireworks.

January 15 The **Fiesta de Cristo de Esquipulas** commemorates an apparition of the Black Christ that an Indian saw in 1595. A statue of the Black Christ has been recognized as having miraculous powers since 1737 and is the main spiritual symbol throughout Guatemala. Tens of thousands of pilgrims walk to Esquipulas from all over the country.

January 23 The **Fiesta de Rabinal** highlights a week of dances, processions and ceremonies drawn from the ancient Maya play *Rabinal Achi*, the town's claim to fame.

FEBRUARY

Early February Candlemas (Candelario), observed as a religious holiday throughout the country, especially in Chiantla, Huehuetenango and San Juan Ostuncalco, marks the midpoint of winter on February 2.

The week before Ash Wednesday Later in the month, many ladino towns revel in a week-long **Carnival** leading up to the austere period of **Lent** (Cuaresma). In odd-numbered years, Antigua sponsors the country's largest Carnival festival during the week before Lent; also in Antigua, religious vigils and large street processions are held each Friday and Sunday during Lent.

MARCH–APRIL

The week before Easter La **Huelga de Dolores** (the Strike of Sorrows), when mobs of student demonstrators hooded for anonymity confront the national government with angry protests and drunken parodies at the University of San Carlos and elsewhere, takes place on the Friday before Palm Sunday as a sort of prelude to Holy Week. In Guatemala, **Holy Week** (Semana Santa)—the week leading up to Easter—outshines the Christmas season as the biggest holiday of the year. Everybody travels then. Expect large crowds and high prices. Semana Santa observances are particularly impressive in Antigua Guatemala. Travelers come from all over the world to witness them.

MAY

Early May Labor Day, May 1, is a Guatemalan national holiday. The **Day of the Cross**, May 2, is observed in Chichicastenango, as well as in Amatitlán, where a fair is held from May 1 to 5.

Late May or early June The **Feast of Corpus Christi** (late May or early June) is marked by celebrations in Guatemala City and many other towns; the most famous and colorful procession is in the village of Patzún east of Lago de Atitlán.

Several villages on Lago de Atitlán mark their patron saints' feast days in June: the **Feast of San Antonio de Padua** is observed in San Antonio Palopó on June 12 and 13. The **Feast of San Juan Bautista** takes place in San Juan La Laguna from June 22 to 24 and the **Feast of San Pedro** is celebrated in San Pedro La Laguna on June 29. June 30 is **Army Day**, a national holiday that closes banks and offices.

JUNE

Mid-July **Fiestas Julias**, the state fair, fills Huehuetenango with revelry from July 12 to 18.
Late July Local fairs take place in Santiago Atitlán on July 23 to 25 and in Momostenango on July 28 to 30.

JULY

August 15 The **Festival of Guatemala**, which marks the founding of the present capital, is observed in Guatemala. Everything is closed.

AUGUST

September 15 September 15 is Guatemala's **Independence Day**. The biggest celebrations can be found in Guatemala City and in Quetzaltenango, where the festivities are the climax of the state fair that runs from September 12 to 16.

SEPTEMBER

The **Feast of San Francisco** is celebrated with local fairs in San Francisco El Alto and Panajachel from October 1 to 4. Later in the month, from October 15 to 18, similar fairs take place in Aguacatán and San Lucas Tolimán to observe the **Feast of San Lucas**. October 20 is **Revolution Day**, a national holiday.

OCTOBER

Early November **All Saints' Day** (Todos Santos) on November 1 and **All Souls' Day** on November 2 are observed throughout Guatemala. The most spectacular celebrations include those in Guatemala City and Chichicastenango. The village of Santiago Sacatepéquez near Antigua observes All Saints' Day by flying elaborate, colorful nine-foot kites. Todos Santos Cuchumatán celebrates All Saints' Day, its main fiesta of the year, with nonstop festivities all week from October 31 to November 5, climaxing in an all-day horse race.
November 25 The **Feast of Santa Catalina** is a major fiesta in Zunil and Santa Catarina Palopó.

NOVEMBER

Early December In a highland tradition of obscure origin known as **Devil Burning** (Quema del Diablo), on December 7

DECEMBER

men costumed as devils terrorize children in Maya town and village streets, followed by bonfires in the streets after sundown.

Mid-December   The **Feast of Our Lady of Guadalupe,** December 12, is widely celebrated throughout the country, especially in Guatemala City, Chichicastenango, Sololá and Santa Lucía Utatlán. The **Christmas** season, from December 16 to January 6, is a religious and family-oriented holiday. It is a heavy travel time (although not as busy as the period around Semana Santa), but don't expect as much in the way of public spectacle as you would find in Mexico. Poverty strips Christmas of the commercialism that fuels holiday frenzy in the United States, and the spiritual idea behind Christmas doesn't seem to fit in as well as Easter with traditional Maya religious practices. Guatemala City, Antigua and some other ladino towns hold *las posadas*, a reenactment of Joseph and Mary's search for lodging, on the nine evenings before Christmas.

December 31   The **Change of Mayors** in Chichicastenango on December 31 is one of the most impressive ceremonies in the Guatemalan highlands.

▼▼▼▼▼▼▼▼▼▼▼▼
Before You Go

VISITORS CENTERS

Guatemala's tourist information agency, the **Instituto Guatemalteco de Turismo,** better known as INGUAT, can provide maps and tourist information. ~ P.O. Box 144351, Coral Gables, FL 33114-4351; 305-442-0651; www.travel-guatemala.org, e-mail inguat@guate.net. For help with specific problems, contact the nearest Guatemalan consulate:

West Coast   548 South Spring Street, Suite 1030, Los Angeles, CA 90013; 213-489-1891

Southwest   9700 Richmond Avenue, Suite 218, Houston, TX 77042; 713-953-9531, fax 713-953-9383

Southeast   300 Sevilla Avenue, Oficina 210, Coral Gables, FL 33134; 305-443-4828, fax 305-443-4830

East Coast   2220 R Street NW, Washington DC 20008; 202-745-4952, fax 202-745-1908

57 Park Avenue, New York, NY 10016; 212-686-3837, fax 212-447-6947

ORGANIZED TOURS

One way to deepen your experience of Guatemala's complex culture and ecosystems is to take a specialty tour. Although these expeditions are not yet nearly as common as in neighboring Belize, adventure travel entrepreneurs have begun to rediscover Guatemala. Their specialty expeditions offer unusual insights into people, wildlife and places few travelers have seen, and encounters with a world virtually unchanged over the centuries.

Many travelers go to Guatemala to study Spanish. While most do their classroom work in Antigua, there are other options for the adventuresome. The **Eco-Escuela de Español** offers Spanish instruction and homestays in the village of San Andres, across Lago

Petén Itzá from Flores on the edge of the Maya Biosphere Reserve. The curriculum integrates classroom work with field project experience. Students learn firsthand about tropical forest ecology, conservation methods, community development projects and sustainable forest use. Interested students can do volunteer work during their stay, and weekend field trips explore conservation projects and archaeological sites. Four hours of daily instruction cost US$50 a week, and lodging and meals with a local family cost an additional $40 a week. ~ Avenida Barrios at Calle Central, Flores, Petén, fax 502-9-501-370; operated by Conservation International, 1015 18th Street NW, Suite 1000, Washington, DC 20036, 202-973-2264, fax 202-887-5188.

A simple way to combine language study with a comprehensive tour of the highlands is to make arrangements through **AmeriSpan Unlimited**. Basically a booking agency for personally approved language schools all over Latin America, AmeriSpan offers language programs in three very different Guatemalan cities—Antigua, Panajachel and Quetzaltenango—allowing students to spend part of their classroom and homestay time in each place. The bilingual staff can further customize a language study/travel tour by helping arrange weekend volcano climbs, horseback rides or trips to Maya ruins and villages. ~ P.O. Box 40513, Philadelphia, PA 19106-0513, 215-829-0996, 800-879-6640, fax 215-829-0418; Antigua office: 6 Avenida Norte No. 34, phone/fax 502-9-323-343.

To combine explorations of the Guatemalan backcountry with a program for fitness and weight loss, contact **Global Fitness Adventures**. This holistic tour company offers active Guatemalan adventures that incorporate morning yoga and meditation, massages, stretch classes and healthy food, along with hiking and other outdoor activities. Seven-day trips focus on volcano climbing around Antigua and Lago de Atitlán. Twelve-day trips also include a four-wheel-drive expedition to highland Maya villages in the Cuchumatán mountains and hiking in the Ixil Triangle and the Mario Dary Quetzal Reserve. ~ P.O. Box 1390, Aspen, CO 81612; 303-920-1780.

Diving Plus organizes scuba diving excursions based in Livingston on Guatemala's Caribbean coast, using English-speaking local guides and dive masters. Tours can include explorations on the Río Dulce and side trips to Copán or Tikal. ~ P.O. Box 1320, Detroit Lakes, MN 56501; 218-847-4441, 800-552-3419, fax 218-847-4442.

The Livingston and Río Dulce area is also a center for nature-oriented sailing trips. **Southeastern Aquatours of Guatemala** operates sailing charters between the Río Dulce and the Belizean Cayes for one to four people on a 32-foot sloop with a bilingual captain who is also the cook. The trips can be extended with a stay in a *palapa* hut on Lago de Izabal, a canoe trip to a canyon and cave near El Estor or a visit to the Maya ruin of Quiriguá. ~ P.O. Box 685, Valrico, FL 33594; 813-685-9545. Sailing and environmental awareness are combined by **Maya Tours**, which conducts ecotours of the Lago de Izabal and Río Dulce area on a 41-foot ketch. Six- to eight-day custom tours for parties of 4 to 12 people focus on wildlife observation and jungle adventures including a swim under hot waterfalls. For physically active persons with medical risks, a board-certified physician tour guide is available. ~ P.O. Box 13175, Charleston, SC 29422-3175; 800-656-2221, fax 803-762-1240.

Far Horizons Archaeological & Cultural Trips, operated by noted archaeologist Mary Dell Lucas, offers trips to Guatemala that incorporate Maya ruins, natural history and Indian festivals. The trips use the services of local guides who can provide an insider's view of each area, introducing tour participants to friends and explaining customs and traditions. Some tours include jungle river trips. ~ P.O. Box 91900, Albuquerque, NM 87119-1900; 505-343-9400, 800-552-4575, fax 505-343-8706.

PACKING   Pack light! A camera plus whatever else you can fit in your day-pack would be perfect. A couple of freedom-loving Californians I met at a Tikal jungle lodge went even further and started their month-long Guatemalan trip carrying nothing but belt packs. Remember that you are going where beautiful handmade clothing is "almost free," as the street vendors say. So are colorful woven bags to carry it in. The less stuff you bring with you, the more stuff you can buy and bring back. There is nothing like lugging 75 pounds of suitcases around in search of a hotel to make one feel the absurdity of materialism.

Bring along a minimum of sporty, summery clothing. T-shirts, shorts, swimsuit, sunglasses and a good pair of hiking boots. A flashlight with extra batteries is a must for exploring caves and for those nights when hotel generators shut down early. You'll want warm clothes for the chillier climate of the Guatemala highlands, but there's no reason to bring them from home. You'll find great selections of sweaters and jackets for sale in the streets and markets of Antigua, Panajachel and Chichicastenango.

For visiting Maya villages in the highlands, where much is dominated by tradition, you will want to keep your clothing modest so as not to offend the locals. There is really no place in Guatemala where short-shorts, string bikinis, tight tops or other Cancún-style attire is appropriate. Nudity is against the law. If you want to sunbathe in the buff, find a very, *very* private place to do so. Never visit a church in shorts. Women should always show respect by wearing a skirt (and in many areas a head covering) in churches, and men should wear a shirt.

When it comes to toiletries, such items as toothpaste, deodorant, shampoo, soap, insect repellant, skin creams and shaving cream can be found in Guatemala City, Antigua, Panajachel, Quetzaltenango and, if you're lucky, Huehuetenango, but not around Copán, Río Dulce or Tikal. Most toiletries sold in Guatemala are inexpensive American brands. Choice is generally limited, so if you're picky about your brand of toothpaste or shampoo, it's a good idea to bring your own. Imported items like tampons, batteries and suntan lotion are also available in *farmacias* in many larger towns, though they cost more than in the States.

Pack a first-aid kit. Include a good insect repellent, aspirin, Band-Aids or bandages, cold capsules, vitamins, motion sickness tablets, calamine lotion or a small bottle of white vinegar (for insect bites), prescription drugs you use, iodine or alcohol for disinfecting wounds, antibiotic ointment, water purification tablets, sunscreen, lip balm and diarrhea medicine. Anyone with a medical condition should consider wearing a medic alert identification tag that identifies the problem and gives a phone number to call for more information. Contact **Medic Alert Foundation International**. ~ P.O. Box 1009, Turlock, CA 95381; 800-344-3226.

Because tourism is a key industry in Guatemala, 35mm film is about as easy to find as suntan lotion. As in U.S. tourist destinations, tourist-trap prices prevail in the places where you're most likely to use up all your film and need more.

Besides *Hidden Guatemala*, bring some other good books. It is becoming easier to find reading material in English in Guatemala, but *new* imported books are almost unheard of. Except for tourist-oriented books on the Maya ruins, books in English are pretty much limited to the haphazard selections of endlessly recycled novels on the shelves of used bookshops and book exchanges in the parts of Guatemala where American expatriates congregate, such as Antigua and Panajachel, as well as in Copán Ruinas, Honduras. In these towns, you'll find a used-book trade-in shelf in practically every restaurant, hotel and laundromat. If you bring along the latest paperback best-sellers from the United States, you'll be amazed at how valuable they are as trade goods in the expatriate community. Carrying around the only copy in Guatemala of the latest by Stephen King, John Grisham or Danielle Steele is sure to attract new friends fast.

Another easy-to-carry item that helps make new friends is pens or pencils. Used ones are fine as long as they still work. In every part of Guatemala, schoolchildren approach tourists asking for *"una pluma para mi escuela"* ("a pen for my school"). Many village families cannot afford such things as writing utensils, and schoolteachers sometimes send their charges out to solicit pens on the street.

PASSPORTS & VISAS   All visitors to Guatemala should have valid passports and must have either a visa (free, obtained in advance from any Guatemalan consulate in the United States or Mexico) or a tourist card (US$5, issued upon entry into Guatemala). Under current regulations aimed at encouraging tourism, citizens of the United States, Canada and Great Britain can enter Guatemala without a passport if they obtain a tourist card in advance from a Guatemalan consulate in their country of origin and have proof of citizenship such as a birth certificate or naturalization papers. In practice, however, foreign nationals still need to show a passport when renting a car, cashing traveler's checks, or, in many cases, checking into a hotel. Travelers who plan to do continuing business, such as import-export trade, in Guatemala, as well as those who plan to use Guatemala as a home base while exploring other Central American countries, may want to apply in advance for multiple-entry visas, which let you leave and reenter the country on the same document.

All visas and tourist cards are normally issued for an initial stay of 30 days and can be extended to 90 days by applying in person at the **migración office**. ~ 41 Calle 17-36, Zona 8, Guatemala City; 4-714-670. You have to apply again for an extension *(prórroga)* beyond 90 days, and the request can take several days to process.

Citizens of certain foreign nations need to obtain visas in advance. For example, the last time I traveled into Guatemala by bus I made the acquaintance of a group of backpack travelers from the British Isles. Those with United Kingdom passports strolled across the border in five minutes for a $5 fee, but the poor soul with the Irish passport had to take an all-day trip back to the nearest Guatemalan consulate in Mexico for a visa. (Wonder what ever happened to him. . . ?) Visitors who drive motor vehicles into Guatemala must also obtain visas in advance.

To cross over to the Maya ruins at Copán in Honduras, you need only your passport. Visitors going no farther than the archaeological site get a special tourist card that does not cancel their Guatemalan visa or tourist card. If you stay longer than 12 hours, you are supposed to wait 72 hours before reentering Guatemala and must pay a new US$5 tourist card fee.

GUATEMALA CUSTOMS   Guatemala's customs *(aduana)* regulations, as they apply to tourists, are minimal and somewhat vague. As a practical matter, instead of physically inspecting your luggage, Guatemalan customs officials at highway border crossings prefer to charge a small fee per bag for a tag certifying that they have inspected it. For passengers arriving at the Guatemala City airport, there is a cursory baggage inspection. Soldiers patrol the airport with dope-sniffing dogs.

In Guatemala, your luggage is more likely to be searched when *leaving* the country. Checked baggage usually runs the gauntlet of drug-detecting dogs, and you and your carry-ons go through at least two x-ray and metal detector security checks—one at the entrance to the international concourse and another at the boarding gate—and bags may also be inspected by hand. This policy stems from an agreement with the United States intended to reduce the northward flow of contraband drugs. Ancient artifacts, such as pre-Columbian statues or colonial art, are considered national treasures—and property of the Guatemalan government. You can bet that if Guatemalan officials searching your gear for drugs find antiquities instead, the treasure will be confiscated and you will find yourself so busy answering questions that you'll miss your plane home.

U.S. CUSTOMS

Even if you live there, the United States can be much harder to enter than Guatemala. When returning home, United States residents may bring $400 worth of purchases duty-free. Anything over this amount is subject to a 10 percent tax on the next $1000 worth of items. In case customs officials question the values you declare, save the purchase receipts for goods you buy in retail stores and record your marketplace and street vendor purchases neatly in a notebook.

Persons over 21 are allowed one liter (or quart) of liquor duty-free.

Sportfish, shrimp and any seafood that can be legally caught in Guatemala can be brought across the border. Many other fresh foods, however, are not allowed into the United States and will be confiscated.

Pirata (pirated copies of copyrighted books, cassettes, CDs, videos and computer programs, as well as clones of trademarked goods like designer jeans) are available in Guatemala City. Bringing these items into the United States is strictly prohibited.

All items made from any part of an endangered species—such as the sea turtle, crocodile, black coral or ocelot—are prohibited in the United States and will be confiscated. Vendors of such items usually will not warn you that you can't take them home.

For more details, contact **U.S. Customs**. ~ 1301 Constitution Avenue, Washington, DC 20229; 202-566-8195; www.customs. ustreas.gov. Another government resource is the **U.S. Fish and Wildlife Service**. ~ Department of the Interior, Mailstop 430, Arlington Square, 1849 C Street NW, Washington, DC 20240; 202-208-5634; www.fws.gov. TRAFFIC, **World Wildlife Fund and the Conservation Foundation** has further information. ~ 1250 24th Street NW, Washington, DC 20037; 202-293-4800.

To avoid confiscation of prescribed drugs, label them carefully and bring along a doctor's certificate of prescription. As for contraband drugs, there's a war on. Smart travelers remain neutral.

Customs checks at the U.S. border can be stringent or swift, depending on how suspicious you look. Air travelers must claim their baggage at the airport where they first arrive in the United States, clear customs with it, and then recheck it before boarding an ongoing flight to their final destination. Those entering the United States by bus or private car can usually expect a more thorough baggage check than air passengers. To avoid problems, dress neatly and declare your purchases.

SHOTS

No inoculations are required to enter Guatemala. Cases of hepatitis, malaria, typhoid, cholera and other tropical diseases do occur but seldom afflict travelers. If you are planning to visit remote areas, your doctor may recommend tetanus, typhoid and gamma globulin (for hepatitis) shots and/or malaria pills. For a health update on areas you're visiting, call the **Centers for Disease Control**. ~ 404-332-4559.

MONEY MATTERS

Traveling Expenses   Travel in Guatemala can be very inexpensive if you eat and sleep like the locals. Not only has the exchange value of the Guatemalan quetzal, which originally traded one-to-one for U.S. dollar, slid to six or eight quetzals to the dollar, but most accommodations and restaurants are quite simple and basic because most of their guests are traveling on lower budgets than many gringos can even imagine. This is one reason for Guatemala's great popularity with international student travelers. You can get a perfectly good room with a bed, a table and a shared bathroom down the hall for about $3 a night in *hospedajes* all over the country. Hotel rooms with private bath and ceiling fan can cost US$12 to $15.

If you prefer a higher standard of quality and comfort in your accommodations, you'll pay at least as much as you would at a comparable place in the United States, generally $60 to $100. Insisting on total comfort can limit your travels, because such accommodations are found only in a few major tourist areas. If you venture into the more remote areas of the Maya highlands, your only lodging options will be places with rock bottom rates and rooms that are worth every penny. Rooms are considerably more expensive *and* often not very comfortable in Flores and Tikal.

Prices of restaurant meals have been on the rise in the last few years. You are likely to spend around $4 per meal in restaurants—a little more if you order beef. There are more expensive restaurants, but only in Guatemala City and Antigua. Serious budget travelers can eat hot meals at the *comedores* found around public markets for a dollar or less or put together a picnic from the fruit and vegetable market for pocket change.

Guided trips in the Petén, whether by four-wheel-drive, horse-back or river raft, cost about $50 for a half-day trip or $100 per full day for a party of up to four. An individual or couple pays the same price if the guide cannot find other visitors to share the trip. The same rate prevails whether you take a regularly scheduled tour or design your own itinerary. Rates are about the same in Antigua for sightseeing tours and volcano-climbing trips.

Bus travel is quite inexpensive. The few first-class bus lines, which travel the major highway routes between Guatemala City and Huehuetenango, Quetzaltenango and Tapachula, Mexico, in the west, Puerto Barrios in the East and San Salvador, El Salvador to the south, cost about $10 one-way. Small shuttle vans take tourists quickly between major destinations—the Guatemala City airport, Antigua, Panajachel and Chichicastenango for market days—also for about $10 one-way. The crowded, crazy second-class buses that travel virtually every road in the country cost only a dollar or two.

Car rentals cost more than in the United States—about US$50 to $60 a day for a Japanese passenger car, twice as much for a four-wheel-drive vehicle. Insurance rates are relatively low, but the price of gasoline is higher than in the United States.

Travelers who like Guatemalan clothing or folk art will find themselves overwhelmed by bargains, even without pushing hard in price negotiations. US$100 or so will buy more gifts and souvenirs than you can carry home. For the best prices on *típica* clothing, shop in Panajachel. For good prices on village *traje*, familiarize yourself with styles and sources at a large, relatively expensive market like Chichicastenango or Antigua, then travel to the villages where the items you like are made. You'll find much lower prices, and you'll take home purchases with more exciting stories behind them. Don't bother shopping for Guatemalan clothing in the Petén or the eastern part of the country; prices there actually run higher than in the United States.

Currency Guatemala's currency, the quetzal, is quite weak against the U.S. dollar. Until the mid-1980s, the exchange rate was one to one, but it has now slid to between six and eight to one. For services and Guatemala-made goods, the price in quetzales tends to run about the same as it would be in U.S. dollars, making this a country of amazing bargain prices. Foreign exchange rates have been held close to the same level for nearly ten years as inflation has raised prices, so Guatemala's currency is considered overpriced in foreign exchange, especially when compared with other Central American currencies.

Coins are rarely seen in Guatemala these days. Paper currency is all the same size and comes in denominations as small as Q0.50 (less than US10¢). Take a few minutes to familiarize yourself with the currency. It's easy to keep track of if you think in terms of corresponding U.S. money. Although not precise, these comparisons help when you need to make quick calculations:

Q0.50 = about a dime

Q1 = a little less than a quarter

Q5 = US$1

Q10 = US$2

Q20 = US$4

Q50 = US$10

Q100 = US$20

Changing Money   Be smart and protect your vacation by carrying traveler's checks. Well-known brands, especially American Express, are easiest to cash. You will need your passport to cash them. Canadian and European traveler's checks and currency can pose problems; some banks will not cash them. When you cash traveler's checks at the bank, you almost always receive Q100 bills. Tellers are often reluctant to count out small change for markets, photos and such. Try to spend these larger bills for change at every opportunity, especially before heading for highland villages.

Keep in mind that Maya villages have no banks, and it is usually impossible to cash traveler's checks there. On market days, there are often money changers around. At other times, only small-denomination local currency will work. It is no coincidence that the half-quetzal note, the smallest denomination of paper currency, is the only Guatemalan money printed with a Maya Indian motif. You can get change for Q0.50, Q1, Q5 and Q10 bills, but you may have trouble spending a Q20 in many Maya villages.

Most banks are open at 9 a.m., close between 12 noon and 2 p.m., and reopen until 6 p.m., Monday through Friday. They often have specified hours, which vary from bank to bank and day to day, for exchanging foreign money. Retail businesses and street hustlers will often buy dollars, and sometimes traveler's checks, at exchange rates lower than at the bank. Most hotels can change at least small ($20) traveler's checks into quetzales for guests.

Credit Cards   Credit cards are just about as widely accepted in major tourist areas and cities of Central America as they are in the United States. MasterCard and Visa are the most popular ones; American Express cards are sometimes frowned upon because of their stiff fees to merchants. The Guatemalan government imposes a 7 percent tax on all credit card transactions.

If you need a financial transfusion while on the road, money transfers can be made through any big bank at home through an affiliate bank in Guatemala City (which can take as long as five working days). Check before you leave home to see whether your bank offers this service.

Bargaining   In Guatemala, everything is negotiable. Haggling over prices is a tradition that unites Old World and New World heritages. When the conquistadores arrived in Guatemala, they found cities and villages with public marketplaces remarkably similar to the ones they were used to in Europe.

Today, Guatemala holds onto the custom of bargaining in public markets, though not so much in retail stores. Price negotiations are a kind of universal language. By writing numbers on a pad of paper, you can do it even if you don't speak Spanish.

Price bargaining can be a lot of fun as long as you maintain a cheerful attitude. Don't look at it as a war of wits because you're bound to lose. From earliest infancy, children watch their mothers sell things. They learn about salesmanship before they can walk. By the age of seven their skill at separating tourists from their money is honed to a fine edge, and they know how to use those big brown eyes to tug on your heartstrings. Foreign visitors who come from societies where prices are fixed and haggling is rare only stand a chance of "winning" a negotiation by viewing each transaction as one where everybody wins.

It's only natural for market vendors to double or triple their asking prices when they see you coming their way. Vendors are well aware that you paid more for your plane ticket to get to Guatemala than they earn in a year. If you lived in a country where the average annual per capita income is $852, as it is in Guatemala, you'd charge "rich" foreign tourists more than you charge your neighbors, too.

It doesn't matter whether you paid 25 quetzales for a shirt someone else might have gotten for only 15 quetzales. It doesn't even matter whether you paid less than you would pay in a store back home (unless you're hoping to make your fortune in the import business). What matters is whether you'll actually wear it when you get back home.

Some people enjoy bargaining. It's an extrovert's game that pays off in savings. Give it a try. What have you got to lose? Cut the quoted price in half and start bargaining from there. Drift away and watch the vendor call a lower bid. But if you reach a good ballpark figure, don't quibble over nickels and dimes. So the vendor makes an extra 50¢. You undoubtedly got a great deal, too. Everybody wins.

If you feel uncomfortable haggling over prices, you'll probably reach the same result if you simply look at an item with longing and ask, "*¿No me da una discuenta?*" (Won't you give me a discount?), then wait patiently. The vendor will do all the work, running through repeated calculations and hypothetical price reductions before naming the bottom-line price.

Bargaining is discouraged in any store that tags the merchandise with fixed prices. Shopkeepers are more likely to negotiate reduced prices for a quick cash sale. In all small retail stores, it's okay to inquire about discounts when purchasing multiple items.

Tipping (and Bribery)   Although *propinas* (tips) are completely personal, the standard tip in Guatemalan restaurants is 10 percent. In Guatemala City, Antigua and sometimes Panajachel, it is customary for restaurants to add a 10 percent tip into the bill. Tip bellboys, porters, chambermaids and anyone else who renders extra service the equivalent of at least 75¢ to $1. Taxi drivers in Guatemala do not expect a tip. Gas station attendants deserve one (25¢ to 50¢) if they wash your windows, check your oil or put air in your tires. Children often assault your car at stoplights or outside restaurants, madly cleaning your windows or begging to watch your car for a tip. Musicians sometimes perform for tips on the town plaza. Even a small coin is much appreciated.

In Guatemala, the custom of the *mordida* persists. Literally, the word means "little bite"; actually, it means bribery of public officials. Guatemala has been making serious efforts to eradicate the practice, at least where tourists are involved, because it horrifies many gringos, who fail to understand that public officials in the Third World are woefully underpaid. If you would tip a waitress for giving you the best possible service, then why not reward a traffic cop or border guard for exercising the discretion of his office wisely?

If you find yourself in the position of having to discuss a bribe, never use the word *mordida* or in any way suggest that you are asking the officer to do anything illegal. The very suggestion is highly offensive and could even land you in jail. Sometimes a small bribe is referred to as a *propina* (tip) or as an unofficial *honorario* (fee). More often, if you ask the officer whether there is another way the matter can be worked out, you will hear the following line of reasoning: "For me to fail to enforce the law would be a serious dereliction of duty and honor. It is for the court, not me, to assess a fine in a case like this. . . . But since you are a visitor in my country, and I like you, if you tell no one, I might let the *delincuencia* pass just this once. Of course, you must understand that in Guatemala it is customary to exchange a favor for a favor. Now that I am doing this favor for you, it would be the right thing for you to give me a *regalo*, a gift. For my wife. The amount is whatever you think is right. . . . Well, a little more than *that*. . . ."

If the idea of bribery bothers you, pay up anyway and report it to the government tourism office later. Anybody who is in a position to solicit a bribe can also cause interminable delay and hassle if you don't hand over the cash.

LODGING   Lodging in Guatemala comes in many forms. This book will help you evaluate them ahead of time. You'll find an amazingly wide range of accommodations, all the way from a handful of "international class" hotels in the capital and charming colonial *posadas* (inns) in Antigua to *hospedajes* that offer very simple, cheap lodging similar to youth hostels in the United States and Europe but are oriented more toward families. Luxury hotels in some major tourist towns such as Panajachel and Chichicastenango are among the best in the country, while at the upper end of the Río Dulce cabañas are built right on the jungle river's edge. When you find yourself unexpectedly spending the night in one of the many backcountry towns where international tourists are not the clientele that hotels have in mind, you'll discover that the finest hotel around has steel doors and a single shared bathroom.

The major Maya ruin of Tikal has what are commonly called "archaeological hotels" within walking distance. In this remote area the amenities can be a little rustic (for example, at Tikal electricity comes from small gasoline-powered generators and may be rationed to a few hours a day), but the experience of staying there is special enough to justify any mild inconveniences you might encounter. Staying in one of these hotels lets you hike into the rainforest around Tikal to hear it burst into noisy life at dawn.

Guatemalans love to travel, and that includes a lot of people who live far below the poverty line by U.S. standards. There are many very cheap lodgings where you can spend the night for the price of a hamburger. I don't make a practice of mentioning unexceptional rock-bottom budget lodging in this guide except in villages where they have the only rooms in town, which I categorize in the "low-budget" range, but those who are willing to sacrifice comfort to save money will have no trouble finding it.

Around Christmas and especially Holy Week, all hotels hike their rates *way* up. Reservations are essential at these times, as the scramble for rooms can be fierce. Hotels at Tikal are increasingly often booked up by tour companies months in advance. Confirm your reservation, preferably in writing, before you go. If the hotel reneges (hotels typically overbook during holidays to make sure they are filled if any parties fail to show), complain to the nearest INGUAT tourist office and . . . well . . . nothing will happen.

Some of the better hotels demand a two-day (but sometimes up to 30-day) cancellation notice before refunding your deposit. Check on cancellation policies at the outset, and remember that cancellation by mail can be fiendishly slow. You can avoid these problems and lingering communications complications by using a knowledgeable Spanish-speaking travel agent.

In most areas, finding a room without reservations is no problem outside Christmas week and Holy Week. The hotel information in this guide should be enough to help you find lodging approximating the kind you want as closely as possible. If you are planning to stay at any of the several Chichicastenango hotels in the deluxe price range, reservations are a good idea because these places sometimes fill up with bus tour groups. Reservations are also a good idea at Tikal National Park because the number of rooms there is very limited. The cheapest way to make hotel reservations is by fax.

Tourist areas in Guatemala are sharply defined. If you stray very far off the beaten path, you'll find that rural towns offer only very simple, very cheap lodging, often noisy and none too clean, and you will have to ask around (in Spanish) to find it. In smaller towns, you'll want to arrive early in the afternoon before market day; *hospedajes* in these places rarely have telephones, and rooms rent on a first-come, first-served basis. In larger towns, if you arrive in the evening, you'll usually find a few local hotel owners or their representatives hanging around the bus station trying to recruit guests to fill their vacancies. You can take one of these rooms (inspect it before parting with your quetzales) to rest up and get oriented, then check out other possibilities at your leisure the next day.

When selecting a hotel, smokers should be aware that Guatemalan law prohibits smoking in enclosed public places. This includes hotel rooms, and many hotel managers enforce the law strictly. If this poses a problem for you, be sure to pick a hotel with a nice central courtyard, one with sitting areas and flower gardens.

In Guatemala, room rates at all hotels are regulated by the government. A notice is posted inside the room door stating the maximum authorized rate per night. Oddly enough, in Guatemala the maximum rates are often posted in U.S. dollars rather than the local currency, quetzales. Rates are always negotiable, and outside peak season, you will often find that the rate you are paying is lower than the authorized rate. If it is higher, you can complain to INGUAT or at least threaten to do so when you discuss the rates with the hotel manager. Government agents often act on price-gouging complaints against hotels—except during Christmas and Easter weeks, when the government is closed.

This book's hotel listings range from budget to ultra-deluxe, with an emphasis on unique or special midrange to upper midrange establishments when available. Hotels are rated as follows:

Budget facilities have rooms for less than $15 a night for two people (the words low budget in the text denote *hospedajes*, hostels and the like that rent rooms for $5 a night or less). Outside a few main tourist areas, virtually all lodging qualifies as budget. Don't expect phones, fans, TV or private baths.

Moderate hotels are priced between $15 and $45. Expect to find good-quality furnishings, ceiling fans or (in lowland areas) air conditioning and color cable TV (with lots of gringo network choices) in towns where it is available. Most jungle lodges in the Petén and Río Dulce areas also fall into this category.

Deluxe hotels offer rates from $45 to $90. They include highrise business travelers' hotels in Guatemala City's Zona Viva and

a handful of elegant inns and resort complexes in Antigua, Panajachel and Chichicastenango.

Ultra-deluxe hotels have accommodations at prices above $90.
Outside Guatemala City, the country has fewer than half a dozen
of them, and each is unique. All of them are described in this guide.

The ratings are necessarily approximate because of fluctuat-
ing currency exchange rates and growing demand for tourist accommodations in Guatemala.

Federal sales tax (called IVA in Spanish-speaking countries)
on lodging is 15 percent in Guatemala, and there is an additional
7 percent government surcharge if you pay by credit card.

DINING

Restaurants are categorized in this guide as follows: *budget* restaurants cost $3 or less for dinner entrées; *moderate* restaurants range
between $3 and $8 at dinner and offer pleasant surroundings and
a more varied menu; *deluxe* establishments tab their entrées between $8 and $15, feature sophisticated cuisines, plus decor and
more personalized service; and *ultra-deluxe* restaurants generally
price above $15. Restaurants add a 15 percent IVA, and in Gua-
temala City and Antigua many add a 10 percent service charge in
lieu of a tip.

In small towns, the only restaurants are likely to be *comedores*
where the fare consists of tortillas, black beans and an egg or
sometimes a bony little chunk of chicken. In these circumstances
it is best to bear in mind that for the locals a meal at one of these
places is a rare dining splurge costing about a day's earnings for
a farmworker.

It is customary in small towns for diners who finish their meals
to wish the other patrons of the restaurant *"buen provecho"* (or
just *"provecho"*) before leaving.

TRAVELING WITH CHILDREN

Should you bring the kids on a Guatemalan adventure? That de-
pends. Lots of Latin American women travel and sightsee with infants in arms, and tourist mothers I've met experienced no problems doing the same. In fact, thanks to the Ladino reverence for
motherhood, a baby is likely to mean special treatment, attentive
service and sometimes lower prices all along the route. Although
for some people traveling by public transportation with an infant
could be one too many stressors, it is also true that many travelers find it fairly easy to enjoy the best of both worlds—parenting
and adventuring.

Older kids? Take them along, by all means. It can be challenging and rewarding as well. Ancient temples and pyramids are great
for climbing and poking into secret passageways, and the mysteries of vanished civilizations they present can tantalize young minds
for weeks on end. The jungle holds limitless fascination. You will
be amazed at how quickly children can become fluent in Spanish.

Guatemalans adore children and are used to dealing with them in restaurants and hotels, though many hotels lack cribs and baby-sitting services. Baby food, medicines and sometimes disposable diapers can be found in bigger towns.

Remember to get a tourist card for each child. Children traveling with only one parent must have notarized permission from the other parent (or, if applicable, divorce papers, guardianship document or death certificate) authenticated at a Guatemalan consulate. Minors traveling alone must have a notarized letter of permission signed by both parents or guardians.

Prepare a junior first-aid kit with baby aspirin, thermometer, vitamins, diarrhea medicine, sun block, bug repellent, tissues and cold medicine. Parents traveling with infants will want to pack cloth diapers, plastic bags for dirty diapers, and a wraparound or papoose-style baby carrier. (In the Chiapas and Guatemala highlands, notice how mothers tie baby carriers from long, narrow handwoven shawls.) If you plan to tour by car with an infant, bring a portable car seat. For children of any age, be sure to bring along toys, books and art supplies to drive away boredom during long trips.

Pace your trip so your child has time to adapt to changes. Don't plan exhausting whirlwind tours, and keep travel time at a minimum. Seek out parks, plazas, outdoor entertainment and short excursions to amuse your child. Guatemala's marketplaces are more fascinating than museums to many children.

WOMEN TRAVELING ALONE

Machismo, the age-old code of manhood that calls for the protection, adoration and domination of women, is alive and well in Guatemala's ladino population, and spousal abuse is reportedly commonplace. Among Indians, domestic violence is rare, but village tradition guides women into subservient roles. Increasingly, both ladino and Indian women are speaking out for their rights.

Torn between the rising tide of Latin American feminism and traditional machismo, ladino men often behave toward North American and European women in bizarre and unpredictable ways. Liberated foreign women are commonly believed to be sexually promiscuous, and many men feel honor-bound to let their interest be known. Fortunately for travelers who find themselves the objects of such attention, these men are also easily intimidated by any assertive woman. Although Guatemalan men can be annoying, they're rarely threatening. The easiest way to handle them is to politely say *"No entiendo"* and walk away. Most men get the message.

Incidents of sexual assault against gringa women whose solo sightseeing takes them to isolated places are on the rise in Guatemala, especially in hiking areas near Guatemala City and Antigua.

However, nowhere in Guatemala is it anywhere near as prevalent as in most U.S. cities.

The best defense is traveling with one or more companions. Two or more women traveling together or a woman traveling with children will almost never be harassed. Today, many North American and European women (as well as many Mexican and Central American women) travel independently by temporarily joining up with other woman travelers.

SENIOR TRAVELERS

While Antigua, Panajachel and Río Dulce have communities of retired *norteamericanos*, Guatemala has been slow to develop as a seniors' vacation and retirement haven because formal immigration procedures make legal resident status difficult to apply for, infrastructure such as transportation, roadways and telephone service is still developing and medical facilities are limited.

Many older travelers to Guatemala join escorted tours, leaving the planning to others. The **American Association of Retired Persons Travel Experience** (AARP) offers escorted tours to Guatemala. ~ 601 E Street NW, Washington, DC 20049; 800-424-3410; www.aarp.org. **Elderhostel** provides educational programs in Guatemala for seniors ages 60 and up. Programs cover Spanish language, Maya history, folk art and archaeology, and include field trips and instruction from university professors. ~ 75 Federal Street, Boston, MA 02110; 617-426-7788, 877-426-8056; www.elderhostel.org.

Be extra careful about health matters. Bring any medications you use, along with the prescriptions. Consider carrying a medical record with you—including your current medical status, medical history, your doctor's name, phone number and address. If possible, include a summary of your medical status and history translated into Spanish. Medicare and many private health insurance plans do not provide coverage outside of the United States, so travelers are wise to contact their insurance agents or service providers for short-term supplemental international coverage.

GAY & LESBIAN TRAVELERS

Homosexual acts, as well as sexual solicitation and same-sex public displays of affection, are crimes in Guatemala. The laws are enforced only in the form of harassment during occasional police sweeps. The laws sometimes provide police officers with an excuse to solicit bribes from apparently gay travelers. The best defense is discretion.

Antigua has established gay and lesbian communities. There are no gay bars, and private parties serve the social scene. Some local gay men cruise the Parque Central in the evening.

In the red-light districts of Guatemala City and rough towns such as Puerto Barrios, a large percentage of prostitutes are male transvestites. If there is a more dignified gay scene in these places, it hides deep underground.

Homosexuality has traditionally been accepted among the Maya people. In highland villages it is fairly common to see public displays of affection between young men, and less so between women. Travelers who fantasize about joining them must remember that the Maya people observe rigid taboos against sexual relations, whether gay or straight, with non-Indians.

DISABLED TRAVELERS   Physically challenged travelers can enjoy Guatemala with proper planning. Most Latin American establishments and transportation systems do not provide special amenities, such as wheelchair access, for people with disabilities. Copán and Tikal, as well as other Maya ruins in Guatemala, have rough, rocky trails or other obstacles that limit wheelchair mobility. For that matter, even the easiest destinations, such as Antigua and Panajachel, have bumpy cobblestone streets and uneven or nonexistent sidewalks that can make getting around a challenge. You may want to get help from a good travel agent to track down hotels and other facilities to suit your situation. You may also wish to consult the comprehensive guidebook *Access to the World: A Travel Guide for the Handicapped* by Louise Weiss (Holt, Rinehart & Winston).

For more information contact the **Society for the Advancement of Travelers With Handicaps**. ~ 347 5th Avenue, Suite 610, New York, NY 10016; 212-447-7284; www.sath.org. For additional valuable tips, contact the **Travel Information Service**. ~ 215-456-9600; www.mossresourcenet.org. **Flying Wheels Travel** is a travel agency specifically for disabled people. ~ 143 West Bridge Street, Owatonna, MN 55060; 800-535-6790. You can also contact **Travelin' Talk**, a networking organization. ~ P.O. Box 1796, Wheat Ridge, CO 80034; 303-232-2979; www.travelintalk.net.

STUDENT TRAVELERS   An exceptionally high percentage of travelers in Guatemala are college-age students. Guatemala has become such a popular place to study Spanish that Antigua, where the majority of language schools are found, often feels a lot like an American college town. It's a great place for solitary student travelers to connect up with new friends and traveling companions for trips deeper into the Guatemalan heartland. Then, too, anyone willing to forego luxury and speed in favor of once-in-a-lifetime experiences will find that traveling in Guatemala can be ridiculously inexpensive. Those second-class "pigs-and-chickens" buses and *camioneta* trucks can take you just about anywhere in the entire country for a fare so low that the rainforest, volcanoes, ancient ruins and exotic Indian villages are within range of even the tightest travel budget.

In public markets, a good, hot *comedor* meal or a big bag of fresh fruits and veggies will set you back less than a dollar.

There are no internationally affiliated youth hostels in Guatemala. You'll find decent hotel rooms for a fraction of the nightly rates of hostels in the United States or Europe. Just about every town has a hotel where backpackers and student travelers congregate. Here are a few:

In Guatemala City, it's the **Chalet Suizo**. ~ 14 Calle No. 6-82, Zona 1; 2-513-786.

In Panajachel, the most popular student lodgings include the **Mayan Palace Hotel** (Calle Principal; 9-621-028) and the nearby **Hotel Primavera** (Calle Santander; 9-622-052).

Chichicastenango's **Hospedaje Salvador** (5 Avenida) may not be the best low-budget bargain in town, but it is the biggest and best known.

In Quetzaltenango, the centrally located **Hotel Río Azul** is simple, safe and student-friendly. ~ 92 Calle No. 12-15, Zona 1; 9-630-654.

The backpackers' inn of choice in Huehuetenango is the dark, funky, very cheap **Hotel Central**. ~ 5 Avenida No. 1-33; 9-641-202.

In Monterrico, the original budget beachcombers' hotel on the beach is the **Hotel El Baule** (on the beach), run by a former U.S. Peace Corps worker.

Cobán's **Hostal de Acuña**, a true hostel with bunk beds in shared dorm rooms, is ecology-oriented and exceptional in every way. ~ 4 Calle at 3 Avenida; phone/fax 9-511-547.

In Livingston, your best bet is **Hotel African Place**, where lush gardens compensate for very basic rooms.

The large campground is where most student travelers stay at Tikal National Park. An indoor alternative in Flores is the waterfront **Posada El Tucan**. ~ Calle Centroamérica No. 45; phone/fax 9-500-577.

To bring a pet into Guatemala, you must have an International Health Certificate for Dogs and Cats (Form 77-043) signed by a U.S. veterinarian verifying that the animal is in good health, as well as a separate certification that it has been immunized against distemper and rabies within the last six months. Some travelers "adopt" stray dogs in Guatemala and try to bring them back to the United States. In a car, a Form 77-043 and vaccination certificate signed by a vet in either Guatemala or Mexico will get you and your new dog across the U.S. border easily. If you are traveling by air, the questions raised by importing a foreign dog can slow your trip through U.S. Customs considerably.

TRAVELING WITH PETS

▼▼▼▼▼▼▼▼▼▼▼▼
Once You Arrive

EMBASSIES

Following is a list of foreign embassies in Guatemala. All of them are located in Guatemala City. There are no consulates elsewhere in the country.

CANADA Edyma Plaza Building, 13 Calle No. 8-44, Niv. 8, Zona 10; 3-333-6102

COSTA RICA Avenida de la Reforma No. 8-60, Zona 9; 3-319-604

EL SALVADOR 12 Calle No. 5-43, Zona 9; 3-343-942

FRANCE 16 Calle No. 4-53, Zona 10; 3-372-207

GERMANY 6 Avenida No. 20-25, Zona 10; 3-370-028

HONDURAS 16 Calle No. 8-27, Zona 10; 3-334-629

ITALY 5 Avenida No. 8-59, Zona 14; 3-374-578

JAPAN 6 Ruta No. 8-19, Zona 4; 3-319-666

MEXICO 13 Calle No. 7-30, Zona 9; 3-337-258

NICARAGUA 10 Avenida No. 14-72, Zona 10; 3-680-785

SWITZERLAND Edificio Seguros Universales, 4 Calle No. 7-72, Zona 9; 3-365-726

UNITED KINGDOM Gentro Financiero Torre II, 7 Avenida No. 5-10, Zona 4; 3-321-601

UNITED STATES Avenida de la Reforma No. 7-01, Zona 10; 3-311-541

TRAVEL AGENCIES

Antigua, Panajachel and other towns where tourists commonly go have numerous travel agencies. You'll also find them in Guatemala City, located in the lobbies of larger hotels. These agencies do a lot more than just sell airline tickets and make hotel reservations. They often serve as clearinghouses for small tour operators and can help you arrange a motorcycle rental, a plane or four-wheel-drive trip to remote ruins, a horseback expedition into the mountains, a jetboat or raft trip down one of the region's spectacular rivers or any number of other adventures. Stop in and see what they have to offer. If nothing else, you'll come away with plenty of friendly suggestions to enhance your visit.

TIME

Guatemala stays on Central Standard Time year-round, so the time is the same as the Central Standard Time Zone in the winter or the Rocky Mountain Daylight Time Zone in the summer.

BUSINESS HOURS & SIESTAS

One of the more famous Latin traditions is the siesta, a midday break lasting two or three hours, when establishments close while workers go home to eat and rest generally from 1 to 4 p.m. or 2 to 5 p.m. Later, stores reopen until 7 or so.

Siesta is a custom prevalent only in hot-climate areas. In the cool highlands, Guatemala, people do not take siestas. Instead, business hours in towns like Huehuetenango are pretty much the same as in the United States.

Whether you're getting gas, checking the thermometer or order-ing a *cerveza* (beer), you'll notice the difference: everything is met-ric. Guatemala is on the metric system, which measures tempera-ture in degrees Celsius, distances in meters, and most substances in liters, kilos and grams.

WEIGHTS & MEASURES

To convert from Celsius to Fahrenheit, multiply times 9, divide by 5 and add 32. For example, 23°C—the average temperature in Cancún during the winter—equals [(23 x 9)/5] + 32 or about 73°F. If you don't have a pocket calculator along (and you prob-ably should), just remember that 0°C is 32°F and that each Cel-sius degree is roughly 2 Fahrenheit degrees. Here are some other useful conversion equations:

- 1 pound (*libra*) = .45 kilo (*kilo*)
- 1 kilo = 2.2 pounds
- 1 gallon = 3.8 liters
- 1 liter (*litro*) = .26 gallon, or about 1 quart
- 1 foot = .3 meter
- 1 meter (*metro*) = 3.3 feet
- 1 mile = 1.6 kilometers
- 1 kilometer (*kilómetro*) = .6 mile

Electric currents are the same in Guatemala as in the United States—110 volts, 60 cycles, compatible with all American port-able appliances. If you need to convert appliances from other countries, bring your own adapters.

ELECTRIC VOLTAGE

Telephones Calling to Guatemala can be a frustrating, all but hopeless experience. However, recent changes have made the process somewhat easier. To call into Guatemala, dial 011 (in-ternational code), 502 (country code), then the seven-digit local number. The country code for Honduras is 504.

COMMUNI-CATIONS

Many establishments in Guatemala have no phones because of the expense and because it can take literally years on a wait-ing list to get one installed. For local or long-distance calls, your best bet is usually to ask your hotel manager for assistance in plac-ing the call. You will pay any long-distance charges plus a small fee for the service.

AT&T and some other U.S.-based long-distance companies have special numbers you can dial in Guatemala and Belize that will connect you with an English-speaking operator and let you charge international calls to your calling card, often at a lower cost than you would pay through the local phone company. Ask your long-distance carrier for a directory of international numbers.

To phone home without a calling card, go to any office of Guatel, the national phone company. You give your calling information to the person behind the desk and wait until the call goes through, which can take a few minutes or several hours depending on how busy international phone lines are. Then you take the call in a private booth and talk as long as you want. At the end of the call, you pay cash for it at the desk. These calls can be very expensive; it's easy to spend a huge amount—in cash—on a phone call home.

For placing calls unassisted, here are some key numbers to remember: long-distance operator: 91; international operator (English-speaking): 98; prefixes for dialing direct to the United States, Canada and Europe: 95 (station to station) and 96 (person to person).

Guatemalans answer the phone by saying, *"Bueno."*

Faxes and E-mail   Recently, entrepreneurs around Guatemala have rushed in with solutions for the high cost of international communications. Quite a few businesses operate international fax services that let you send a message home for just a few dollars and receive faxes through them for a few dollars more. You say your mom doesn't have a fax machine? No problem. Some places will fax your message to an associate in Miami, who will stick it in an envelope addressed to your mom and drop it in the U.S. mail.

Many hotels, restaurants and bookstores have trade-in sections of old English-language paperbacks.

For travelers whose moms have computers with modems, the fastest and cheapest way to send a message home is via the Internet. The going rate for e-mail is Q25 for 2500 characters—more than a page of typed text. All these services are made possible by independent satellite access companies that bypass Guatel's high rates. The same places can save you money on long-distance phone calls, sometimes costing as little as one-third the rate the Guatemalan phone company charges. Some of the businesses that now offer discount phone, fax and e-mail services to travelers are

Antigua: **World Wide Calls** ~ 1 Calle Poniente No. 9, 8-325-666, fax 8-320-662, e-mail wwcall@infovia.com.gt; **Cybermania** ~ 5 Avenida Norte No. 25B; 8-326-556; or **Conexion** ~ 4 Calle Oriente No. 14, 8-326-641, fax 8-322-676, e-mail zoee@conexion.com.gt

Panajachel: **c@fe.net** ~ 7-622-426; or **Panajachel Tourist Services** ~ Calle Santander, 7-622-122, e-mail panamail@guate.net

Chimaltenango: **MegaTel** ~ 2 Calle No. 4-25, Zona 2, 8396515, fax 8397053, e-mail mgchim@c.net.gt

Quetzaltenango: **Maya Communications** ~ 7-612-832, fax 7-651-203, e-mail mayacomm@infovia.com.gt

Cobán: **Access Internet Café** ~ 1 Calle 3-13, Zona 1; 9-521-883

Flores: **Tikal Net** ~ Calle Centroamérica, 9-260-655, e-mail tikalnet@guate.net; or e-mail **c@fe.net**, Avenida Barrios, 9-261-409

Snail Mail   Mail from Guatemala takes two to three weeks, and letters or packages that look as if they might contain something valuable are at some risk of vanishing in the mail system.

The postage rate for packages from Guatemala to the United States is expensive enough so that it doesn't make much sense to mail purchases home—a good reason to travel light and leave plenty of luggage room for purchases. If you do mail packages home from Guatemala, you'll find it much less frustrating to use one of the shipping agencies in Panajachel or Antigua instead of trying to deal with the post office and Guatemalan customs on your own.

United States customs regulations let you mail items of less than $50 duty-free to a particular address (but not your own) as often as every 24 hours. Mark the parcel "Unsolicited Gift Value Under $50" and be sure to enclose a sales receipt.

While you are on the road, you can receive mail in Guatemala at the main post office in any city through Lista de Correos (similar to General Delivery in the United States). Use this address format: [Your Name], Lista de Correos, Name of City, State (or Department), Country. The post office holds Lista de Correos mail for only one month in Guatemala, and then returns it to the sender. The post office will charge you a small fee, and you will need identification to pick up your mail. For more security, American Express offices hold mail for cardholders and persons carrying American Express travelers checks.

PRINT MEDIA

Two English-language weekly newspapers, the *Guatemala Weekly* and the *Guatemala News*, are published in Guatemala City and distributed free all over the country. Both contain Guatemalan news of interest to gringo tourists and expatriates, with a much less conservative slant than any of the major Spanish-language newspapers presents. In Antigua, where a lot of expatriates from the United States live, the *Miami Herald*'s English-language Latin American edition is usually available. The *Revue*, a free monthly English-language magazine published and distributed in Antigua, carries tourist information, editorials and short articles on everything from pop psychology to mountain biking. Back issues of the *Revue* can be read on the internet at www.revue.conexion.com.

LAUNDRY

Your wash can be taken care of overnight at your hotel (sometimes quite costly) or in a few hours at a laundromat (inexpensive; the attendant puts your laundry into the washer and dryer and folds it for you) in any city along your route. In small towns and villages, women will often wash your clothes by hand for extra cash. Dry cleaners are rarely seen outside Guatemala City.

If you're staying in remote areas, bring liquid detergent to wash your clothes. Laundry facilities are scarce in the jungle!

PICTURE TAKING

As you visit villages anywhere in the Guatemalan highlands or stroll through the public markets in larger towns, cities and tourist areas throughout the country, you will most likely admire the colorful, elaborately handcrafted clothing worn by traditional Maya people, and perhaps exotic facial features in which it is easy to imagine a full range of qualities from peaceful simplicity to stoic nobility to ancient, mysterious wisdom. And it is almost irresistibly tempting to try to capture indigenous people in photographs. It can also be frustrating to try.

Maya people often seem to have a preternatural sense that warns them of tourists with cameras. They will wag fingers at you in warning not to try to take their picture, and if you look through the viewfinder you're likely see everyone in the market turning their backs to you. Then, too, I have often been amazed at the way photos of Indians I've taken without asking permission first come out so unfocused that faces are unrecognizable. (There must be a rational explanation for this phenomenon; I just don't know what it is.) Sooner or later, travelers get the message: Many traditional Maya people don't want their picture taken— a taboo that we, as visitors, ought to respect.

The image is a vitally important thing to traditional Maya people. Note how, in highland Maya churches, mirrors are hung around the saints' necks. When one's image is reflected in the mirror, the people believe, it establishes a direct spiritual link with the saint. Little wonder, then, that the same people do not want their images "stolen" by the machines of pale, rich foreigners.

I once overheard a bus tour guide explaining, with a faintly patronizing attitude toward Indian "superstitions," that the purpose of this custom was to ward off the "evil eye." When we asked a young mother why she hid her baby's head, though, she explained that it was simply to protect him from having his picture taken. Maybe, in traditional cultures, the camera *is* the modern, high-tech equivalent of the "evil eye."

Yet there is more involved than mere superstition. To aim a camera at a person without consent and shoot is an assaultive act. After so many centuries as victims of armed invasion by foreigners, it is not unreasonable for the Maya people to take offense at photo assaults by gringos. Then, too, stories abound of village people who, while visiting the city, have been understandably horrified to find their own pictures in magazines or tourist brochures, accompanied by strange, incomprehensible foreign writing.

Camera-shyness also wears other faces in Guatemala today. In one village in the Ixil region, where people suffered terrible persecution by the army during the 1980s, a local guide explained to me, "People see you here with a camera and they don't know you are a tourist. They think you are a journalist, and they're afraid to have their picture appear in the newspaper. Not so long ago, people would be shot for talking to journalists."

In many villages, attitudes toward cameras are changing. Some adult vendors and most children are more willing than in the past to pose for photographs, usually for a small payment; Q2 for a person, up to Q5 for a group, seems to be the going rate just about everywhere. In particular, people who sell or beg in the streets of Antigua and Panajachel, who wear the traditional dress of their former villages but are more accustomed to foreigners' strange ways—and in dire need of money—are almost always willing to be photographed for a fee. And if you converse with them for a while and let them get to know you, many people who would deeply resent having their likeness captured by a stranger are more than willing to offer it as a gift to a new friend.

Photography is best done in market towns, and not in people's own villages. Chichicastenango, with its huge, tourist-friendly twice-weekly market, presents probably the best photo opportunities.

Most towns and a surprising number of villages have camera shops or professional portrait and event photographers that also sell film to tourists. These are both an indication that photography is allowed and a good place to ask about restrictions. Otherwise, in villages be sure to visit the administrative office to familiarize yourself with official photography restrictions and prohibitions before you even reveal that you have a camera in your possession. Some villages have strict laws against photography, with punishments that can range from confiscation of your camera to imprisonment. The best policy is to leave your camera back at the hotel when you visit traditional Maya villages.

Many Maya women cover the heads of their infant children in arms with special cloth sacks, towels or blankets whenever they are in public. The purpose is to develop the child's spiritual self free from the distractions of the outside world. In villages where this practice is followed, it is offensive to photograph these infants or mothers holding them. Public breast-feeding of infants is common in all Maya towns and villages, and photographing this activity is not appropriate.

Although the Maya are very modest in most circumstances, communal nude bathing (men in the morning, women and children in the afternoon) is practiced in rivers or hot springs near many villages. Photographing people while bathing is also offensive.

Finally and most important of all, taking a photograph inside a church is a serious offense in all Indian areas. People who try will have their cameras smashed and may be fined or even physically beaten.

By the way, Indians aren't the only ones who can be touchy about photography. Soldiers are trained to be suspicious of anyone photographing a military installation, so a snapshot of one of the goofy guardhouses and grandiose gateways in front of some highway-side army posts can result in minor but unnecessary hassles.

HEALTH & SAFETY

Hospitals, medical clinics, dental offices and other health care providers, as well as the Red Cross, can be found in Guatemala City and Antigua. There are also health centers in most department capitals, though they are generally open for limited hours and may or may not have a doctor on staff. Most backcountry villages have pharmacies (*farmacias*) where the proprietor will either tell you what medical help is available in town or diagnose your condition and dispense the appropriate drugs without a prescription.

Visits to doctors are relatively inexpensive, and hotels can usually recommend English-speaking physicians. In Guatemala City, the best inpatient care for problems that don't call for expensive technology is in small privately-operated hospitals, often with a dozen or fewer beds, which take patients referred by physicians. Hospitalization is quite inexpensive by U.S. standards and provides much more personal attention than you get in big U.S. hospitals, and the food is better. Contact your health insurance carrier before you leave to find out the extent of your coverage while abroad.

Still, Guatemala has only about one-fifth as many doctors per capita as the United States, and hospital facilities are primitive by North American standards. Central Americans who can afford it go to Miami or Houston for major surgery. For true emergencies, a San Diego–based service called **Critical Air Medicine** provides air ambulance service to anywhere in Central America—24 hours a day, every day of the year. ~ Toll-free from Mexico, 95-800-010-0268; from Guatemala, call collect to 619-571-8944.

Intestinal Distress   The illness most people encounter is diarrhea, euphemized as turista, due to food and drink carrying unfamiliar strains of bacteria. A bout can range from a 24-hour case of mild cramps to an all-out attack with several days of fever, chills and vomiting, followed by a lousy feeling that lingers on for weeks. I have suffered both kinds, and they are truly no fun.

But not everybody gets sick in Guatemala. Those who stay healthy use the best defense: prevention.

Avoid drinking tap water or ice that is made from tap water (commonly used in Guatemalan restaurants, so ask!), and don't brush your teeth with tap water. Ask if your hotel has bottled *agua purificada* (purified water). Always drink bottled liquids—mineral water, sodas, fruit drinks, soft drinks or beer—whenever possible. Remember, one drop of bad water can make you sick for weeks. The easiest and most reliable ways to purify water are to add chlorine bleach—two drops per liter of water—or boil the water for at least one minute. Water purification filters eliminate bacteria and amoebas but not viruses.

Eat with discretion. Consume only thick-skinned fruits that you peel yourself, such as oranges and bananas, and vegetables that are cooked through. Nuts with shells, such as peanuts and coconuts, are pretty safe bets too. Avoid milk products; unpasteurized milk is frequently served in Guatemala. Steer clear of raw seafood—*ceviche* is renowned for causing turista—as well as garden salads. Even if the produce was rinsed in purified water, it may have been fertilized (in the fields) with human waste, a common practice in Guatemala.

Look carefully at small *comedor* restaurants before eating there. A lot of the food from market stalls is delicious and very well prepared. Although Guatemala has no effective health regulations on food service, cooking areas are open to public view, giving you a chance to visually inspect it and see whether the meat looks fresh, the cook's hands are clean and the cookware is washed with soap. If the *comedor* looks clean and the food is hot off the grill, it's probably okay. You can minimize the risk by focusing on corn-based main dishes such as tamales and passing on the meat.

Many people believe in preventive medicine. Some take a slug of Pepto-Bismol before every meal; others, a shot of *aguardiente* (Central American distilled spirits similar to white rum), believing it will extinguish any threatening organisms. The antibiotic Doxycyclin is commonly prescribed as a preventative, although it causes sensitivity to the sun—not a good situation in the tropics—and can lead to other sorts of digestive difficulties. We met several people, including former residents of Central America, who swear by garlic pills as the best prevention. Lime juice is also a traditional preventative for stomach problems.

If you take all the necessary precautions and still get hit with turista, try these remedies: Lomotil, the stopper-upper. Use sparingly. Not a cure, it's a morphine derivative that induces a kind of intestinal paralysis. Stop the dosage as soon as symptoms disappear. Paragoric, Kaopectate, Kaomycin, Imodium AD and Pepto-Bismol help keep the cramps down. Diodoquin, Mexaform, Streptomagnum and Donamycin are stronger over-the-counter cures available in Guatemalan drugstores. For diarrhea with a fever, you can take Septra or Bactrium if you are not allergic to sulfa drugs. But remember that prolonged use of any antibiotic is not good for your immune system and can make you more susceptible to other tropical diseases.

Manzanilla (chamomile) tea, available from herbalists at many public markets, soothes the stomach and often works wonders. Yerba buena (peppermint) tea is also soothing. Papaya restores the digestive tract. Light, easy-to-digest foods like toast and soup keep your strength up. Lots of nonalcoholic liquids—any kind— prevent dehydration. Carbonated water with juice of a *lima* (a Mexican lime, different than the kind sold in the United States) is another popular stomach soother. A concoction of water with lime juice, sugar and salt is easier to absorb and retain than plain water, and helps replenish lost nutrients.

Rest and relaxation will help your body heal faster than if you run around sick and wear yourself down further. The symptoms should pass within 24 hours or so, and a case of turista seems to have an immunizing effect—any subsequent bouts you may have will be less severe, and eventually your body will adjust to the foreign water. If you spend a month or more in Central America, you may find that you have similar problems with the water back home when you first return—just like Mexican tourists, who suffer from turista when they visit the United States.

In rare cases, diarrhea may be a symptom of a more serious illness like amoebic dysentery or cholera. See a doctor if the diarrhea persists beyond three days, if your stool is bloody (appearing with black splotches) or foamy, or if you have a high fever.

Infections   Guatemala boasts an amazing array of animal and plant species, so it should come as no surprise that bacteria, viruses and other microorganisms also flourish in much greater abundance and variety than in temperate climates. Any wound, however slight, should be bandaged and cleaned frequently with soap and water. If hot swelling, red streaks or throbbing pain develops, don't wait and see; start looking for the nearest doctor or *farmacia* immediately. Some bacteria such as streptococcus A (the common pneumonia virus, which can also infect open, unbandaged wounds) can prove fatal in a day or less.

Most seasoned travelers know that in tropical lowland areas, even the most minor of scrapes, scratches and bites tend to grow into oozing sores that take weeks to heal. This is often caused not by bacteria entering the wound itself but by microorganisms in the bloodstream that migrate to any part of the body. One of these, leishmaniasis, is endemic in the Guatemalan lowlands, where it is spread by insect bites. The condition is more annoying than dangerous, except that as with any open wound it exposes you to the risk of serious secondary infections from strep and staph bacteria. Leishmaniasis stays in your bloodstream even after you return home, however, and a course of oral antibiotics over several weeks is required to get rid of it. If after your trip you find yourself plagued by frequent, slow-healing sores, see your doctor promptly.

In many parts of the United States and Canada, doctors know very little about even the most common tropical disease. If you wander into an emergency room in Philadelphia or an urgent care center in Seattle with a jungle infection, you're likely to find yourself hospitalized for observation as doctors run an extensive battery of tests ranging from skin biopsies to bone scans in a vain attempt to come up with a name for what you've got. Once doctors find the name under which to look up a disease, the rest is easy; but until they have identified it, they cannot discharge you from the hospital, and the only way you can get out is to leave "AMA"—against medical advice. To avoid being held hostage by the medical system for days or even weeks, demand to be seen first by a doctor—or a physician's assistant or nurse—who has worked in Latin America. Plenty of people in the medical community have spent a year or two at the beginning of their careers as Peace Corps or medical mission volunteers. If you can locate one, he or she may be able to diagnose your condition at a glance, saving you from a stint in the hospital as a medical curiosity.

Venereal Disease/AIDS   AIDS (*SIDA* in Spanish) is reported to be epidemic up and down the Caribbean coast, including Puerto Barrios. It is still uncommon in Guatemala City and unheard of in rural areas. Most cases here are said to be transmitted through drug use. Take whatever precautions are appropriate for you. Condoms, though much less commonly available than in the United States, are found in some Guatemalan pharmacies. Blood plasma may not be screened for the HIV virus.

The standard nonlethal venereal diseases, especially gonorrhea and syphilis, are endemic among ladino and Maya alike. It is wise to assume that any Guatemalan willing to have sex with a gringo is high-risk for contagious diseases and take whatever preventive steps seem appropriate.

Mosquitoes and Other Pests   Ask anyone who's spent a night in the jungle and they'll tell you: The most ferocious animal is not a jaguar but a mosquito. Mosquitoes protect their territory in the hot, damp lowlands. The little buzzers are thickest in rainforests, swamp areas and along the coastal bush. They are fewest in the cities and the highlands. The best defenses are long sleeves and pants along with a good repellent.

What works for you may not work for someone else. People who wish to avoid DEET, the active chemical in most commercial mosquito repellents, may want to investigate other methods.

Herb shops and health food stores sell good-smelling and more or less effective insect protection lotions made from oils and herbal essences. Some people swear by daily doses of vitamin B_6 or garlic, others by tobacco smoke. The new electronic mosquito repellent devices, which emit a sound pitched at the high edge of human hearing, are supposed to drive mosquitoes away. I tried one out on a recent trip into the Petén rainforest (toward the end of the dry season, admittedly, when mosquitoes are fewest) and emerged from the jungle unbitten.

Campers will find that mosquito netting is more important than a tent or sleeping bag. Hang a mosquito net over a hammock under a *palapa* in a campground like the ones at Tikal National Park and sleep comfortably (if not exactly privately) in paradise. Whether you're camping or spending your nights indoors, mosquito coils will keep the bugs away while you sleep.

For mosquito and other bug bites, lime juice takes the itch out, disinfects your wounds and acts as a repellent too. Limes (*limones*, not *limas*) are sold in every village. An ointment called *andatol*, sold in pharmacies, also helps reduce itching. Clean bug bites daily, using an antiseptic on bad bites to avoid infection.

Another annoyingly itchy bug is the chigger. As common in many parts of the United States as in Guatemala, this tiny, nearly invisible bug burrows its way into your skin and can tunnel around for weeks, slowly driving you crazy with the urge to scratch. Chiggers prefer tight places, especially around the tops of socks. An effective way to get rid of them is to paint open chigger bites with clear nail polish, cutting off the chiggers' oxygen supply.

Drugs   Marijuana, cocaine, crack and other drugs are widely available and sometimes used publicly up and down the Caribbean coast, including Livingston and Puerto Barrios. Foreign visitors will rarely have access to drugs elsewhere in the country, except that in some areas such as Panajachel, American expatriates sometimes deal marijuana or magic mushrooms to other Americans—at considerable risk.

The United States government pays Guatemala a lot of money to enforce drug laws, and these substances are highly illegal. In fact, since leftist guerrillas are not perceived by the U.S. government as an international Cold War menace the way they were a few years ago, the main justification for the large sums of U.S. military aid dispensed to the Guatemalan army is to combat international drug smuggling. Since rumor has it that Guatemala's elite security forces are into the drug trade up to their eyeballs, the army must appear to be enforcing the drug laws (by busting drug users or small-time dealers they consider undesirable) without actually enforcing the law against the big-time traffickers. Drugs are sometimes used as an excuse for bloody attacks on the estates of local political figures who are identified as enemies of the military.

Possessing, using or exporting drugs can land you in jail, where getting out can take a lot of time and money. The legal system in Guatemala presumes the accused guilty until proven innocent. Foreigners are not allowed bail or a trial by jury and can be kept in jail for up to a year before trial. Prison sentences for possession may run 15 years, and there is no parole or other early release program. All things considered, it's probably better to stay out of the war on drugs. Unless you want to invite trouble from customs officials, be sure to carry prescription drugs in their proper containers. Remember, they sometimes search you for drugs when you leave Central American countries.

Crime   Guatemalans often ask me, "Aren't you afraid to live in the United States?" They're serious. It's not only the shootout-and-car-chase action movies exported to Third World countries that convinces many Latin Americans that the United States is riddled with organized crime, gun violence, racial prejudice and promiscuity. It's also the news. In 1992, I remember, I was cooling off under a Guatemalan waterfall when I heard the news about the Los Angeles riots that followed the acquittal of the police officers who beat Rodney King. Three years later, I was strolling among silent Maya ruins when I heard that the federal building in Oklahoma City had been bombed. It is small wonder that Guatemalans believe the United States is far more dangerous than their own country.

Yet travelers from the United States typically have a mental picture of Central America as a dangerous place peopled by bandits, leftist guerrillas, brutal or corrupt police, torturers and midnight death squads. Guatemala is the quintessential "banana republic," the land where the word *desaparacidos* ("disappeared" political prisoners) was invented. In remote corners of the country, Maya villages were massacred by the army for their land in the 1970s and 1980s. There has only been a democratically elected civilian government since 1985, and a powerful coalition dominated by the military and its wealthy sponsors still controls the president, not vice-versa as in truly democratic countries.

Oddly enough, the end of Guatemala's civil war in 1996 increased, rather than decreased, the risk to international visitors. As military aid dwindled and the army shrunk, some soldiers deserted with their uniforms and weapons to start new careers as highway robbers. In the past three years, though, the government's new tourist police agency together with regular police surveillance in trouble areas has brought about a 50 percent decrease in crime rates. Of more than 240,000 Americans who visited Guatemala in 1998, less than one percent had any problem with crime.

In any city throughout the country, it makes sense to watch out for theft. The crime rate in Guatemala runs high, especially in Guatemala City, where it is about the same as in major U.S. cities. The difference is that foreign tourists are natural targets for theft because they stand out in a crowd and seem wealthy in a country where the average income amounts to around US$80 a month.

Be aware that whenever you are in public, any *ladrón* (thief) who happens to be around will be checking you out. Use common sense. Watch out for pickpockets, purse snatchers, and pack slashers, especially in public markets and other crowded places. By far the worst place for this kind of theft is the second-class bus terminal and adjacent public market in Guatemala City. Carry your trip funds, passport and other important documents in a money pouch or hidden pocket inside your clothing. Keep cash in your side pocket, never a back pocket. In cities, carry day-packs under one arm rather than on your back. Don't leave wallets or cameras lying on the beach while you go for a swim or sitting on a café table while you go to the restroom. Better hotels offer safe-deposit boxes at no extra charge. Always lock your hotel room and car. Park in a secured lot at night. Don't leave radios, gifts, cassettes or other temptations visible inside the car. Never flash a large amount of cash. Dress with humility; a thief will focus on the best-dressed, richest-looking tourist around, so make sure it's not you.

Just like in the United States, certain cities have a well-deserved reputation for crime, and travelers should use extra caution when visiting them. Guatemala City is known for its *ladrones*. All hotels recommended in this book are located in safe neighborhoods. As a general rule, downtown areas where there is a lot of activity after dark are safer than outlying neighborhoods of the city. Don't tempt fate by wandering around dark back streets late at night. If you're camping out, avoid lonely roadside stops or isolated beaches unless you're with a group. Stay away from drug deals. In short, exercise the same caution you would use at home. Observe these common-sense precautions, and feel fortunate that you are not in New York City, where unlike in Guatemala the petty criminals carry guns.

STAYING LONGER

Quite a few gringos establish permanent homes in Guatemala, and most of them keep their paperwork current simply by leaving the country for 72 hours every 90 days in order to obtain a new tourist card. Legal resident status is available only to foreign nationals of age 51 or older and those who have been married to a Guatemalan citizen for at least two years *and* have a child with that person. The legal formalities to become a Guatemalan resident are quite burdensome. You need your birth certificate approved by the Guatemalan consulate closest to where you were born, a police report showing that you have no criminal record approved by the Guatemalan consulate closest to the last place you lived, and proof of at least $300-a-month income from outside the country; the approval process takes about a year, during which the applicant is not allowed to leave Guatemala. It can often be simplified for those in a position to pay substantial legal fees and bribes.

For most travelers, the best way to get from the United States to Guatemala is to fly. Various commercial airlines operate daily (or in a few cases every other day) international flights to Guatemala City from Miami, New Orleans, Houston, Dallas and Los Angeles.

▼▼▼▼▼▼▼▼▼▼
Transportation

AIR

La Aurora International Airport is set beside a barrio packed to overflowing with tiny, makeshift houses perched on the edge of a gorge in the southern part of Guatemala City, on the boundary between Zona 9 and Zona 13. Most flights from the United States, Europe and other parts of the world connect through Miami, Houston, Dallas/Fort Worth or Los Angeles. They include American, Air France, British Airways, Continental, Iberia, Japan Air Lines, KLM Royal Dutch Airlines and Lufthansa. Guatemala's national airline, Aviateca, has flights from Los Angeles, Houston, Miami, Cancún and Mérida. Other Latin American airlines that fly into Guatemala City include Aeroquetzal (Guatemalan), Aerocaribe and Mexicana (Mexican), Aeronica (Nicaraguan), COPA (Panamanian), LACSA and TACA (Costa Rican), and SAHSA (Honduran).

During special events, holidays and the November-to-May high season, make flight reservations at least two weeks to a month in advance. Air delays are common. So are flight cancellations—be sure to confirm your flight 48 hours before departure. Canceled flights seem to be a particular problem at Flores (the airport for Guatemala's Tikal National Park), where the next flight out may not be for several days.

Guatemala has an airport departure tax equivalent to a little less than US$10, which must be paid in local currency when you check in at the airline desk.

When booking your international airline tickets, if you will be taking a connecting flight on your return trip, be sure to allow plenty of time. At the hub airport where you first land in the United States—probably Los Angeles, Dallas, Houston, New Orleans or Miami—you will have to wait for and claim your baggage, clear U.S. Customs, and recheck your bags before boarding your onward flight. Allow one-and-a-half to two hours.

From the airport When you arrive at the Guatemala City airport on an international flight, shuttle van drivers will probably approach you before you even clear customs to offer transportation to Antigua, a one-hour trip. Both taxi and shuttle vans wait outside the terminal, where competitive drivers may try to snatch your luggage to get your business. Passengers arriving from Santa Elena/Tikal, who don't need to go through customs, may actually find cab drivers mobbing the runway to get passengers as they descend the stairway from the plane. Be sure to discuss the price they want to charge before you let go of your luggage. Shuttle fares to Antigua are standardized at Q60 (about US$10); taking the same shuttle from Antigua to the airport costs a couple of dollars less. Taxi fares from the airport to Guatemala City destinations vary wildly. Drivers typically ask about US$10 to take one or two people to a Zona Viva hotel but may settle for half that if there are a lot of other cabs around.

Within Guatemala   The only commercial air passenger service within Guatemala is between Guatemala City and Santa Elena, the nearest town to Tikal National Park. Aviateca, Guatemala's national airline, purports to offer scheduled flights to Santa Elena and back three times a week. In reality, departures are wildly erratic. Flights may be canceled if there are too few passengers, and additional flights may be announced on short notice as demand (either passengers or cargo) materializes. Travel agencies in Guatemala City and Antigua, as well as in a few expensive hotels elsewhere, know about the special flights. Passengers won't learn of a flight cancellation until check-in at the Guatemala City airport. Remember, if your flight to Tikal is canceled, Aviateca is obligated by international treaty to put you up in a Guatemala City hotel, normally on the Zona Viva, until the next flight. If this happens to you, turn to Chapter 4.

CAR   Traveling from the United States to Guatemala by car is a challenging and time-consuming adventure. Not that it's particularly dangerous—just demanding. It involves traveling most of the length of Mexico. Mexican highways usually offer a choice: older two-lane roads called *libres* that take longer to drive than you would expect, and limited-access toll freeways called *cuotas* that cost a startling amount—typically about 10¢ a mile. The drive to Cancún from Brownsville, Texas, the closest border crossing, to Guatemala City is 1525 miles (2540 kilometers). It can be done in roughly 48 hours of actual driving time. To make the journey comfortably, without arriving in Guatemala exhausted, allow at least a week. (Realistically, most people driving from the United States to Guatemala take weeks to do it, savoring the various regions of Mexico along the way.) From El Paso, Texas, it's a 2150-mile (3600-kilometer) trip requiring 70 hours of driving, and from San Diego it's 2780 miles (4635 kilometers)—more than 85 hours of driving.

If you are driving to Guatemala from the U.S. border, plan well ahead for refueling and evening stops. Gas stations in Mexico are a government monopoly, and in much of the country they are few and far between. Never pass up an opportunity to fill your vehicle's tank. Driving after dark can be dangerous (the most common hazards are vehicles stopped in the traffic lane without lights and vehicles traveling without lights well after dusk—sometimes considered a display of machismo). In northern Mexico, especially, it can be a long way between towns large enough to have hotels or restaurants. For those with trailers, RVs or motor homes, private campgrounds abound in most parts of Mexico, and even in the smallest villages there are always informal sites where self-contained RVs can be parked—inquire locally. In Mexico, unleaded gasoline is available at all Pemex stations. Gas is sold by the liter and costs significantly more than in the United States. Fuel prices run about the same in Mexico and Guatemala. In Guatemala, where buses and cargo trucks are far more common than cars, diesel fuel costs much less than gasoline and is more readily available in remote areas.

The rules of the road are very informal. Few Guatemalans own cars. This means that on main highways, particularly Route 9 between Guatemala's capital city and the Caribbean shipping ports, passenger vehicles are outnumbered ten to one by big trucks carrying professional drivers with more than their share of macho hormones. Although driving the truck-clogged two-lane blacktop highways may seem suicidal at first, you'll soon notice that a certain odd kind of courtesy comes into play. Other drivers assume that you, too, will drive like a maniac. If you start to pass a slow truck around a blind curve on a mountain road only to find a bus barreling toward you, for instance, you'll be amazed at the way the oncoming bus slows to a crawl and the truck pulls over to within inches of the precipice to open up a passing lane just for you. Of course, other drivers expect the same kind of courtesy from you. Defensive driving here means always being ready for the next motorist to do something completely stupid. In other words, watch out for them and let them watch out for you.

The best adventures are found along unpaved back roads through the highlands and jungles. There is so little traffic that you can hear a bus coming from miles away. Most of these back roads are used by passenger buses on a daily basis, and if *they* can make it, so can your rental car. Probably. Bear in mind, though, that those buses have much higher clearance than passenger cars. Always ask about road conditions up ahead whenever you get a chance. Show people your vehicle and ask whether the road is good enough for it. It's usual enough to find yourself swerving around rockslides and fording rivers when you venture far from the main highways. Avoid driving after dark if you possibly can, or you'll find your headlights suddenly, at the last minute, revealing strange nocturnal creatures right in front of you—from drunks and their pet pigs to swarms of giant toads. Wherever you are in Guatemala, always park in a guarded lot at night.

The main highway through Guatemala is Route 1, the Pan-American Highway. The Guatemalan portion of this international highway starts at the border station of La Mesilla, where it enters Guatemala from San Cristóbal de las Casas and Comitán in the Mexican state of Chiapas. Route 1, a well-maintained two-lane paved highway, takes you on a winding, mountainous trip past Huehuetenango, Quetzaltenango, Lago de Atitlán and Antigua Guatemala before arriving in Guatemala City. From the capital, the Pan-American Highway veers south into El Salvador.

The main highway to eastern Guatemala destinations such as the Río Dulce, Quiriguá, and the turnoff to Copán, Honduras, is Route 9, known as the Carretera Atlántica, or Atlantic Highway. Two-lane, paved Route 9 twists up and down mountains for the first 60 miles (100 kilometers), then descends into the Motagua River Valley and follows the river all the way to the sea.

Getting to Tikal by car is a formidable challenge. Unpaved, mountainous Route 5 north from Guatemala City takes forever and should be attempted only by adventurous souls in high-clearance vehicles. A shorter and easier way is to drive to the Río Dulce area and take Route 13 north past Castillo de San Felipe. The first one-third of this route is paved, but for the last 100 miles (168 kilometers) it becomes a rocky dirt road that is very rough in spots. Start with a full tank of gas and allow at least eight hours to drive the unpaved portion of this route. Few travelers opt to go to the Petén by car, and for good reason.

Motor Vehicle Requirements   The documentation you need to take your vehicle into Mexico is more than sufficient to bring it into Guatemala. Car permits in Guatemala are normally issued for 30 days. Auto insurance policies issued in the United States are not valid in either Mexico or Guatemala. Guatemala does not require liability insurance, but as in Mexico, it means hassles, delay and expense—and possibly jail—if you are involved in an accident without insurance. Insurance costs considerably less in Guatemala than in Mexico—as little as US$1 a day. It is sold in border-town mom-and-pop shops *inside* the Guatemalan border.

If the vehicle is registered in another person's name or a company name, you need a notarized letter from the owner authorizing you to take the vehicle to Guatemala for a specified time. The owner or driver who has the car permit stamp on his or her visa must be in the car whenever it is being driven.

Because of a recent change in the law designed to make it harder for foreigners to live as long-term residents in Guatemala without proper documents, your foreign driver's license is only good for driving in Guatemala during your first 30 days in the

Street Addresses

Confused by street names and directions? Relax. In Latin America, few places are neatly laid out. Maps almost always disagree. Spellings often differ. Streets may have more than one name—or no name at all. Some buildings have street numbers while others on the same street do not, and addresses are not always consecutive.

In nearly all Guatemalan cities and towns, the *parque central* (main plaza or town square) is the key landmark. It almost always fronts the main Catholic church, whose towers are usually visible from all over town.

In Antigua and some other department capitals, city streets have both a number designation, with *avenidas* (avenues) running north–south and *calles* (streets) running east–west, and a street name, which changes upon passing the *parque central*, dating back to Spanish colonial times. For example, in Antigua, Avenida 4, one of the streets that runs past the main plaza, is also called Calle del Obispo Marroquín north of the plaza and Calle del Conquistador south of the plaza. Street signs may give the avenue number, the name, neither or both. To make it easier to find your way around, I use street and avenue numbers instead of the colonial street names whenever possible.

A few years ago, the government issued an official mandate requiring all towns and villages to be divided into zones with numbered streets and avenues. This worked better in some places than others. In Panajachel, for instance, the signs marking main streets such as Calle Santander and Calle Principal were taken down, but no new street signs were put up, and few locals know streets by number.

country. If you are stopped by the police, besides your driver's license you must show a passport, visa or tourist card activated within the last 30 days. If you remain in the country longer than 30 days, each time you go to Guatemala City for your visa extension you must also apply for a temporary driver's license at the central police station (6 Avenida at 3 Calle, Zona 1), window #7. The application must be accompanied by two copies of a passport-type photograph along with photocopies of your passport, visa and foreign driver's license.

Car Rentals   Renting a car eliminates the need for your own insurance and car permits as it lets you leapfrog over the thousands of miles between your garage and the Guatemalan border. Car rentals are widely available in Guatemala City. In Antigua and Panajachel, travel agencies can arrange a rental car for you. It may take several hours' advance notice, or even several days, depending on the season. Advance reservations can be made through several international car-rental agencies including Avis, Budget, Dollar, Hertz and National Interrent.

Anyone 25 years or older, with a credit card, can order a car in advance through one of the international rent-a-car companies and have it waiting in Guatemala. To rent a car upon arrival, you will need your tourist card or passport, a driver's license and a major credit card.

Take the optional extra insurance that lowers your deductible for damage to the vehicle. Rental cars in Central America lead hazardous existences. Having a car is a hassle but much faster than riding the bus.

Rental rates have increased dramatically in recent years and are generally higher than in the United States. In Guatemala, Japanese and Korean cars are preferred. The rates for four-wheel-drive vehicles (necessary for the super-rough and rocky roads in remote areas of the highlands and the Petén) are astronomical.

It is not currently possible to drive a Guatemalan rental car into Mexico, Belize or El Salvador, or to drive a car rented in another country into Guatemala. Written permission from the rental agency is required to drive across the border to Copán, Honduras; this is a common enough request that such permission can often be obtained, especially if you rent your car through a local travel agency in Guatemala City or Antigua.

CARS FOR HIRE   In Guatemala City, a car and driver can be arranged through the travel agent in the lobby of any large Zona Viva hotel. Expect to pay about US$100 a day.

Away from Guatemala City, most taxi drivers seem to have plenty of idle time and are overjoyed to hire out for the day as tour guides. Hourly or daily rates are highly negotiable; a fair rate is about US$25 for a half-day or $40 for a full day.

Guided tours run regularly from Guatemala City and Antigua to Lago de Atitlán, Chichicastenango, Copán, Quiriguá and Río Dulce. The numerous independent travel agencies around Antigua can also arrange custom tours by car or van on a day or two advance notice. Gringo students frequently reserve a van and driver a week or so in advance and then advertise for four to six passengers to share the cost; check the big bulletin board at Restaurant Doña Luisa and the smaller one at the Rainbow Reading Room—or organize your own custom tour, using *Hidden Guatemala* to select some destinations that aren't on the standard guided tour routes.

TAXIS

Taxis can be found everywhere in Guatemala City's downtown and Zona Viva areas. The most reliable places to catch them are in front of a large hotel and near the downtown plazas. Antigua, Quetzaltenango, Huehuetenango, Cobán and most other department capitals also have plenty of taxis, though they are likely to be unnervingly decrepit by U.S. Standards, sometimes missing such essentials as hoods, windshields and even doors. (In places like Huehuetenango that were caught in the middle of El Conflicto during the 1980s, you may even notice old bullet holes.) In all these towns, the taxis wait for passengers around the *parque central* or the town plaza. Cab fares are expensive in Guatemala City and very reasonable in other parts of the country.

HITCHING

Hitchhiking, especially on commercial trucks (since private passenger cars are uncommon away from the Guatemala City–Antigua area), is a widely accepted way of getting around in Guatemala. As a foreigner, most Guatemalans who offer you a ride will ask you to pay a small amount for the lift—usually Q5 for long trips, less for shorter ones. However, local bus or pickup transportation is so widely available and so inexpensive that most international travelers neither need nor want to hitchhike.

Conversely, if you are driving a car in Guatemala, you will find that wherever you go, local people—from soldiers and Spanish teachers to whole Maya families, including pets or livestock—will ask you for a ride. Unlike in the Unites States, picking up hitchhikers in the backcountry is reasonably safe. For many Guatemalans, money saved by avoiding a small bus fare can literally mean eating instead of going hungry. In such circumstances, driving with empty seats in your vehicle seems unconscionable—and the rewards of sharing your mobility can be substantial. I am grateful to Guatemalan hitchhikers for many cultural insights, off-the-beaten-path discoveries and positive adventures.

BUSES

Buses are one of the cheaper modes of transportation in Guatemala. Because few Guatemalans own cars, the bus system is used much more than in the United States, so you can generally get just about anywhere. Bus tickets are sold at the stations for cash (local currency only) on a first-come, first-served basis. First-class tickets can be purchased in advance at the bus line's private station (ask your hotel clerk how to find one). For second-class buses, you simply get on board and a conductor will eventually come around to collect the small fare. Avoid bus travel around big holidays (Christmas and Easter) unless you are able to buy tickets well in advance, which can't be done from the United States. Buses are categorized as *primera clase* (first class), which travel only the main highways, or *segunda clase* (second class), the legendary Third World "pigs-and-chickens" buses. If you are arriving in Guatemala after traveling by bus through Mexico, where the first-class buses are some of the most luxurious anywhere, you will quickly discover that in Guatemala this is not the case.

A few comfortable, reserved-seat first-class buses operate out of individual garages hidden away on side streets of some larger towns. In Huehuetenango, **Transportes Los Halcones** runs daily buses to Guatemala City and connects with second-class buses to Quetzaltenango, Lago de Atitlán and Antigua Guatemala. ~ 7 Avenida No. 3-62 in Huehuetenango; 7 Avenida No. 15-27, Zona 1 in Guatemala City; 3-081-997. **Rutas Orientales** operates first-class buses to Esquipulas near the Honduran border and can let you off at Chiquimula, where you can catch a minibus to the border crossing for the Maya ruins of Copán. ~ 19 Calle No. 8-18, Zona 1, Guatemala City; 3-537-282. **Transportes Litegua** has daily buses to Puerto Barrios that connect with shuttles to the Lago de Izabal/Río Dulce resort area. ~ 15 Calle 10-40, Zona 1, Guatemala City; 3-538-169. **Transportes Fuente del Norte** operates first-class buses to Santa Elena, near Tikal National Park. ~ 17 Calle No. 8-46, Zona 1, Guatemala City; 3-513-817.

Second-class buses, the notorious Third World "pigs-and-chickens" kind, are much slower and less comfortable. Lack of onboard restrooms makes second-class buses a dubious choice for long-distance travel. Considering the low cost of first-class bus tickets, budget is seldom a reason to settle for a second-class bus.

Visitors experiencing Third World travel for the first time will find Guatemala's public buses appalling, and even the most seasoned of globetrotters will find them by turns frustrating and hilarious. With increasing tourism, some comfortable first-class buses can now be found in larger towns, but trips to most places in Guatemala—including such popular tourist destinations as Panajachel, Antigua, Chichicastenango and Tikal—involve riding second-class buses.

A typical second-class bus is of the same type as old school buses. Independently owned and operated, many are 30 to 40 years old and may have rust holes in the floor or broken windows. They pick up passengers at the public market and leave whenever all the hard bench seats are full, then drive around town picking up more passengers from street corners until the aisles are also full. Once on the road, they stop to load and unload passengers at every tiny crossroad. Baggage, from slabs of sheet metal roofing and baskets full of live chickens to your suitcase, are thrown onto a luggage rack on top of the bus. If the inside of the bus gets too crowded and claustrophobic, most drivers will let you ride on the roof, too. An old joke goes:

"What's the capacity of a Guatemalan bus?"

"I don't know. What *is* the capacity of a Guatemalan bus?"

"Four more."

Many Guatemalan towns and cities have no central bus terminal buildings. Second-class buses, which can take you virtually anywhere in Guatemala, always originate in streets or open lots around the public market. Drivers shout their destinations. In Guatemala City's chaotic outdoor marketplace/terminal, where 50 or more buses may be loading at one time, the uproar can be overwhelming. To ride a second-class bus, whether you board at the market or flag one down along the road, just find a place to sit or stand. After a while, the conductor will clamber back to sell you a ticket for a few quetzales.

BOATS

Passenger ferries are the main transportation mode for residents of the villages surrounding Lago de Atitlán. Ferries also provide the only access to isolated fishing spots such as Livingston on the Caribbean coast and Monterrico on the Pacific coast. Fares are quite reasonable by U.S. standards. For instance, Lago de Atitlán ferries cost between US$3 and $4 for a round-trip cruise taking about an hour each way.

TWO

Land and Outdoor Adventures

The worldwide environmentalist community is pouring a lot of energy into protecting Guatemala's natural areas these days. There's a lot that's worth defending, and a lot of development pressures to defend it from. Tropical rainforest, cloud forest, volcanoes, lakes, caves—the variety of Guatemala's natural landscape is amazingly rich. More different mammals, birds, trees and plants live in Guatemala than in any other area of similar size in North America.

Environmental protection in Guatemala means any project for which a foreign government or international conservation group will provide funding. The Guatemalan government usually cooperates with ecological efforts, but, let's face it, it has no money. Fortunately, dozens of public and nonprofit organizations from Europe, North America and Asia have come to Guatemala to help save the environment. Over the past decade, Guatemala has established no fewer than 25 national parks and protected wildlife areas, including the 4,300,000-acre Maya Biosphere Reserve, the largest contiguous expanse of tropical rainforest remaining in North America.

Efforts at environmental protection have had uneven success. A few years ago, for instance, the Guatemalan government with the cooperation of the University of San Marcos, the U.S. Peace Corps and the World Wildlife Fund created the Monterrico-Hawaii Biotope to protect sea turtles that nest on the beaches of the Pacific coast—especially the giant, 1500-pound leatherback turtles, which rank among the earth's most endangered species. Since the people who live along the south coast have traditionally eaten sea turtle eggs, workers at the Monterrico research center set up a public education program coupled with a rule requiring anyone who found a turtle nest to turn half the eggs over to the center. They could sell or eat the other half. The research center's half were hatched, and the young turtles were released into the open ocean safe from predatory birds who would otherwise devour many of the hatchlings before they reached the water. The program worked fairly well for a few years, until a scandal erupted over charges (trumped up, some say) that underpaid employees of the research center were stealing some of the eggs to sell for profit. Political foes of conservation succeeded in eliminating the research center's staff except for a single caretaker. The Peace Corps volunteers were reassigned elsewhere. Public education ceased. Today, while the Monterrico-Hawaii Biotope continues to be a protected area, well worth visiting for its abundant bird life and long, wide beach, the sea turtles it was designed to protect slide closer to extinction each time a beachcomber finds a new nest—and takes the eggs home for dinner.

A recurring problem in Guatemala's conservation movement has been animosity between the ultraliberal University of San Marcos and government factions backed by timber and agribusiness interests. Although opposition between the university and the government over various policy matters can be traced at least as far back as 1898, the friction over conservation started in 1981 with the creation of the Mario Dary Quetzal Reserve south of Cobán. The biotope's namesake, Dr. Mario Dary, was the founder of the environmental studies department at the University of San Marcos. His greatest conservation success was to persuade the government to set aside this 2849-acre cloud forest park in 1980 as habitat for Guatemala's endangered national symbol, the quetzal. A few months after the quetzal reserve was created, Dr. Dary was assassinated—allegedly by Guatemalan secret police at the behest of timber company executives close to military dictator General Fernando Lucas García. The message was not lost on Guatemalan environmentalists, who even now are extremely careful not to step on powerful toes. Most new environmental preservation efforts today are initiated by international organizations, while internal activism remains subdued. (Incidentally, though the quetzal reserve continues to be Guatemala's most accessible remnant of virgin cloud forest, quetzal sightings there are rare. Soon after the reserve was established, a new paved highway was routed through the portion that is open to hikers, chasing most wildlife to the other side of the mountain. For serious trekkers, the best place to see quetzals is the new Sierra de las Minas Biosphere Reserve.)

Guatemala's most ambitious and publicized environmental effort has been in the Petén rainforest, where the government in collaboration with UNESCO, the U.S. National Geographic Society and other international organizations has set aside millions of acres of contiguous ancient forest as the Maya Biosphere Reserve, Tikal National Park, Mirador–Dos Lagunas–Río Azul National Park and El Zotz–San Miguel–La Pelotada Biotope. As the country's only underpopulated area that is accessible by road, the Petén now appears to be the inescapable choice for resettling the many thousands of refugees who are returning to Guatemala. The UNESCO Man and the Biosphere Program, under which the region is protected, does not prohibit human settlement; instead, it limits the land to sustainable uses (which do not include timber cutting), with a buffer zone where people live and one or more untouchable core areas.

But in Guatemala the rainforest faces an unprecedented threat. This small country has not only more people per square mile than any other in Latin America but also an estimated 150,000 citizens living as refugees outside its borders. Many of them are now returning home after as much as a generation in exile. It is unrealistic to expect Guatemala City, already overcrowded, crime-ridden and terribly poor, to absorb the returning refugees. Pressure is mounting to open more and more of the Petén wilderness to homesteaders.

The UNESCO biosphere plan can hardly have anticipated anything like the present Guatemalan refugee situation. In a pilot resettlement project, the government financed the purchase of El Quetzal, a remote 14,900-acre plantation on the edge of the Petén buffer zone, where 238 returning refugee families have been resettled to form a forest products cooperative, which will be required to repay the government for the purchase of the land beginning in five years. Under present environmental protection regulations, only sustainable-use activities such as rubber tapping and spice and nut gathering are permitted at El Quetzal; however, a new study has concluded that under these rules El Quetzal can support only 189 families, not the 238 that have homesteaded there, and will never generate enough profits to repay the government-backed loan. As a result, the government's National Commission for Refugees (CEAR) is petitioning to rezone El Quetzal, lifting environmental regulations to permit timber and slash-and-burn farming. Another government agency, the National Commission of Protected Areas (CONAP), opposes the move but admits that due to its lack of manpower to patrol this remote area, timbercutting, poaching and other activities are already going on at El Quetzal. If all of the 40,000 refugees now slated to return from camps in Mexico are allowed to homestead in Petén communities patterned after El Quetzal, it is likely to mean not only opening about 600,000 acres—15 percent of the total protected area of the Petén—to development within the next few years, but also setting an ugly precedent for alleviating Guatemala's internal population pressures.

A classic struggle between development and conservation may be taking shape in the country's northern jungle. Models for sustainable, environmentally sound economic growth have been tested and proved in other Latin American countries—but never before on such a large scale in the face of such fearsome odds.

Thus it is easy to adopt a "see it before it's gone" attitude toward the Petén rainforest. Easy, but not necessary. In Costa Rica, Belize and to a lesser extent the Mexican states of Quintana Roo and Campeche, ecotourism has proven able to supplement the income of sustainable forest communities while providing an immediate reason to preserve the environment. The Guatemalan government is presently fragmented over this issue, and the economic benefits of ecotourism are an increasingly powerful argument for CONAP and the ecological position. We can make a difference not only by supporting international conservation organizations that are working for environmental protection in Guatemala but also simply by traveling in an ecologically sound way, proving the value in tourist dollars of saving the rainforest. (And if worst comes to worst, at least you *will* have a chance to see it before it's gone.)

GEOLOGY A series of dichotomies divide Guatemala's terrain into a number of dramatically different environments. There are highlands and lowlands, each with its wet side and dry side, each region changing suddenly between the rainy season and the dry season.

In the southern two-thirds of the country, most of the interior is highlands known as the Altiplano, made up of rugged, ridge-like mountain ranges and a total of 40 volcanoes, of which only three—Volcán Fuego near Antigua, Volcán Pacaya south of Guatemala City and Volcán Lacandón near Quetzaltenango—are active. The tallest of Guatemala's volcanoes, Volcán Tajumulco near the Mexican border in the department of San Marcos, rises just over 14,000 feet (4220 meters) above sea level. Of the mountain ranges that form the Altiplano, the highest—in fact, the highest mountain range in Central America—is the Cordillera de los Cuchumatanes north of Huehuetenango, with peaks rising as high as about 12,800 feet (3837 meters).

Altitude has a profound effect on climate. Any traveler who believes the tropics are always hot (or even warm) is in for a surprise. Midrange elevations, around 5000 to 7000 feet, enjoy mild temperatures, typically mid-70s in the daytime and chilly at night, giving rise to Guatemala's motto, "Land of Eternal Spring." That's why the past and present capital cities and most other major towns are built at these altitudes. At higher elevations, such as around the Maya town of Todos Santos high in the Cordillera de los Cuchumatanes, cool daytime temperatures give rise to nights so cold that you can see your breath.

When it comes to climate, altitude is only half the story. The difference between the wet side of the mountains and the dry side is equally startling. Moisture spills from the Caribbean Sea southwest across the rainforest of Belize and the Petén until it strikes the coolness of the Altiplano, where it condenses into misty rain at the rate of 80 inches per year, making for a climate more than three times as rainy as Seattle, Washington. The rainfall on the north side of the mountains creates an arid rain shadow on the south side so suddenly that in many places when you cross a mountain ridgeline the environment changes from drizzly cloud forest to barren, rocky desert within a distance of 12 steps. Much of southern Guatemala including most of the land you see on the way to Copán, Honduras, is chaparral and big-cactus wasteland.

The lowlands of Guatemala come in different varieties, too. The one thing the different lowland regions have in common is that they're very hot. The northern one-third of the country, the Petén, is a region of low, rolling hills and ridges covered by luxuriant rainforest that reaches far beyond the borders of Mexico and Belize. The Petén receives huge, thunderous downpours of rain in the summer wet season and virtually none in the dry season. Though the region was heavily inhabited 1200 years ago, the seasonal shortage of water, the lack of incentives to build roads and the steamy climate have kept the Petén almost unpopulated in modern times.

The hot lowland valleys of eastern Guatemala, particularly along the Río Motagua en route to the Caribbean seaports of Puerto Barrios and Santo Tomás de Castilla, have been so thoroughly agriculturalized into vast banana plantations that only a few tiny natural areas like the grove of lofty hardwoods left by clear-cutters as a backdrop for the Maya ruins of Quiriguá hint at the luxuriant forest that once covered the region. From these valleys come most of the 2.5 billion pounds of bananas Guatemala exports each year—almost all to the United States, where bananas are the best-selling fruit in supermarkets. The coastal plains that lie between the highlands and the Pacific in the southern part of the country are also heavily agriculturalized, not only with banana plantations but also with clear-cut pasturelands where zebu cattle from Africa graze.

Both coasts have sand beaches where sea turtles lay their eggs and mangrove wetlands where egrets, herons, pelicans and many other wading birds surround the visitor. Except for the faded port town of Puerto Barrios, no place on the Caribbean coast is accessible by road, and the beaches lie on the far side of a long wilderness peninsula you can reach only by hiring a fishing boat. Highways and ranch roads make access easy to the Pacific coast, where long, straight bars of dark, hot volcanic sand hold the sea back from quiet estuaries teeming with life.

FLORA

The steep mountainsides of the Guatemalan highlands are bare of trees nearly to the top ridgelines. Landowners often clear-cut the mountain slopes, leaving the trees for local Indians who harvest the wood for cooking and heating fuel as they have for countless centuries. Hikers who follow a forested ridgeline find a tall, open, homogenous forest of tropical pines and cedars, usually with the lower branches hacked off as high as a wood gatherer can reach. The mountain forests were once lush with hardwoods that have since been cut down. Today ancient forest groves can still be found in remote areas. These places are held sacred by local Maya people, whose religious practices include leaving offerings at the base of particularly old trees.

Evergreens also form the foundation of the cloud forest that grows high on the wet north-facing slopes of the highlands. Unfortunately, this chilly, dark, rain-soaked microclimate has also proved ideal for growing coffee, so only a few protected areas of natural cloud forest are easily accessible, while larger areas survive in remote mountains where no road goes. Besides huge pines, so thickly covered with moss, lichen and epiphytes that the trees' bark often cannot be seen at all, the cloud forest has stands of hardwoods including cypress, pepper and walnut trees. Since most cloud forest that remains today is on slopes too steep for agriculture, the upper boughs of the trees do not form a solid canopy like that of the lowland rainforest, where undergrowth is restricted because little light reaches the forest floor. The beams of light that filter through the cloud forest enable a dense undergrowth of palms, ferns and flowering vines to grow. It is in the cloud forest that Guatemala's national flower, a rare white orchid called *monja blanca* (white nun), can be found, along with many other orchid and bromeliad species that have evolved to thrive in cool climates and high altitudes. Other flowers found in the cloud forests (as well as in areas that were once covered with cloud forest) include hibiscus, bird of paradise, red ginger and bougainvillea vines that bedeck tropical pines with magenta blossoms, giving them the aspect of lofty, fantastic Christmas trees.

Of course, the real botanical showpiece of Guatemala is the rainforest, which Guatemalans call *el monte*. Its thick green canopy hovers more than 100 feet up with solitary orchid- and bromeliad-covered guanacaste trees standing twice that height. The rainforest is magnificent in the diversity of its plant life. It contains more than 700 types of trees and 4000 known types of flowering plants. The diversity is so great that some plant species are found within only a single square mile of the rainforest and nowhere else on earth.

Most of the rainforest around Tikal is almost certainly less than a thousand years old. Using satellite mapping to reveal the outlines of ancient farmers' fields, archaeologists have determined that virtually all the land within a 62-mile radius of Tikal had been cleared for cultivation 1100 years ago. After the abandonment of the city began, around A.D. 900, it is difficult to estimate how long it took for the lofty ceiba, mahogany and sapodilla trees to take root among the ruins. The jungle existed in something like its present form when Spanish conquistador Hernán Cortés visited the region in 1525.

Among the common trees of the rainforest are the sapodilla, from which chicle comes. *Chicleros,* who earn money by collecting the sapodilla sap for sale to chewing gum manufacturers, climb these trees to a height of 50 feet or more and work their way down, using a machete to slash slanted grooves in the bark through which the chicle sap oozes down the trunk. Then there's the strangler fig tree, whose seeds germinate after the wind or birds drop them into the high branches of the forest canopy. The seed first dangles tendrils down to the ground a hundred feet below, where they take root. Slowly, inexorably, the tendrils grow into a light-colored trunk that wraps itself around the host tree, slowly cutting off its light, air, water and soil nutrients until after many years the older tree dies and the mature strangler fig stands independently. The innocuous-looking poisonwood tree poses a concealed hazard. The slightest skin contact with the black sap that oozes from the tree's bark and twigs raises painful, burning blisters that persist for two weeks. Fortunately, instant relief is found in the sap of the gumbo limbo, easily identified by its constantly

Text continued on page 62.

Tourism &
the Environment

Ecotourism means environmentally and culturally sensitive pleasure travel. It is based on the idea that protecting ecosystems and the traditions of indigenous cultures can go hand in hand with appropriate kinds of economic development, especially tourism. True ecotourism implies community involvement. Conservationist experience in Costa Rica and Belize over the past decade has shown that the keys to protecting rainforests, ancient ruins and endangered species are local people and tourist dollars. If local villagers learn to depend on visiting sightseers for a living, they no longer have an incentive to burn the forest for food or hunt jaguars and crocodiles for the price of their skins. They are less likely to loot pre-Columbian ruins if they can get paid to guide tourists there for picture taking instead.

Some environmentalists believe that ecotourism is a contradiction in terms. The best thing you can do for a threatened habitat, they say, is to stay home and leave it alone. But these environmentalists do not live in Guatemala, where industries far more destructive than tourism are lurking in wait for opportunities to destroy unprotected wilderness in the name of profit. Belize, just over the border from Guatemala's Petén province, has worked hard to develop ecotourism as the largest sector of its national economy; yet the country remains so poor that recently its government could not resist an offer equivalent to just US$7500 from an international timber company for the right to clear-cut 200,000 acres of virgin rainforest. Belizean conservationists finally blocked the project by showing (on paper, at least) that future ecotourism development in the area could generate more profits than timber leasing would.

In Guatemala, the government is alert to the powerful message nature-oriented travelers send by supporting the value of wilderness. International tourism is the country's largest single income source, and since no international resort developer has been eager to make a long-term investment in historically unstable Guatemala, tourism here generally means the kind of travelers who don't mind braving "pigs-and-chickens" buses, jungle huts or funky hotel rooms and generous doses of confusion for the chance to experience tropical forests, ancient ruins, native markets and friendly, traditional people.

To help visitors enjoy and contribute to the environment of Guatemala, the author and publishers of *Hidden Guatemala* have compiled a short environmental code of ethics:

1. **Do not disturb wildlife or natural habitats.** Stay on the trails, avoid using machetes or collecting plants or wildlife. Bird nests should be viewed from a safe distance with binoculars, and nesting sea turtles should be observed only with a trained guide. Do not feed monkeys or other wild animals: feeding by humans alters their diets and behaviors. Raccoons, which normally live alone, become pack animals when fed and spread diseases that kill them. The stomach fluids of deer that eat human food change so they can no longer digest leaves or other wild food sources, and they starve to death during the off-season.

2. **Do not litter.** If you'll be in remote areas, take along a sack to carry out your garbage. Just one food wrapper or aluminum can is all it takes to ruin a remote trail or little-known ruin for the next visitor. Many kinds of trash—plastic six-pack holders, for instance—can be deadly to wildlife.

3. **Be conscious of helping local communities.** Use the native tour guides—they are the best—and patronize locally owned lodges, restaurants and markets. Buy souvenirs from native craftspeople; Maya villagers make marvelous handicrafts.

4. **Be culturally sensitive.** Remember that you are a guest in the Maya world. Make an effort to learn basic customs and follow them. Try to communicate in Spanish whenever possible. Don't judge Guatemala by hometown standards. Respect local tradition and bear in mind that some gringo tourist habits may be offensive to village people.

peeling, copper-colored bark. Forest folk healers, who have included the gumbo limbo in their storehouses of forest remedies and miracle cures since time immemorial, point to the unexplained fact that poisonwood and gumbo limbo trees always seem to grow close to one another as proof that the forest contains a plant medicine to treat every illness or injury that may befall a human there.

Perhaps the most fascinating flora in Guatemala's rainforest are orchids. These flowering epiphytes, or air plants, grow on tree trunks and limbs, sometimes near the ground but more often in the top reaches of the forest canopy. As a class, orchids are unique in the plant kingdom because of the amazing diversity of species. Nearly a thousand orchid species have been identified in the Petén rainforest, but botanists claim that this may represent only 2 to 3 percent of the total species that exist. Orchids evolve into new forms so rapidly that a species may exist in the branches of a single giant tree and nowhere else on earth. The secret to orchids' diversity and fast evolution is that different types do not cross-breed because each orchid species is pollinated by a different insect that is attracted only to the flowers of that particular species. For a newly evolved orchid to develop into a sustained species, a unique new insect must evolve too. Rare and newly discovered orchids are of particular interest to scientists because each species contains different, complex chemical compounds that may provide models for the development of new, life-saving pharmaceutical drugs. Some researchers believe that the orchids of the rainforest canopy hold great promise for discovery of new medical treatments for cancer, AIDS and other diseases.

FAUNA   **MAMMALS**   Most wild mammals in the Guatemalan highlands are the same ones found in pine forest and small-farm areas of the United States. Raccoons, skunks, rabbits, squirrels, weasels, opossums and porcupines are among the woodland animals that have learned to adapt to encroaching cornfields by raiding crops or scavenging household garbage. Thanks to the winterless tropical climate and farmers' lack of means or desire to kill them, these forest creatures are much more common than in most woodland areas in the United States. The deep fern undergrowth of the cloud forest provides the domain for the *guatusa*, a midget species of deer, the coche de monte, or collared peccary, and the agouti.

The rainforest of the Petén supports the richest array of wildlife to be found anywhere on the North American continent. Mammals that live in the forest include several species of predatory cats—margays, jaguarundis, ocelots, cougars and jaguars. To the ancient Maya, the jaguar symbolized the forces of darkness and primeval nature. Jaguars were the first gods recorded in stone by Preclassic Maya sculptors. Known in Spanish as *tigre* and often translated as "tiger" by English-speaking guides, the endangered jaguar is now rare throughout its range, which once spanned from Argentina to Texas and the American Southwest. Jaguars are more abundant in the Petén rainforest than anyplace else on the continent—in fact, conservationists estimate that more jaguars inhabit Tikal National Park than all the rest of North America. Yet a visitor's chances of seeing one of these elusive nocturnal predators are just about zero. Cougars (called *pumas* in Guatemalan Spanish) are even rarer than jaguars. Other rare and elusive species in the Petén include anteaters, kinkajous and tapirs.

Most visitors to Tikal National Park and other protected areas can expect to see monkeys. The medium-sized monkeys commonly seen around Tikal are spider monkeys, easy to spot because of the rattling, crashing noises they make as they leap from branch to branch. You can also tell when they have been around by the debris of partially eaten fruit at the base of trees. Local guides usually have no trouble spotting monkeys because they frequent certain trees, particularly the sapodilla tree, whose sweet fruit smells and tastes like custard. Black howler monkeys were on the verge of extinction in the Petén just a few years ago following an epidemic of yellow fever that killed them by the millions. They have made a remarkable comeback, though, and are now common in Tikal National Park and other protected areas of the Petén. You're less likely to see them than spider monkeys, since they are small and mainly nocturnal, but if you spend a night at Tikal you'll almost surely hear them. Their "howl" is actually a deep, booming roar that sounds like a lion. Howlers often hang out in the trees near the campground *comedores*, where their vocalizations continue all night long. In southern lowland forests, and especially around the ruins of Copán where they are protected, you may see a much smaller species, the white-faced monkey.

The most common large animals in the rainforest are whitetailed deer, which are hunted by the local people of the Petén for meat to feed their families and sell to restaurants. Other mammals that are traditionally hunted, eaten, and served in restaurants in Flores and other Petén towns are armadillos and tepescuintles. The latter, known as a paca in English, is considered a great delicacy. Coatimundis may be seen in the underbrush toward dusk, as may white-lipped peccaries (called *jabalis*), a small piglike beast that forages around the roots of bushes. Visitors often catch glimpses of silver foxes, known to the locals as *"gatos de la selva"* ("forest cats") gliding through the ruins of Tikal.

The Petén rainforest is also home to more than 20 species of bats, including various kinds of fruit bats and insect-eating bats as well as the nightmarish, though fairly rare, vampire bat. They really do drink blood from both animals and people, so it can't hurt to keep windows closed, screened or shuttered after dark. A mosquito net also discourages them, or so I'm told.

BIRDS About 700 bird species, from tiny tropical hummingbirds to vultures and eagles, live in Guatemala at least part of the year. Several are among the world's rarest birds. The *pavón,* or horned guan, a turkey-sized black-and-white bird with a red hornlike cockade on its head, lives only on the slopes of Guatemalan volcanoes. The five-foot-tall jabiru stork, the largest flying bird in the Western Hemisphere, is sometimes seen in the spring around breeding areas in the wetlands of the Petén and the Pacific coast. The colorful keel-billed motmot is believed to be extinct everywhere except Guatemala, where sightings are extremely rare; its relative, the blue-crowned motmot, is often spotted by birdwatchers. Until recently, birders flocked to Lago de Atitlán in hopes of spotting the flightless Atitlán grebe, which lived solely among the reeds on the lake's shore. Sadly, these unique birds became extinct in the early 1990s as a result of the government's stocking the lake with bass, which ate infant grebes as they swam on the surface of the lake.

Another elusive and unmistakable endangered species is Guatemala's national symbol, the quetzal. Its image is everywhere—woven into the patterns of *típica* clothing, sculpted in bright-painted clay figurines, printed on tourist brochures and posters, incorporated into the national seal. The main unit of currency is called the quetzal. The highest honor the government can bestow is admission to the Order of the Quetzal. Reverence for this green and bright red bird with its long, flowing tail feathers is rooted deep in Maya tradition. Stelae at the ruins of Tikal, Quiriguá and Copán show noblemen or priests bedecked in huge headdresses of quetzal feathers, and it is the quetzal that provided the plumage for the Plumed Serpent, known in Guatemala as Gucumatz, whose legend spread throughout the ancient Maya and Toltec world. The quetzal was chosen as the national symbol because it cannot survive in captivity. To the Guatemalan people, its image means "Live free or die." Ironically, it is this same trait that may doom the quetzal to extinction, for it nests only in the trunks of wild avocado trees that grow in the cloud forest, an environment that is also, unfortunately, perfect for growing coffee beans. Guatemala's quetzal population is estimated at 40,000, but most of them live in the remote cloud forests of the Sierra de las Minas in Baja Verapaz, the Sierra de Santa Cruz in Izabal and the north slope of the Cordillera de los Cuchumatanes in Huehuetenango.

Another bird that is both colorful and endangered is the guacamaya, or scarlet macaw. Often seen gliding in pairs above the rainforest canopy in the Petén, the largest member of the parrot family is threatened by the shrinkage of its habitat and by poaching for the international pet bird market. The bird has been hunted since ancient times both for its feathers and because forest people consider its flesh a delicacy. The Petén is also home to eight species of parrots, parrokeets and loros, as well as to the colorful keel-billed toucan.

Also unique to the Guatemalan rainforest is the Petén turkey, which is commonly seen roaming around the campground and lodging areas of Tikal National Park. It looks much like a peacock and has a warty golden crown. And keep an eye out for such other exotic rainforest birds as the keel-billed toucan, the *loro*, or green parrot, and the *oropéndola*, a kind of tropical oriole that colonizes giant trees with hundreds of hanging nests.

Birding enthusiasts visiting Guatemalan forests—or even driving along backcountry roads—can expect to see raptors (hawks, falcons and eagles), including the azacuán, or Swainson's hawk, which was revered by the ancient Maya because its northward migration coincided with the start of the rainy season, giving rise to the legend that it was a messenger to the rain god. After dark, large owls called *búhos* glide among the trees in search of prey.

REPTILES AND AMPHIBIANS In the backcountry after dark, anywhere there is even a single puddle of standing water nearby, you'll probably encounter huge toads, often reaching a foot in length. Stagnant ponds swarming with insects harbor bullfrogs of similarly impressive size. Both the toads and the bullfrogs are harmless to humans. The most unusual amphibians in the region are the various species of small tree frogs that inhabit the Petén rainforest, including the red-eyed tree frog, whose bright-colored eyes stand out in contrast to its white-and-blue skin, and the glass frog, whose underbelly is so transparent that you can see its internal organs through the skin.

Sea turtles climb out of the water to lay their eggs in the beach sand along both coasts of Guatemala. Green ridley, hawksbill and loggerhead turtles nest on the pristine, remote beaches of the Caribbean coast. Both loggerheads and green ridleys can reach 300 pounds in weight. Olive ridley and leatherback sea turtles nest on Pacific beaches. The leatherback, the largest of the seagoing reptiles, can reach 1200 pounds and more than 6 feet in length— a truly awesome sight. Unfortunately, leatherbacks have become so rare that only a dozen times a year is one spotted on the Guatemalan coast, and some scientists believe that they are already "technically extinct"—that is, so few in number that the gene pool is no longer large enough to sustain future generations.

Around Lago Petén Itzá and other large bodies of water in the hot lowlands, a type of small crocodile called a cayman is common, as is its larger cousin, the Morelet's crocodile. Other common species of large reptiles include iguanas, which are caught and cooked as a meat delicacy in ladino regions of the country, and basilisk lizards, which run on their hind legs like miniature dinosaurs.

Okay, there *are* snakes in Guatemala. Boa constrictors, for instance. You never realize how big a snake can look until you unexpectedly see one of these rainforest dwellers in the wild, but they are benign. The most feared snake is much smaller: the fer-de-lance, the deadliest snake in Central America and one of the most common. This pit viper prefers to use its long, spiked, poisonous fangs on mice, its favorite food, and to avoid humans, which it knows it cannot eat. Unfortunately, mouse-hunting draws the snake to places like barns, wells and storehouses, where humans are likely to take it by surprise, so people worry more about them than about rattlesnakes or coral snakes.

The good news is that the great majority of snakes are neither aggressive nor poisonous. To be on the safe side, when walking in natural areas, try to step heavily and make noise, warning snakes that you are coming so they can leave quietly, and do not put a hand or foot where you can't see it. If you see a snake, retreat as quietly as possible. If someone in your party is bitten by a snake, it's important to capture or kill the snake immediately if you can, to let a doctor determine whether it is poisonous and, if so, what antivenin is appropriate. Quickly take the victim and the snake to the nearest town and find the local doctor or *farmacia*. Along the way, you may have a chance to ask someone whether the snake is poisonous *(venenoso)*. Most venomous snakes in Guatemala are rear-fanged, and although they are as likely as their deadly cousins to bite a human, their venom is specific to small animals and reptiles and is not harmful to humans. Only front-fanged snakes are dangerous to hikers, and antivenin is the only cure. *Do not* slice the wound open and suck it. *Do not* give the victim alcohol. Just head for the nearest outpost of civilization as fast as possible.

INSECTS No survey of tropical life systems would be complete without at least a brief acknowledgment of the insect kingdom. Bugs abound in coastal and jungle areas, and no trip should be without chiggers, sand fleas, mosquitoes, scorpions or even, perhaps, one of the gigantic tarantulas that frequent both rainforest and banana plantations. Before you cancel your trip, however, remind yourself that most insect species are not only benign, they're also fascinating—especially in rainforest areas, where watching bugs can be more fun than TV. There are bugs that disguise themselves as vegetation and others that are gaudy in their brilliant hues and elaborate markings.

Ants—particularly leaf cutter ants, which can strip a bush of virtually all its leaves in a matter of a few hours and transport the vegetation a fragment at a time along a line that can stretch unbroken along the jungle floor for miles—can be interesting to watch, especially when you realize that an ant colony functions as a single mind, capable of transmitting remarkably complex messages rapidly by leaving trails of scent chemicals called pheromones.

One of the most spectacular phenomena in the Petén rainforest is an invasion of army ants. These carnivorous insects travel in vast hordes that can cover up to one square mile of ground. Villagers in some parts of the Petén expect the ants to come through their communities about once a year. When that happens, the villagers must vacate their homes, taking their household pets and livestock with them, until the ants have passed. The silver lining is that the army ants effectively exterminate any snakes, frogs, insects and other pests in and around the village.

Bees are also abundant throughout Guatemala. Honey has been a staple food of the Maya since ancient times, and beekeeping is an important industry in the highlands today. African "killer" bees have colonized lowland areas in large numbers. Chapter Four includes mosquito-repellent hints. Regarding scorpions and tarantulas, just remember to shake your shoes out before you put them on in the morning.

▼▼▼▼▼▼▼▼▼▼
How to Help

ECO-TOURISM TOURS

Guatemala has an abundance of tour outfitters who specialize in environmentally oriented expeditions. Guides and outfitters who operate in national parks and other protected areas are licensed by the government, controlling competition and limiting most guide services to one or two areas. Other tour companies, as well as travel agencies, may sell space on the same tour—not always at the same price. It pays to shop around.

Guatemalan outfitters will routinely cancel a tour if fewer than a minimum number of people (normally four) show up. Booking a Maya-ruins-and-caves trip into the Petén rainforest before you buy your plane tickets, and putting down a cash deposit before you leave home, is probably a wise move if you're traveling during the January-through-Easter tourist season. At any other time of year, the risk of a trip being canceled is far greater than the risk that it will be sold out. The most reliable plan is to request information in advance, then sign up at the last minute. Another option is to sign up with a U.S.-based company that furnishes complete arrangements including lodging, meals and equipment. Here are a few of the best companies, both Guatemalan and North American, specializing in ecotourism expeditions:

Maya Expeditions, 15 Calle No. 1-91, Zona 10, Guatemala City; 3-634-955, fax 3-374-965; e-mail mayaexp@guate.net

MesoAmerica Explorers, 7 Avenida No. 13-01, Zona 9, Guatemala City; phone/fax 2-325-045

Panorama Guatemala Cultural, 5 Avenida No. 8-57, Zona 9, Guatemala City; 2-314-174

Izabal Adventure Tours, 7 Avenida No. 14-4, Zona 9, Guatemala City; 2-340-323, fax 2-340-341

Servicios Turísticos del Petén, 2 Avenida No. 7-78, Zona 10, Guatemala City; 3-346-235, fax 3-346-237.

Tropical Tours, 4 Calle No. 2-51, Zona 10, Guatemala City; 3-323-3748, fax 2-323-748

Guayacán Eco-tours and Adventure, 11 Calle No. 3049, Zona 1, Oficina 8, Guatemala City; 2-515-489, fax 2-510-981

Adventure Travel Center Viareal, 4 Calle Oriente No. 14, Antigua, Sacatepéquez; phone/fax 8-320-162; e-mail viareal@guate.net

Amerispan Guatemala, 6 Avenida Norte No. 40, Antigua, Sacatepéquez; 8-320-164; www.amerispan.com/guatemala, e-mail amerispan@guate.net

Archaeology Ecotours, 6 Avenida Norte & 3 Calle Poniente, Antigua, Sacatepéquez; phone/fax 8-324-879; e-mail jebar99@emailgua.com

Epiphyte Adventures, Apdo. Postal 94-A, Cobán, Alta Verapaz; phone/fax 9-512-169

Far Horizons Archaeological & Cultural Trips, P.O. Box 91900, Albuquerque, NM 87119-1900; 505-343-9400, 800-552-4575, fax 505-343-8706

Guatemala Travel Representatives, 720 Worthshire Street, Houston, TX 77008; 713-688-1985, 800-451-8017, fax 713-869-2540

Exito Latin American Travel Specialists, 5699 Miles Avenue, Oakland, CA 94618; 510-655-2154, 800-655-4053, fax 510-655-4566; e-mail exito@wonderlink.com

ENVIRON-MENTAL PROGRAMS   For information on conservation and environmental programs and opportunities to participate in developing ecotourism enterprises in Guatemala, contact these organizations:

Fundación Defensores de la Naturaleza, Avenida las Americas 20-21, Zona 14, Guatemala City; 23-373-897; e-mail defensores@pronet.net.gt

Consejo Nacional de Areas Protegidas (CONAP), Calle 6-28, Zona 1, Guatemala City; 2-500454.

Centro de Estudios Conservacionistas, University of San Carlos, Avenida de la Reforma No. 0-63, Zona 10, Guatemala City; 2-028-531

Proyecto Ecológico Quetzal, 2 Calle 14-36, Cobán; 9-521-047; e-mail bidaspeq@guate.net

United Council of the Protected Areas of the Petén (UNEPET), 8 Avenida 2-92, Zona 3, Flores, Petén; 9-500-196, fax 9-500-197

Proyecto Petenero para un Bosque Sostenible (PROPETEN), Flores, Petén; 2-501-370.

Conservation International/Eco-Escuela, 1015 18th Street NW, Suite 1000, Washington DC 20036; 202-973-2264, fax 202-887-5188; www.conservation.org/ecoescuela

A number of international environmental organizations are also involved in conservation efforts within Guatemala. Among them are **Greenpeace International,** the **Nature Conservancy,** the **World Wildlife Fund,** the **Audubon Society, Lighthawk** and the **Rainforest Alliance,** as well as the German **Green Party.**

In the Guatemalan countryside, "outdoors" is a relative concept. Most people cook, eat, bathe and sometimes sleep outside and travel on foot

Outdoor Adventures

along country lanes and forest trails. If you like to do these things too, needless to say, you've come to the right place.

Whether it's a misty early morning jog through the rainforest from your hotel room door or a four-day trek from the nearest village to an ancient Maya city along rubber-tappers' trails, a backcountry route people have walked for millennia can take you deep into a primeval landscape. A journey along footpaths between highland Maya villages lets you see traditional peasant life without motor vehicles or electricity. Other trails lead to legendary birdwatching spots or to the craters of fuming volcanoes.

If your idea of outdoor recreation involves renting expensive equipment, you've come to the *wrong* place. There is probably not a single jet ski all-terrain vehicle for rent in the whole country. There's yet no place where you can ride a chairlift to the top of a volcano, though bungee jumping has been coming into its own recently. If you ask about where to find such popular gringo pastimes as tennis and golf, anyone except the concierge of a major Guatemala City hotel will respond with dumbfounded disbelief.

But if you're content to forfeit all the bells and whistles of resort tourism in exchange for the pleasures of walking softly through an exotic land where nature is always close enough to reach out and touch, Guatemala is the place you've been looking for.

By no means the organized activity that it is up north, camping in Guatemala takes place mainly in a handful of national parks and nature reserves, plus a few archaeological sites. Campgrounds in national parks such as Tikal are operated by concessionaires and charge small nightly fees.

CAMPING

Many campers in lowland parks eschew tents and sleeping bags in favor of hammocks and mosquito nets, and some campgrounds offer *palapas,* thatch-roofed open-air structures under which to sling your hammock. This hot-weather mode of camping doesn't offer much privacy, but the necessary gear is lightweight and very compact. Insects are likely to share your campsite. Bug spray, mosquito nets and insect coils can help make camping more enjoyable. Locals burn coconut husks to smoke out bugs.

Hammock camping is a bad idea in the highlands, where a sleeping bag helps ward off the night chill.

FISHING

The Pacific coast boasts the world's best deep-sea fishing for sailfish. Marlin and sawfish are also plentiful. Giant tuna and *dorado* (dolphinfish or mahimahi) are the top catch for eating. *Sierra* (mackerel) are a common catch. Sportfishing charters on yachts and *pangas* are available in Iztapa and Likín. Deep-sea fishing trips can be arranged in advance through **Guatemala Offshore Fishing**, located in Guatemala City's only fishing tackle shop, **Kurican**. ~ 5 Avenida No. 11-63, Zona 9, Guatemala City; 2-317-222. There's bass fishing in Lago de Atitlán; considering the quantities of sewage and insecticides that pour into the lake, I wouldn't recommend eating a fish caught there, even though restaurants serve them and the local people depend on them as their main source of protein.

BIRD-WATCHING

Major destinations for birders include Tikal National Park, Laguna Lachua National Park and the Mario Dary Quetzal Reserve in Alta Verapaz, Río Dulce National Park in the eastern part of the country and the Monterrico-Hawaii Biotope in the south along the Pacific coast.

A number of Guatemalan tour operators organize special bird-watching trips. Among them are **Aventuras sin Limites** (11 Avenida No. 9-30, Zona 1, Guatemala City; 2-228-452, fax 2-947-293), **Expedición Panamundo** (6 Avenida No. 14-75, Zona 9, Guatemala City; 2-317-621, fax 2-317-565) and **Izabal Adventure Tours** (7 Avenida No. 14-4, Zona 9, Guatemala City; 2-340-323, fax 2-340-341).

SWIMMING

Along the south coast of Guatemala, the Pacific Ocean stretches ink-blue to the horizon. Add to this the many lakes found in Guatemala (many of which, sadly, are now polluted by untreated sewage) and you have a number of possibilities for taking a dip.

Nude sunbathing is against the law in Guatemala. Travelers get away with it on deserted beaches, where no one can be offended, but remember that Catholic traditions reign in Latin America and ladino and Indian families find flagrant nudity disrespectful. Be discreet and cautious.

RIDING STABLES

Horse trips are a popular activity in some parts of Guatemala, especially in mountain areas. You will find few resorts with riding stables in these areas, but a number of expedition outfitter, small

Guatemala's
Natural
Treasures

Guatemala has more than 20 national parks and nature reserves. Many of the latter are designated as *"reservas biósferas"* in accordance with the regulations of UNESCO's International Man and the Biosphere Program. Others are *"biotopos"* that focus on habitat protection for endangered species.

Some Guatemalan national parks rank among the world's great destinations. Tikal National Park, for instance, presents the ruins of the greatest known ancient Maya city surrounded by a vast expanse of rainforest wilderness. Atitlán National Park encompasses the deepest lake in North America and the volcanoes and Indian villages that surround it. When it comes to magnificence, Yellowstone and the Grand Canyon have nothing on these places.

At the other extreme, some Guatemalan national parks and reserves, such as Cerro Bisís Natural Reserve in the rugged mountains north of Chajul or the Machaquilá Reserve several days downriver from Poptún, have remained pristine because they are nearly impossible to get to. In this book I have included material only on areas that are accessible to independent travelers, sometimes with the help of a local guide.

In addition to national parks and reserves, Guatemalan conservation laws protect the slopes of most of the country's major volcanoes and the immediate area surrounding most archaeological sites.

For official information on archaeological sites, contact the **Instituto Guatemalteco de Antropología e Historia**. ~ 12 Avenida No. 11-65, Zona 1, Guatemala City; 2-531-570. National parks, reserves and other protected natural areas are administered by the **Consejo Nacional de Areas Protegidas (CONAP)**. ~ 2 Avenida No. 0-69, Zona 3, Guatemala City; 2-322-671.

stables and freelance guides are eager to guide visitors into the backcountry on horseback. To find out about them, inquire at the nearest INGUAT (tourist information) office or a local travel agency or check tourist-oriented bulletin boards.

SPELUNK-ING   There are hundreds of caves in Guatemala, many of them virtually unexplored. Visitors with candles or flashlights can see Lanquín Cave in Alta Verapaz on their own, while a guide is necessary for a raft trip (see below) into the larger Candelaria Cave. Electric lighting is provided at the cave called Actun Kan near Flores in the Petén. Farther to the east, near the village of Poptún, guides can be arranged at **Finca Ixobel** to visit various nearby caves, possibly including Naj Tunich, a partially flooded cave in which the walls were elaborately decorated by Maya priests who revered the cave as an entrance to the underworld and held ceremonies there in the 8th century A.D. (Public trips to Naj Tunich are infrequent to minimize wear or damage to the artwork in the cave.)

BIKING   Long-distance road tours of Guatemala and neighboring Belize are organized by **Paradise Bicycle Tours**. ~ P.O. Box 1726, Evergreen, CO 80439; 800-626-8271.

THREE

History and Culture

In the long, slow pageant of Guatemala's history lie ancient glory, profound tragedy and newborn promise. Millennia ago, during the time when Europe witnessed the decline and fall of the Roman Empire and the feudal oppression of the Dark Ages, the ideas emanating from great forest cities such as Tikal distinguished the Maya as the most sophisticated civilization ever known in pre-Columbian America. Then, inexplicably, it collapsed.

Six hundred years later, Spanish conquistadores came to Guatemala to build one of the most elegant capital cities in the Western world and a network of grandiose mission churches that sought to connect the descendants of the ancient Maya with the spiritual traditions of Europe. After three centuries, the Spanish empire collapsed for equally puzzling reasons having to do with political machinations an ocean away.

THE PRECLASSIC MAYA (2000 B.C.–A.D. 250)   Traditional Maya people believe that their first ancestors were made from corn, explaining why they eat little else. Modern-day ethnologists say this creation myth is probably accurate on a symbolic level. The ethnologists believe early inhabitants of Guatemala and neighboring areas were the first people to cultivate corn. Their development of agriculture would revolutionize the civilizations of tribal people throughout North America who traded a nomadic existence for permanent farms and towns.

HISTORY

The supernatural creators of the first Maya worried that their new corn-beings might become too powerful to hold the gods in awe, so they gave humankind a handicap—"shortness of sight." In other words, humans were allowed to see what was happening nearby at the moment but not what took place in faraway parts of the world or distant times. That's the problem experts face in understanding the Preclassic Maya. Few clues remain to help us see across the huge interim of time between their era and our own.

Most archaeologists believe that the Preclassic Maya lived in villages of oval, thatch-roofed huts not much different from those in which the northern Maya people of the Yucatán still live in today. The villages were set around central plazas with thatch-roofed temples elevated on low dirt mounds. Not many remains of such villages have been found, however; over the centuries, some grew into cities with much larger stone-faced pyramids built over the original low temple mounds, while others were abandoned to decay rapidly and became overgrown with tropical forest, leaving no stonework to mark their former sites. Most of what archaeologists have learned about Preclassic times has come from studying smaller artifacts such as pottery, bone and obsidian tools and clay effigies. In many areas of Guatemala, from the Petén rainforest to the highlands of El Quiché, scientists have unearthed such artifacts dating back at least as far as 1500 B.C.

On the whole, it appears that the Preclassic Maya enjoyed a simple, comfortable, tropical way of life. They reaped the bounties of forests rich with fruit and game, played games and slept in hammocks. They worshiped the god who brought rain. They grew corn, runner beans and tomatoes, as well as cocoa beans, which would come to be accepted as money throughout Mexico and Central America. The early Maya spoke a single language from which all modern Maya languages derive.

Kaminaljuyú, located in what is now the western outskirts of Guatemala City, may have been one of the largest and wealthiest Preclassic Maya communities in Guatemala. Although from ongoing excavations it appears so far that any evidence of early inhabitants there has been obscured by later occupation, Preclassic artifacts carved from jade traced to the mines at Kaminaljuyú are found throughout the Maya world. Jade was the most precious of treasures to the ancient Maya people, who believed that it possessed the power to stop pain and prevent or heal injuries.

The first seeds of cultural sophistication are thought to have come from the neighboring Olmec, a civilization that appeared in the region of Veracruz, Mexico, around 1200 B.C. and lasted until 400 B.C. No Olmec burial remains have ever been found, and their dwellings were swallowed up by swamplands millennia ago. All that is known about the Olmec people comes from their art, which includes giant stone heads, round clay pyramids, sculptures, altars and finely carved jade jewelry. The jaguar god, later revered by the Maya as the symbol of earth and night, first appeared in Olmec art. The Olmecs developed a crude form of writing and the foundation of the calendar system later used by the Maya and other Mexican cultures.

The exact connection between the Olmec and the Maya is not known. Some experts believe that both the Maya and the Toltec of central Mexico were direct descendants of the Olmec, while others think the Olmec and Maya cultures exchanged knowledge and perhaps blended together during Preclassic times. The discovery of giant Olmec-style stone heads at La Democracia in southwestern Guatemala has led some scientists to speculate that the two cultures may have merged in this Pacific lowland area. Recently, however, laboratory testing has shown the stone heads at La Democracia to be around 4000 years old—older than either the Olmec or Maya cultures—leading some to hypothesize that Olmec and Maya alike may have descended from common ancestors. The Polynesian appearance of the features on Olmec and La Democracia stone heads has even spurred speculation that these forgotten ancestors may have arrived from across the Pacific Ocean by boat.

The Preclassic Period ended around A.D. 250 as the Classic Maya civilization blossomed throughout the region—a development that archaeologists refer to as the Maya Fluorescence. The conventional belief is that it happened suddenly, seemingly out of nowhere, around the time of the Roman Empire's decline. Yet it is equally possible that the scientific and cultural achievements of the Classic Period had been evolving for millennia before artists began recording them for posterity. Maya priests may have written glyphs in the dirt for a thousand years before carving them on stone monuments. Astronomers may have grounded their calculations in natural landmarks long before elaborate observatories were built in accordance with cosmic alignments. Because so few artifacts remain from that distant time, modern scholars will never know for sure.

Many theories have attempted to explain why the Maya civilization blossomed from a seemingly unremarkable farming culture into the glory and splendor of the Classic Period. Early theorists speculated that Maya civilization sprang into existence as the result of contact with ancient Egyptians, Phoenicians, Cambodians or even the people of lost Atlantis. More recent theorists point to puzzling details in ancient Maya sculptures as evidence that travelers from outer space visited earth long ago.

The Church of Jesus Christ of Latter Day Saints, founded in 1830 at about the same time ancient Maya civilization was being "discovered," believed that the Maya were members of the lost tribes of Israel who had learned to build pyramids in the time of the Egyptian pharaohs; their life in the New World is the subject of the Book of Mormon.

None of these theories have been proven false, really. All share a common, unspoken premise that "mere Indians" could only have achieved such feats of architecture, astronomy and art with outside help. The truth may be even more amazing: perhaps a single insight of genius on the part of an Indian whose identity remains unknown inspired a burst of creative energy that spread throughout a region larger than modern Italy to shape human accomplishment over a span of nearly seven centuries.

Exactly what revolutionized the Maya world, neither descendants of the ancient Maya nor archaeologists who study the question know for sure. The catalyst may have been a fundamentally new way of understanding time. It may have come from the invention of the Maya "long count" calendar, which enabled priests to conceive of enormously large time spans and make predictions thousands of years into the future. This new perspective may have made permanence more important, inspiring the creation of art and architecture designed to last into the distant future.

THE CLASSIC MAYA (A.D. 250–900)   The Classic Period lasted much longer than the time that elapsed between Columbus' first landing in the New World and the end of the 20th century. Something mysterious ushered in this golden age of massive, ornate, brightly painted architecture, exquisite works of art, astounding advances in mathematics and astronomy, and the most sophisticated system of writing ever devised in the Western Hemisphere. The Classic Period dawned with the first hieroglyphic dates carved on Maya stelae, or carved stone monuments, and ended six-and-a-half centuries later with the last dates carved before stone sculpture halted so abruptly that artists at Tikal walked away leaving the last monuments unfinished.

The northern lowlands known as the Petén formed the center of the Classic Maya world. The awesome architecture of Tikal was mirrored in other great cities of the rainforest—Uaxactún, El Ceibal, Yaxchilán and particularly El Mirador, a hard-to-reach site in extreme northern Guatemala that has the largest pyramids ever built by the Maya. Artistic magnificence spread through the Maya world like a flower unfolding, to Palenque (Chiapas, Mexico) in the west, Cobá (Quintana Roo, Mexico) in the east, Uxmal (Yucatán, Mexico) in the north and Copán (Honduras) in the south. All these and many other Maya centers were abandoned within a span of a few years between A.D. 800 and 900.

By the beginning of the Classic Period, dialects of the original Maya tongue had evolved into as many as 11 different languages, and communication had become more difficult between the lowland people of the Yucatán and the highland people of Chiapas and Guatemala. Written language was the same throughout both regions. It consisted of about 1500 hieroglyphic elements, most representing spoken syllables. The writing may have developed in Preclassic times as a means to hurdle language barriers. It was widely used in the Classic era in stone inscriptions on stelae, columns, altars, doorways, stairways and walls. Archaeologists do not know whether peasant farmers could understand the stelae inscriptions or whether reading and writing were the exclusive province of the ruling elite.

According to scholars who analyze pre-Columbian thought processes, the worldview of the Maya was so different from that of traditional Western civilizations that any parallels drawn between their culture and those of ancient Egypt, Greece, Rome or medieval Europe are likely to be misleading. At the beginning of the 20th century, H. G. Wells wrote in his masterwork, *The Outline of History:* "It is as if the Maya mind had developed along a different line from that followed by the Old-World mind, had acquired a different twist to its ideas, was not, indeed, by Old-World standards a strictly rational mind at all. . . ."

Recent investigations into Maya thought, based on expanded understandings of Maya hieroglyphs, archaeoastronomy and symbolism, reveal that, far from suffering from the crippling mental aberration Wells had imagined, Maya priests subscribed to a philosophy that people of European descent find hard to comprehend. The concept of duality—true vs. false, form vs. substance, mind vs. body—was foreign to Maya thought. Time and space formed a unified whole. Science and religion were one and the same. Earthly accomplishments mirrored cosmic purposes. The individual merged with the infinite.

It's no wonder that modern travelers experience a sense of awe upon visiting a ruin from the Classic Period. The more we learn about the ancient Maya, the more we realize that theirs was a world of surpassing strangeness. We ponder lesser riddles—how they achieved such flawless and intricate stone carvings without metal tools; why some ball courts were much larger than others; how they derived astronomical formulas unknown to Western science until the 20th century; whether or not they practiced human sacrifice. Yet what we feel while confronting artifacts left behind from a culture that evolved in directions alien to our own poses the fundamental mystery.

The Maya of the Classic Period were ruled by lords who claimed authority through legendary god-king ancestors. The throne was passed down from father to son. Each region had its lord, and most royal families lived in palaces flanked by temples at the center of the city. The lord employed priests, scientists, artists and warriors to govern the common people, most of whom lived in huts scattered across a broad agricultural zone on the outskirts of the city. Alliances between cities were apparently formed through marriage. In Copán, for example, hieroglyphs commemorate marriages of the city's rulers with daughters of the royal dynasties of Palenque and Uxmal.

Many Maya rulers attained great wealth and flaunted it. They ate meals smothered in chocolate sauces made from cocoa beans, which served as money among the common people. Their jewelry and masks were fashioned from jade, the most precious commodity of the Maya world. They wore headdresses graced with another nearly priceless material, quetzal plumes.

There were rigid class divisions. The nobility flattened the skulls of their children at birth to distinguish them from the masses. Some experts suggest that this practice may have altered not only their appearance, but the functioning of their brains as well. Knowledge was probably passed along in teacher-student relationships, but whether peasants could gain enough education to join the ruling class is unknown.

Most of the major ceremonial sites had been occupied for hundreds of years before the reigning lords of the Classic Period transformed them into elaborate urban centers. In many cities, a single lord supervised the construction of the great plazas and pyramids we see today—and in the process the destruction of the older, smaller temples that were buried beneath them. Building these centers meant quarrying stone blocks that weighed as much as 65 tons, transporting them despite the lack of wheels and beasts of burden, and hauling huge volumes of earth to fill the pyramids. One can only wonder if these astounding feats were accomplished by conscripted labor, like the pyramids of Egypt, or through religious devotion, like the Gothic cathedrals of France.

The Classic Maya civilization, from beginning to end, was set in stone, the most permanent of nature's building materials. As a result, bas-relief sculptures, hieroglyphic inscriptions and astronomical alignments detailing this cultural epoch have survived more than a thousand years of weathering and jungle overgrowth. Much of the long-forgotten stonework of the Maya has been discovered; much more has yet to be found.

THE POSTCLASSIC MAYA (A.D. 900–1523)   Just as no one knows what triggered the flowering of Maya civilization, nobody knows what caused it to collapse. In fact, scientists know less about the centuries that followed the carving in stone of the final hieroglyph than they do about the years that went before. Most speculate that the Classic Period ended at once throughout the Maya world with the abandonment of the great ceremonial centers, giving rise to the perception that ancient Maya civilization collapsed because of some universal flaw or cataclysmic event such as war, disease, famine or environmental disaster. A current theory, supported by new discoveries at El Mirador in northern Guatemala, is that widespread deforestation led to soil erosion until the land could not grow enough crops to feed the population. Whatever the reason, virtually all great Maya cities of the Classic era south of the Yucatán were abandoned one after another, beginning with Copán around A.D. 800 and continuing through Tikal around A.D. 900.

With the collapse of the Classic Maya civilization came large-scale migrations to the Guatemalan highlands from the Petén and Toltec-influenced Maya areas that are now the Mexican states of Tabasco and Campeche. The migrations brought the technology of the lowland Maya to the less sophisticated people who had traditionally lived in the highlands. New ceremonial centers were built in defensive positions on mesatops throughout the highlands, including the Cakchiquel capital Iximché, the Pokomam capital Mixco Viejo, the Mam capital Zaculeu and the Quiché capital K'umarcaaj. The ruins of each of these Postclassic highland sites can still be visited today.

After the last inscription was carved on a stone monument, Maya priests began writing in books, a new technological development that allowed for the recording in portable form of much more voluminous and detailed information. Nearly all of these books were destroyed after the Spanish arrived. Of the four original examples that have been found, at least three are from the Yucatán; the fourth may have come from there or from Tayasil, the site of modern-day Flores, in the Guatemalan Petén. Not a single highland Maya book is known to exist. Soon after the Spanish conquest, however, as Catholic missionaries began teaching selected Indian students to read and write, at least two ancient books were secretly translated from hieroglyphs to Maya languages written in the Roman alphabet. The *Annals of the Cakchiquels*, an account of the lineage of the lords of Totonicapán, consists of dry historical facts that paint a picture of constant conflict between the warlords of highland Maya territories throughout the Postclassic era.

The *Popol Vuh*, a comprehensive history and mythology of the Quiché Maya, has come to be recognized as the greatest of the Maya books that have survived to modern times. Equal in scope to the Old Testament of the Bible, the *Popol Vuh* describes how the world was created. It tells how the human race was made from corn after abortive experiments at making people out of other substances. The book goes on to tell of the creation of the sun and the moon, the origins of sacrificial rites, and the history and genealogy of Quiché rulers beginning with their departure from the Toltec city of Tula (which many scholars today believe is myth, not historical fact) and continuing through the arrival of the Spanish conquistadores a thousand years later. The *Popol Vuh* was written, probably by more than one anonymous Quiché scribe, 30 years after the defeat of Tecún Umán—that is, in 1554. The new Roman alphabet edition was kept hidden until almost 150 years later, when a Quiché shaman showed it to a Spanish missionary who, fortunately, chose not to destroy it as other clergymen had done with previous Maya books, but rather to copy it to use as an appendix to his own book. The myths and history contained in the *Popol Vuh* are still passed on in writing and through oral tradition to form the basis for Quiché Maya spiritual beliefs today. As for the book itself, it is in print today in 41 languages.

THE SPANISH CONQUEST (1524–1541) Just three years after Cortés conquered the Aztecs in central Mexico and assumed control over the colony of New Spain, he sent conquistador Pedro de Alvarado to take control of the southern highlands known as Guatemala, which included the area that is now the Mexican state of Chiapas, as well as the southern territory including present-day Honduras, El Salvador and Nicaragua. (Alvarado would never set foot in the southern part of his legal realm.) Alvarado arrived in Guatemala in December of 1523 with a force of 420 Spanish soldiers and 200 Mexican Indian warriors. At the time, the region was ruled by Quiché warlords under the leadership of Tecún Umán, whose court was in the city of K'umarcaaj. (Today the ruins of this ancient capital near Santa Cruz del Quiche are also known as Utatlán.) The Quiché empire extended from Chichicastenango all the way to Xelajú (now called Quetzaltenango).

Alvarado's arrival was no surprise to Tecún Umán, who had been receiving reports for months of the Spaniards and their conquest of Mexico. Tecún Umán had assembled a huge army made up of 30,000 warriors from most of the highland Maya city-states except for the Quiché's enemies, the Cakchiquel. Tecún Umán's army met the Spaniards on a battlefield near Xelajú on February 20, 1524. Incredibly, even though outnumbered 70 to 1, the Spanish force fought the Maya army to a standoff, whereupon Tecún Umán challenged Alvarado to resolve the battle by single combat. Alvarado killed Tecún Umán and, in that moment, assumed control over the largest of the highland Maya empires.

During 1524, the Spanish army burned the city of K'umarcaaj. Then Alvarado turned against the Cakchiquel and seized their short-lived new capital at Iximché and established his first capital, which he called Santiago de los Caballeros de Guatemala, at nearby Tecpán. Alvarado reigned there for only three years before a Cakchiquel uprising forced him to withdraw to a safer location as he waged a six-year campaign to subdue the Cakchiquel rebels. In 1525, Pedro de Alvarez seized the Pokomam capital at Mixco Viejo by treachery, while Gonzalo de Alvarado, Pedro's brother, laid siege to the Mam capital at Zaculeu and finally captured it, placing the entire highlands in the hands of the Alvarado brothers within 18 months after they first arrived in the region.

Alvarado established his second capital, which he again named Santiago de los Caballeros de Guatemala, at the foot of Volcán de Agua. He ruled from that city until his death 14 years later, in 1541. Upon his death, his widow, Doña Beatriz, declared herself Guatemala's new Captain-General and, as her first official act, ordered that the entire cathedral be painted black in mourning for Alvarado. Legend holds that this command offended God and doomed the city. The reign of Doña Beatriz ended two days later, when an earthquake struck, bursting a natural dam that contained a lake in the crater of Volcán de Agua. Water and mud surged down the volcano's steep slope and washed away the capital city, drowning Guatemala's first woman ruler. The site is now called Ciudad Vieja ("old city").

A third Santiago de los Caballeros de Guatemala was built at a more discreet distance from the volcanoes. Known today as Antigua Guatemala, it stood as the greatest city in Central America for more than two centuries.

SPANISH COLONIALISM (1542–1821)   In the history of Latin America as in the United States, nothing much seems to have happened between the founding of a colony and its independence centuries later. Prospectors combed the mountains for small, isolated deposits of metals from copper to gold, but no great wealth was ever found. The Guatemalan economy depended on exporting cotton, chocolate and tobacco to Spain. Guatemala remained a provincial colony in the rugged backcountry of the Spanish empire.

The Maya people struggled to live at the bottom of the social heap. During Pedro de Alvarado's reign, the conquistador failed in repeated attempts to pacify the Rabinal and Kekchi people of the central mountains that are now Baja Verapaz and Alta Verapaz. Alvarado ultimately accepted the bargain offered by Fray Bartolomé de las Casas, a former owner of Indian slaves who had experienced a spiritual enlightenment and devoted his life to missionary work, for which he was the first man to be granted the official title Protector of the Indians. Las Casas agreed to bring peace to the central mountains on condition that the government treat the Indians as human beings possessing fundamental human rights. This was a hard idea for the military and slave owners to accept; they were better served by the prevailing view of Indians as wild animals. Las Casas converted the Maya to Catholicism by the simple expedient of allowing them to worship their old gods as long as they also participated in the forms of worship of the church. Catholicism swept the Maya highlands as fast as missionaries could build churches—more than 700 of them in all—while older Maya ceremonies were also practiced openly and sometimes blended with Catholicism in strange ways. Las Casas was eventually sent back to Spain to stand trial for his pro-Indian attitude. The court found in his favor and authorized his return to the New World to continue his work among the Maya as Bishop of Chiapas.

Tensions built up between Spaniards and *creolos*, people of Spanish blood born in the colonies, because the kings of Spain invariably sent Spanish nobles to fill important jobs instead of promoting Guatemalans to positions of power. The *creolos* eventually became a leftist opposition party that spoke out against the triumvirate of the Catholic Church, the king of Spain and the nobility that had become Guatemala's landed gentry.

While American-born Spaniards squabbled with European-born Spaniards over social status, a new kind of Guatemalan was growing in numbers. Suddenly there were many more *mestizos*—people of mixed Spanish and Indian blood—than pure-blooded Spaniards in Guatemala's population. According to the Maya version of history, the *mestizos* were descendants of Indian women raped by Spanish soldiers, and this is undoubtedly part of the truth. Another part of it is that Spanish soldiers were in the New World for ten years or more, often for life. Only Spanish officials of high rank were allowed to bring wives with them to the New World, so common soldiers were forced to take wives from the Indian population. Since the Maya have always been notoriously unwilling to marry outside their own people, many soldiers found wives among the Indians of central Mexico and brought them along to Guatemala. By the declining years of the Spanish empire, *mestizos* had come to outnumber Guatemalans of pure Spanish descent by nine to one.

In 1697, a military patrol was surprised to stumble across Tayasal, a previously unknown city on an island in Lago Petén Itzá, the site of present-day Flores in the Petén rainforest. The city was the last stronghold of the Itzá Maya, who had ruled the northern Yucatán peninsula for centuries before retreating to the Petén to avoid confrontation with the Spaniards. Martín de Ursúa, leader of the small Spanish force, ordered the siege and destruction of Tayasal, thereby putting an end to the last independent Maya city-state.

In 1773, the capital of Guatemala was virtually destroyed by a series of earthquakes. Walls three feet thick buckled like crumpled paper. Massive brick archways came crashing down. Buildings snapped in two. The stately old capital city was left in ruins—but ruins of such formidable structures that today, more than two centuries later, they look much as they did just after they came crashing down. In 1775, the king of Spain ordered the capital moved over the mountain to the site of present-day Guatemala City.

UNITED CENTRAL AMERICA (1821–1847) The Spanish empire came to an end peacefully as the king of Spain, beset by crippling economic and political problems in his own country, relinquished Spain's claim to the colonies of the New World in 1821. Although independence came peacefully, a lot of blood would be spilled over the question of who would rule the new nation.

Guatemala was annexed to Mexico in 1822 but seceded the following year to become part of the United Provinces of Central America, a new federation created by a constitution modeled on that of the United States. Unfortunately, no leader was able to maintain control over all the provinces of Central America for long. Francisco Morazán, an army general from Honduras with liberal ideas, became president of the United Provinces of Central America and promptly set about abolishing religious orders, slavery and the death penalty while instituting public schools, trial by jury and a new, progressive legal code. But within a year, Rafael Carrera had arisen as a pro-church revolutionary leader with the support of the Maya people throughout Guatemala. The charismatic Carrera deposed Morazán by military coup and established his own government, restoring the authority of the Catholic Church and canceling most of the social reforms of his predecessor. Morazán and his army became a leftist guerrilla force that plagued Carrera's government for more than 20 years.

In 1837, the American explorer John Lloyd Stephens and his sidekick, British illustrator Frederick Catherwood, arrived in Central America. Although his main purpose was to "discover" ancient Maya cities and write a book about them, Stephens had also secured an appointment from the president of the United States as ambassador-at-large, assigned to determine whose government—Carrera's or Morazán's—controlled the United Provinces of Central America for diplomatic purposes. Stephens' two-volume account of the trip, *Incidents of Travel in Central America, Chiapas and Yucatán*, describes traveling through war-torn Guatemala with letters of introduction from the president to both Carrera and Morazán, switching them quickly depending on whose patrol confronted him. In his final report, Stephens told the president of his conclusion that *nobody* held a clear claim to leadership of Central America.

In 1847, Carrera declared Guatemala to be an independent nation and in effect dissolved the United Provinces of Central America. No sooner had he done this, however, than the western highlands declared their independence from Guatemala and formed a new independent nation called Los Altos, with its capital at Quetzaltenango. The breakaway republic lasted less than two years before it was again annexed to Guatemala. Carrera would rule Guatemala for another 18 years until his death.

BANANA REPUBLIC (1847–1944) In the years following Carrera's death, several liberal revolutionary leaders attempted to seize the Guatemalan government by coup. Some of the insurgents were executed, while others went into exile in Mexico. In 1871, two of the exiled leaders, Marcia García Ganados and Rufino Barrios, returned to Guatemala with a revolutionary force of just 45 men. Thousands of people from the countryside joined the rebels as they marched on Guatemala City. Following a siege and fierce fighting, they captured the capital on June 30, 1871. García Ganados became the new president of Guatemala, but the liberal reforms he had promised were slow in coming. The following year, the president's former partner, Rufino Barrios, who was now the general of the army in the western highlands, led his troops in a siege of the capital, demanding an immediate presidential election. García Ganados agreed to the demand, and Barrios was elected president—a position he held for 13 years before an assassin's bullet put an end to his rule.

Barrios is remembered in Guatemalan history as his nation's counterpart to Abraham Lincoln. In the most notorious of his social reforms, he imposed severe restrictions on the church. For his effrontery, the pope excommunicated Barrios, who responded by exiling the Archbishop of Guatemala, effectively shutting down the organized church for more than a decade. The role of the clergy was taken over by lay religious groups called *cofradías*, creating the unique brand of folk Catholicism that continues to play a central role in Maya village life today.

The achievement for which Barrios is most remembered was a peculiar kind of land reform. Confiscating excess land that was not under cultivation from the church and wealthy colonial families, Barrios opened the doors to foreign land ownership for the first time, reselling the land to German immigrants to grow coffee. The coffee boom tripled Guatemala's gross national product in less than ten years, while the land sales financed reorganization of the education system, construction of railroads and establishment of Guatemala's national banking system. The German coffee planters quickly took their place among the most powerful political forces in the country.

Despite his impressive achievements, Barrios also had a very dark side that laid the groundwork for most of the social and political problems that still face Guatemala today. In his zeal to finance development by selling land to outsiders, he soon turned to confiscating land used by Maya communities, touching off Indian revolts in the highlands that were ruthlessly put down by the military. In 1876, to provide cheap farmworkers for the burgeoning coffee industry, Barrios imposed a system of forced labor that amounted to part-time slavery (150 days a year) of the Maya population. Growing more paranoid as social unrest threatened his new order, Barrios created a vast secret police network to insure his continued political power and eliminate opposition. These ills—confiscation of peasant lands, abuse of Indians and government dependence on secret police—would persist long after Barrios' death, leading to Guatemala's worst political crisis a century later.

The assassination of Rufino Barrios in 1885 was followed by years of political turmoil, during which control of the government changed by military coup no fewer than 30 times. Only two leaders in the next 60 years held office for long; both were ultraconservatives, and both became insane while in office. The first, Manuel Estrada Cabrera, is best remembered as the president who opened Guatemala's doors to the United Fruit Company, a United States–based corporation that had a monopoly on tropical fruits imported to the United States. The multinational corporation moved into Guatemala in 1901. It started out buying land on which to grow bananas and soon became the country's largest landowner and employer. The company built and at one time owned all the railroads, shipping ports and public utilities in Guatemala. As World War II began, the company persuaded Guatemala's president to expel Guatemalans of German descent, who owned most of the coffee plantations, and place the plantations under United Fruit Company control. So widespread was the company's power that it came to be nicknamed *El Pulpo* (The Octopus).

Following the overthrow of Cabrera in 1920, a string of other rulers seized power, but none lasted more than a year. The United Fruit Company—with the backing of the U.S. military—consistently supported ruthless generals who in turn overthrew and were overthrown by left-wing rebel leaders. Finally, in 1930, when the Guatemalan government had sunken into such financial ruin that nobody seemed inclined to seize control of it, Jorge Ubico was elected to the presidency. This corrupt populist, who believed himself to be the reincarnation of Napoleon Bonaparte, was essentially a puppet for the United Fruit Company, which asserted absolute control over Guatemala.

The extent of U.S.-based control over Guatemala was demonstrated when the United States entered World War II and immediately called for all German nationals to be expelled from Guatemala as security risks. This meant deporting the owners of most Guatemalan coffee plantations, called *fincas*. The *fincas* were auctioned off, and most of the land was bought by the United Fruit Company at bargain basement prices.

THE OCTOBER REVOLUTION (1945–1954) Rioting in the streets forced an end to Ubico's rule in 1944. Although Ubico tried to pass his power on to another ultraconservative when he stepped down, civil disobedience reached a level that made government impossible. The collapse of the government came to be known as the October Revolution. An interim junta of military and civilian representatives adopted a new constitution, which among other reforms gave women the right to vote for the first time, and the first truly free presidential election in Guatemala's history was held in 1945. Schoolteacher Juan José Arévalo, a self-styled "spiritual socialist," won with 85 percent of the popular vote.

Arévalo instituted ambitious reforms in education, literacy, health care and human rights. He abolished the old forced labor laws and implemented a new labor code that gave workers—including Indian agricultural workers—the right to organize and strike. He even turned over some of the plantation lands that had been seized from German owners to Indian groups for communal use. Large landowners and old-time military officers tried several times to overthrow Arévalo, but without success. The United Fruit Company remained neutral. The perception of political stability in Guatemala was good for the value of the company's stock. Another liberal reformer, Jacobo Arbenz Guzmán, won the 1950 presidential election by a landslide, and Guatemala was hailed as Latin America's finest model of democracy, civil rights and economic development. (The fact that Arbenz's right-wing opponent had been assassinated by unknown persons shortly before the election was conveniently ignored.)

The new Guatemala was too good to last. President Arbenz launched a series of attacks on foreign corporations, particularly the United Fruit Company. He nationalized the fruit company's railroads and created new government-owned power companies and shipping ports in direct competition with United Fruit. He filed suit against United Fruit and other international corporations doing business in Guatemala to recover millions in unpaid taxes. Finally, he instituted a sweeping land reform law providing for condemnation of land not being used for agriculture. Landowners would be compensated for the seized land with government bonds, and the land would be leased or sold at low prices to peasant families and communes. Over the next two years, more than two billion acres of land were turned over to small farmers.

The land reform measures outraged United Fruit Company, which was stripped of about half its holdings in Guatemala. While the government seized only unused land and compensated the company with bonds, the value of the condemned land was determined by its assessed value for tax purposes, which was a tiny fraction of the value shown on United Fruit Company's financial statements. The result? The price of United Fruit Company stock plunged.

The seizure of United Fruit Company land touched off one of the most cynical abuses of power in the often-sordid record of U.S. dealings in Latin America, dashing hopes for peace and democracy while shaping the course of Guatemalan history to this day.

The Eisenhower administration had close ties with the United Fruit Company. John Foster Dulles, the fruit company's former legal counsel and a substantial shareholder, was Eisenhower's secretary of state, and his brother, Alan Dulles, a member of United Fruit's board of directors, had recently been appointed director of the Central Intelligence Agency. In the anti-Soviet paranoia of the 1950s, the Dulles brothers promoted the idea that the Arbenz government was nothing less than the vanguard of world communism in Latin America.

Ultimately, President Eisenhower authorized the CIA to start "Operation Success," a U.S.-sponsored military invasion to overthrow the Arbenz government. On June 27, 1954, Arbenz stepped down. His resignation was accepted by the U.S. ambassador to Guatemala.

EL CONFLICTO (1954–1990)   After the fall of Guatemala's constitutional government, the stage was set for the conflict that would tear the country apart for decades. Arbenz supporters in the Guatemalan military, who faced prosecution for fighting back against the CIA-sponsored expeditionary force, grabbed what weapons and supplies they could and fled into remote jungle areas beyond the mountains. They would become the nucleus of Guatemala's guerrilla movement.

The events of the years that followed were confusing, treacherous, misunderstood and ultimately tragic for the people of Guatemala. Only in retrospect has the chain of events referred to as the Guatemalan civil war, or "El Conflicto," become clear. The following summary is based on reports by Amnesty International, the Central American Education Project, the Inter-Hemispheric Education Resource Center, the *Miami Herald* and the *San Francisco Examiner*.

Following the overthrow of the Arbenz government, the CIA installed Castillo Armas as president of Guatemala. A weak ruler, completely subservient to U.S. and United Fruit Company interests, he was assassinated by right-wing extremists in 1957. The presidency changed hands by coup three times in the next six years. During the same period, Guatemala's poorly armed fugitive rebels followed the lead of Cuban Revolutionary leader Fidel Castro, espousing Marxist doctrine in hopes of receiving military aid from the Soviet Union. Though the hoped-for aid did not come, the fugitives launched their first guerrilla offensive in 1960, marking the beginning of Guatemala's long, silent but deadly civil war. In 1963, U.S. president John F. Kennedy sought to stabilize Guatemala's government with another CIA-backed coup, which installed Guatemalan defense minister Alfredo Enrique Peralta Azurdia as president. One of Peralta's first official acts was to suspend the constitution and impose military rule once more.

Under pressure from the United States, a new constitution was put into place, and new democratic elections brought Julio Cesar Montenegro to power in 1966. Before the army would allow Montenegro to take office, however, he was required to sign a document consenting to military control and granting army leaders absolute decision-making power. Although Montenegro aspired to be a populist reformer in the tradition of Arévalo and Arbenz, his hands were tied, and both death squad activity and military terrorism against the Indian population reached unprecedented levels during his administration. During Montenegro's term in office, Colonel Carlos Arana Osorio with the help of United States Special Forces launched Operation Guatemala, a counterinsurgency campaign that killed at least 8000 people—about twice the U.S. intelligence estimate of the total number of guerrillas in Guatemala. The guerilla forces were believed to have been completely destroyed. Colonel Arana assumed control of the Mano Blanco, the most notorious of the government's radical right "security forces" (also called secret police or death squads). In the 1970 elections, thanks to widespread vote fraud and intimidation, Colonel Arana became president of Guatemala. Arana's security forces were credited with 15,000 political assassinations during his presidency.

General Efraín Ríos Montt, who was destined to become a major political player in future years, lost the 1974 presidential election to right-wing spokesman Kjell Laugerud García by a narrow margin. Laugerud's administration was preoccupied by tension over the independence of neighboring Belize (formerly British Honduras), which Laugerud claimed to be Guatemalan territory wrongfully stolen by British pirates in the 19th century. Great Britain sent troops, planes and gunships to defend the independence of its former colony. The flap over Belize was upstaged on February 4, 1976, when one of the biggest earthquake's in the country's history devastated the capital, leaving 22,000 dead, one million homeless, the city leveled and the government bankrupt. To make the situation even more difficult, the following year U.S. president Jimmy Carter cut off military aid to Guatemala because of the army's dismal and worsening human rights record. There was a resurgence of guerrilla activity as the tattered remnants of the 1960s rebellion sought to topple the weakened, distracted Guatemalan government.

In the 1978 presidential election, again plagued by massive fraud, no candidate won a clear majority, and the congress named right-wing general Fernando Lucas García as the new president. He responded to the country's social, economic and political woes by initiating a wave of military violence in the highlands. Although the actual guerrilla forces at that time numbered only in the hundreds, an estimated 25,000 Guatemalans, mostly Maya Indians and striking miners, were killed during Lucas' four-year reign on the excuse that they were providing aid and comfort to the guerrillas. And the terror was just beginning.

In 1982, election fraud gave the presidency to another right-wing secret police boss, General Angel Anibal Guevara, but he was immediately overthrown by military coup and replaced by General Efraín Ríos Montt. Responding to continued atrocities in the highlands, small guerrilla factions and Maya Indian rebel groups banded together to form the Unidad Revolucionario Nacional Guatamalteco (URNG), which soon grew to a maximum strength of 6000. Because it remained greatly outnumbered by the Guatemalan army, however, the group was never able to get military aid from Cuba or the Soviet Union, so there were never enough guns to arm all the rebel troops. But in the United States, the formation of the URNG convinced the Reagan administration that Guatemala's strategic importance as a buffer against the spread of communism in Central America outweighed human rights considerations. Reagan ordered the restoration of U.S. military aid to Guatemala, to the tune of more than $55 million a year. The Guatemalan army grew to a troop strength of more than 40,000—the largest military force in Central America—and launched a renewed counterinsurgency campaign against the rebels. By the end of 1983, the URNG had been reduced to fewer than 500 people and was completely out of ammunition. Yet the army continued to attack. By the end of 1983, about 400 Maya villages suspected of harboring guerrillas had been annihilated. An estimated 100,000 civilians had been massacred, while an even larger number had fled across the border to refugee camps in Mexico.

General Efraín Ríos Montt, who served as president of Guatemala for just over a year from June 1982 to August 1983, remains perhaps the most powerful man in the country today—and one of the most enigmatic figures in Central American politics. A born-again Christian known for his fire-and-brimstone Sunday morning presidential radio sermons, Ríos Montt steadfastly proclaimed his opposition to the excesses of the radical right. He played a key role in the Contadora meetings sponsored by Costa Rica and aimed at bringing lasting peace throughout Central America. Yet he also presided over the most ruthless slaughter of civilians in the history of Guatemala. Ríos Montt's strategy, known as the Beans and Guns Campaign, was to polarize the countryside by encouraging villages to form civilian self-defense militias as a show of loyalty to the government. Villages that did not participate in the program were assumed to hold antigovernment sentiments and so were terrorized or destroyed by the army. There was also an unspoken belief among Guatemala's peasants that one way to safety was to leave the Catholic faith and join an evangelical church.

During Ríos Montt's brief rule, about 30 percent of Guatemalans converted to Mormon and fundamentalist Christian sects. Since then, aggressive missionary tactics have translated into continued growth of evangelical Christian churches. So far, about half of the country's population has converted, and it is widely predicted that by the year 2000, Guatemala will be 30 percent Catholic and 70 percent evangelical. To the horror of many Christian preachers, however, most highland Maya people continue to practice their ancestral religion as always and reject the idea that it is in conflict with imported religious beliefs.

Opposed by the Catholic Church, the army and the business community, Ríos Montt was deposed by defense minister General Oscar Humberto Mejía Víctores in August 1984. Atrocities against the peasants continued. At the end of 1984, the World Council of Indigenous Peoples issued a report accusing the Guatemalan government of following an intentional policy of genocide against the Maya Indians. At the same time, pursuant to a recommendation by the Kissinger Commission, the U.S. government increased the amount of military aid to Guatemala.

Guatemala began its slippery climb toward governmental integrity and lasting peace in 1986 as new elections monitored by international watchdog groups brought moderate candidate Marco Vinicio Cerezo Arévalo to power. Widely hailed on the international scene as a triumph for democracy, the election's glow faded as it became clear that President Cerezo lacked authority over his nation's military. In 1987, army units began staging atrocities in the countryside and blaming them on the guerrillas. The guerrillas, meanwhile, grew in numbers and stepped up sniper fire on army bases. Though many feared a new outbreak of war, the violence remained at much lower levels than before. In 1989, URNG political spokesmen, who had been in exile in Mexico for the past five years, declared a cease-fire and entered into peace negotiations with the Guatemalan government in Mexico City.

YEARS OF HOPE (1987–PRESENT) International applause greeted the 1990 election of President Jorge Serrano, whose campaign pledges included investigation and punishment of human rights abuses and an end to official corruption. Although the number of guerrillas living as outlaws in the backcountry grew to more than a thousand, violent guerrilla activity continued to decline. Corruption actually increased, however, as inflation ate away at public officials' already low salaries (around $85 a month). Law enforcement and crime detection became virtually nonexistent.

In October 1992, exactly 500 years after Columbus first set foot on an American beach, the Nobel Peace Prize was awarded to a Maya woman of humble origin, Rigoberta Menchú Tum. The daughter of a village healer and midwife, Menchú grew up near Uspantán in the highland department of Quiché, one of the most violent areas during the civil war of the 1980s. In 1981, her father was among 39 protesters burned to death in the Spanish Embassy in Guatemala City while demonstrating for land rights. Soon afterward, her mother and younger brother were arrested by the military and tortured to death. Menchú fled to Mexico, where she wrote a book, *Yo, Rigoberta*, about her family's ordeal and the plight of Guatemala's Maya people. Published in 1983, the book is in print in Spanish and ten other languages. The English edition is *I, Rigoberta Menchú: An Indian Woman in Guatemala* (New York: Verso, 1984).

Rigoberta Menchú worked with other refugees along the Guatemalan border throughout the 1980s and now speaks out for the rights of native people throughout the Americas. The Guatemalan military filed a protest when her Nobel Prize was announced, charging that she was a spokesperson for a leftist guerrilla group to which several of her relatives belonged. At the time, peace negotiations between the government and the guerrillas were deadlocked because of a single issue—the government's refusal to recognize human rights for Guatemala's Indians. When the honor bestowed on Menchú was greeted with unanimous praise in the world press, the Guatemalan government withdrew its protest. Following announcement of the award, her book became an international best-seller and focused worldwide public pressure on ending the massive human rights violations of "El Conflicto."

Public discontent mounted in the capital, bursting into mass demonstrations in 1994 with news stories that accused President Serrano of soliciting bribes and embezzling from the national treasury. Faced with impeachment, Serrano declared a state of emergency, suspended the constitution and ordered the dissolution of the congress. Under pressure from the United States, the army refused to support Serrano, and within two weeks he was forced to resign and leave the country. To fill out Serrano's term, the congress named Ramiro de León, the government's chief human rights advocate, as president. Like his predecessors, de León had difficulty controlling the military or prosecuting army, civil patrol or secret police officers for human rights abuses. He did score a public relations coup, however, by proclaiming 1995 "El Año de la Maya," to recognize the human rights of Indians, which had long been the major stumbling block to a permanent peace settlement.

In the November 1995 national elections, de Leon was replaced by moderate Alvaro Arzú, whose campaign slogan, "Obras, No Palabras" ("Works, Not Words") appears on signs announcing new roadbuilding and public works projects all over the country. Arzú's negotiators finally signed a peace accord with the URNG on December 29, 1996, ending the Guatemalan civil war at long last.

The effect of peace on Guatemala's economy and society has been immediate and dramatic. The capital is full of new cars and new American-style shopping malls. Roads throughout the country are being widened and paved. Tourism has reached unprecedented levels, and international investment is flowing into the country. The army's ranks have shrunk and many military bases have been abandoned. For the first time, the court system has begun convicting and sentencing military leaders for their roles in wartime atrocities.

Yet although the army's power has diminished, the government remains under the de facto control of a handful of rich families and representatives of special interest groups who are content to live in luxury behind fortresslike walls while most of Guatemala's citizens continue to suffer one of the lowest standards of living in the Western Hemisphere. Any genuine redistribution of wealth or political power seems unlikely in the foreseeable future.

Meanwhile, Guatemala's government faces a host of problems surrounding the resettlement of the largest refugee population in the Western Hemisphere. Thousands of refugees who fled Guatemala during the conflict have returned to face an uncertain future in their homeland, while thousands more remain in United Nations–sponsored camps in Mexico awaiting repatriation. Many others who live as undocumented aliens in Mexico and the United States are also seeking to return to Guatemala. Thousands of members of Communities of Population in Resistance (CPRs)— groups of refugees in hiding in the Ixcan and other remote areas of Guatemala—are also emerging under a government amnesty program. Altogether, the resettlement effort is expected to continue well into the 21st century, and its ultimate impact on the economy, environment, culture and political climate of Guatemala cannot be predicted with any certainty.

One thing about Guatemala's new, kinder and gentler image *is* certain: tourism, already the largest source of international revenue (surpassing coffee, bananas and military aid), is likely to become even more important in the coming years. The Guatemalan government, as well as private citizens of all cultures and walks of life, are enthusiastic about the promised flow of tourist dollars. Big-city businessmen fantasize about building international-class resort developments, while villagers daydream more mundane dreams of boosting their standard of living by working as guides or bringing better prices for their beautiful handweaving. But the reality is that the tourist industry in Guatemala will evolve in ways that deliver whatever the traveler is in the market for. By such basic decisions as where and how to travel, where to stay and eat and what to buy, every traveler who visits Guatemala at this point in history plays a very real role in shaping the nation's future.

Since the end of Spanish colonialism, Guatemala has rarely known peace or political stability. Increasingly throughout the 20th century, the United States has asserted its power to control Guatemalan political affairs in the name of national security, only to see anarchy escalate. Torn by racial divisions hundreds of years old, three cultures coexist in delicate balance in Guatemala: Maya, ladino and gringo.

Until recently, Maya Indians have officially comprised about 55 percent of Guatemala's people, making this the only nation in the world where American Indians were the majority of the population. Unfortunately, this fact hindered the development of democracy and the recognition of Indians' human rights, because many non-Indians feared that a majority of Indian voters might result in an Indian-dominated government, which could lead to a bloodbath in retaliation for centuries of oppression. In 1995, to set the stage for peace accords, President de León announced that Maya Indians had become a minority—48 percent of the population. He arrived at this figure by taking previous figures and subtracting the estimated 200,000 Indians massacred during the 30-year civil war. Of course, since most Indian births and deaths are undocumented, the new population figure was merely a public relations ploy with no solid evidence to support it. As refugees return and international health workers help extend Indians' life expectancies, there can be little doubt that the Maya will continue as Guatemala's ethnic majority.

The Maya are by far the largest indigenous group in North America, inhabiting not only Guatemala but also the neighboring Mexican states of Yucatán, Quintana Roo, Campeche and Chiapas and, in smaller numbers, Belize and Honduras. (The Maya world also included El Salvador until the 1980s, when the last Maya Indians were exterminated in that country by military counterguerrilla activities that masked genocide.) Today, the Maya people number 20 times more than the Navajo, the largest Indian tribe in the United States; in fact, there are three times more Maya today than the total Native American population of the United States, and about four-fifths of them live in Guatemala, where they are separated into 22 different language groups.

In English, we often use the term *Indian*, which most American Indian tribes prefer to *Native American*. But in Spanish, *indio* is a highly offensive racial slur. Instead, the politically correct word is *indígena*. (Students in Latin American countries are taught that the English word *Indian* is a corruption of *indígena*, meaning "native," and has nothing to do with Columbus' supposed belief that he had reached the East Indies.) In Guatemala, *Maya* is also used to mean any traditional Indian. Another word for Indian commonly used in Guatemala by Maya and ladino alike is *natural*.

Ladinos account for most of the other half of Guatemala's population. This term has slightly different connotations in various parts of the Spanish-speaking world; in Guatemala, where there are virtually no citizens of purely Spanish heritage, a ladino is any person of mixed Spanish and Indian ancestry whose primary language is Spanish. Since the highland Maya people have always considered intermarriage with non-Indians taboo, there is a cultural disagreement as to exactly how the mixture of blood came about. Maya tradition holds that ladinos are descendants of conquistadores' rape and slave-owners' sexual exploitation. Ladinos, however, claim that their ancestors were Aztec and Toltec people from Mexico who came to Guatemala as warriors or as wives of Spanish soldiers. Guatemalan ladinos generally disavow any kinship with the Maya, an odd form of racism that is expressed in the common saying *Tal vez soy pobre, pero a lo menos no soy indio* (I may be poor, but at least I'm not an Indian).

The term *ladino* has a long, strange history in the Spanish language. As one of the 16 *castas*, or racial classes, recognized by Spanish colonial law, it denoted a person of Spanish descent who was married to an Indian and thereby committed to spend the rest of his life in America. *Ladino* originally derived from a Latin word for Romans living in the outlands of the empire. In Spanish it has been used over the centuries to mean various kinds of outsiders—Spaniards living among Moors, Jews living among Spaniards, or Spaniards living among Indians; in slang, it also means tricky or "street-smart." A synonym for ladino that is widely used by both Maya and ladino is *Guatamalteca* (or, if you're talking to a gringo expatriate, "Guatemalan"). In the kind of backhand paradox often found in this country, the descendants of Spanish invaders are called Guatemalans, while the people who have always lived here—and from whose language the word *Guatemala* derives—are not.

About three percent of Guatemala's population consists of *gringos*, or foreigners. Sizable numbers of expatriates from the United States and other English-speaking countries live in Antigua and Panajachel, and despite mass deportations during World War II there are still many people of German descent in the central Guatemalan department of Alta Verapaz. Altogether, gringos would be a culturally insignificant minority were it not for their tremendous economic and political power, which has been a central fact of life in Guatemala throughout the 20th century. For decades, most agricultural land, most jobs and virtually all public transportation and utilities were owned by the U.S.-based United Fruit Company. Throughout recent history, the U.S. Central Intelligence Agency has been one of the most powerful forces controlling the Guatemalan government. Today, both tourism and international relief efforts make gringos an everyday sight on the streets of every Guatemalan town and village.

The word gringo comes from the Spanish *griego,* literally meaning Greek or, in the broader sense, incomprehensibly foreign. The slang word came into vogue in Mexico during the mid-19th century as a pejorative term loosely meaning "rich white honky," a usage that soon spread throughout Central America. But today it is generally not intended as an insult; instead, it has come to mean "tourist." Applying the word to oneself (*"Lo siento. Soy gringo."*) will excuse just about any social blunder.

CUISINE

Most Maya people eat almost exclusively corn. In part, this is a religious matter, since Maya tradition as recorded in the *Popol Vuh* holds that human beings were created from corn. Maya families shun other grains except on the Thursday before Easter, when many eat wheat bread to commemorate the Last Supper.

The mainstay of the Indian diet is the tortilla, smaller and plumper than the ones made in Mexico and the United States. Most of the time, Maya people only eat tortillas, seasoning them with condiments such as salt or chile salsa, but if you are fortunate enough to be invited to dinner in a Maya home you will probably be served a more special corn entrée such as *box-bol*—corn meal wrapped in tasty, edible chayote leaves, cooked like tamales and served with a spicy red sauce. Another favorite special-occasion meal is tamales stuffed with beans and cooked in banana leaf wrappings.

Corn is also used for beverages. *Atol,* a thin souplike drink made by boiling finely ground corn flour, is served with most Maya meals. It may be flavored with honey, powdered chile or cardamom. The favored homemade alcoholic beverage in the highlands is *cuxa,* a fermented corn beer fortified with a little clear moonshine corn whiskey. Imbibe at your own risk.

Other traditional Maya foods include honey and fruit. The two are often combined to make *miel de frutas,* a tropical fruit cocktail stewed in honey and water. In lowland areas, Indian and ladino alike eat bananas with most meals. These may either be the long, green *plátanos* that are favored throughout Central America but rarely seen in the United States, or yellow bananas that are sold locally because they are too small for commercial export. (Try them for yourself: the smaller a banana is when it ripens, the sweeter it is.)

Although most Maya households include chickens, turkeys and pigs, the Indians rarely eat meat. A chicken may be shared at a big family feast, usually to celebrate a marriage, but the rest of the time livestock is raised only to sell at the market. Most chickens are sold to restaurants or to people who are preparing for traditional ceremonial sacrifices to the old gods. More costly than other ritual offerings such as incense, fresh flowers, liquor and Pepsi, chickens are reserved for the most important prayers.

Meat is essential to ladino meals. In fine restaurants, the classiest menu selections are usually *bistek* (that is, "beefsteak"), usually thinner-sliced and tougher than that served in the United States but flavorful and hormone-free, and *parrilla mixta* (mixed grill), a charbroiled sampler of chicken, beef, pork and sometimes German-style sausage. Guatemala's most famous regional dish is *pepián de pollo*, chicken smothered in a greenish sauce made from pumpkin seeds and spices. Restaurants in Flores and elsewhere in the Petén often specialize in wild game meats such as venison, tepescuintle (a large rodent), armadillo and pheasant.

In a manifestation of the anti-Maya prejudice that pervades ladino life, non-Indian Guatemalans consider tortillas and other corn products low class and prefer wheat or rice instead. No distinctively Guatemalan cuisine has evolved around these. Instead, ladinos have developed a taste for "international" foods, particularly pizza and spaghetti with any of a wide assortment of often-unusual sauces and toppings. A new import that is currently in vogue in many parts of Guatemala is *chao mein*, which is made from local market vegetables, served over rice and usually bears little resemblance to Chinese cuisine.

Many tourist restaurants, especially in Panajachel, now cater to gringo tastes by offering vegetarian menu options, nearly always made with tofu. Years ago, some idealistic young Americans in the town of Solalá near Panajachel built a tofu factory, thinking that it could provide a much-needed source of low-cost protein for local Indians who could not afford meat. But the Indians, who had never accepted even such staple "foreign" foods as bread made from wheat, could not be interested in eating tofu. Eventually the Americans gave up on the project and left town, but the equipment remained, along with a few locals who had been trained to operate it. Today the Indians still don't eat tofu, but the factory does a good business making it for tourists to eat.

Soft drinks are called *aguas* in Guatemala, not refrescos as in Mexico. You order an *agua de fresa* (strawberry soda), for instance, or an *agua de Pepsi, agua de Coca* or *agua de limón India Quiché* (lemon flavor of the local brand of soft drink with a Maya Indian girl on the label). In Guatemala, *refrescos* are the flavored waters served by street vendors from big glass jars containing ice cubes; they're known in Mexico as *aguas*. Another popular beverage is *tiste*, a concoction of *achiote* pepper, sugar and cinnamon that is sold in paste form (just add water) in many public markets.

As for the nation's alcoholic beverages, the most common brand of Guatemalan beer is Gallo, served everywhere. Made without hops, it lacks the flavor of even the most unexceptional Mexican and North American beers but serves as an adequate thirst quencher after a steamy jungle hike. A tastier alternative is Moza, a sweet dark ale made by the same brewery and served only in high-class restaurants and nightclubs. Hard liquor, distilled from sugar cane, ranges from the low-priced, throat-burning Quezalteca *aguardiente* to smooth Colonial rum.

Surprisingly, although coffee is Guatemala's largest export product, the coffee served in most restaurants outside the main tourist areas is just awful. Most so-called coffee is made from roasted ground wheat with a small amount of genuine coffee added. In Antigua and Panajachel, many restaurateurs have found that good coffee is the secret to success in the gringo tourist trade, and a number of entrepreneurs have gone into the business of buying beans directly from small farmers, roasting and grinding them and selling the gourmet coffee to restaurants. In the backcountry, the Spanish word *café* still seems to mean simply "brown liquid."

Of course you'll get more out of a trip to Guatemala if you speak fluent Spanish. But what if, like most people who live in the United States, you don't? Many people who have never studied Spanish worry more than they ought to about traveling to Guatemala and other Latin American destinations. One of the fundamental lessons foreign travel teaches is that it's perfectly possible for people to communicate even though they don't know a word of each other's language. Words help, but it's your tone of voice, the expression on your face and gestures or sign language that often count for more when it comes to making yourself understood.

LANGUAGE

People will relate to you better if you attempt to speak Spanish, no matter how poorly. Even if you know little or no Spanish, it's a good idea to practice a handful of basic, polite phrases. Don't be shy about saying, *"Hola"* (Hi), *"Buenos días"* (Good morning), *"Me llamo _____"* (My name is _____), *"Por favor"* (Please) *"Gracias"* (Thank you) and *"Adios"* (good-bye) at every opportunity. Trying to say something in Spanish gives the person you're speaking to an idea of how much Spanish you know (or don't know) and that's good. It lets that person know how slowly and simply he or she must speak for you to understand. Many Guatemalans know a few words of English, too, and mutual efforts to speak in each other's language often leads to a pidgin English-Spanish conversation that somehow works just fine.

It also pays in smiles if you study for your trip by practicing a few useful phrases like *"¿Cuánto vale esto?"* (How much is this worth?), *"La cuenta, por favor"* (The check, please), *"¿Tiene usted una habitación para la noche?"* (Do you have a room for the night?) and *"¿No habría modo de resolver el problema de otra manera?"* (Isn't there some other way to resolve the problem?). You'll find these phrases and many others to build your repertoire in any of the dozens of Spanish phrasebooks sold in U.S. bookstores. I like Lonely Planet's pocket-sized *Latin American Spanish Phrasebook*, which contains regionalisms of Mexico, Guatemala and other countries.

Spanish-language instructional cassette tapes can help you learn Spanish pronunciation, which is much more straightforward than English. Even if your Spanish is good, tapes can help you reattune your ear and "brush up" before your trip. The most enjoyable and practical practice tapes are the basic *Spanish on the Go* and more advanced *Spanish on the Road* sets published by Barron's Educational Series and sold in most bookstores.

The most useful questions to learn are those that can be answered yes or no or with a number. It can be very frustrating to ask for directions, for example, and receive a cheerful reply so long, fast and complicated that you can't make sense of it. It is usually better to ask questions like, "Is this the right way to . . . ?" and "How many blocks?" and "On the right or left?"

Many people who have studied Spanish in school find themselves helpless when it comes to actually communicating in Mexico. Once you've learned it, Spanish vocabulary stays stored in the deep recesses of the mind, but it's often hard to bring it to the surface after years of disuse. Before you leave for Guatemala, you may find that a few weeks of using tapes or other aids can help attune your ear and tongue. A painless way to tune into Spanish is to spend your TV-viewing hours watching Spanish-language cable channels or rented Spanish videos. Although the Guatemalan motion picture industry is, in a word, nonexistent, Mexican filmmakers have been achieving international stature recently with such acclaimed films as *Como Agua Para Chocolate* (*Like Water for Chocolate*), well worth watching repeatedly in Spanish with or without the English subtitles. Other Mexican films to look for include *Cabeza de Vaca, El Patrullero (The Highway Patrolman)* and *Carmesí Profundo (Deep Crimson)*. Most U.S. video stores can order Mexican films and Spanish-version videocassettes (subtitled or dubbed) of almost any popular Hollywood film. Last but not least, don't miss John Sayles' *Men With Guns*, a surrealistic view of life in the Guatemalan backcountry in the last days of the civil war, scripted in an authentic polyglot of Spanish, English and Maya.

End of
the World?

The Maya calendar served not only to record past events but also to predict the future. Its complex system of cycles within cycles let priests determine the unique character of each day over a span of 52 years—and to predict events on corresponding future dates.

Archaeoastrologer José Argüelles's 1987 book *The Mayan Factor* popularized the New Age belief that ancient Maya prophecy predicts the end of the world as we know it on December 23, 2012, which Argüelles calculated to be the end of the final cycle on the Maya calendar. Since then, more than two hundred other books have elaborated on this prophecy.

Present-day Maya spiritual leaders have rejected this notion as a misunderstanding of their divination methods. New Age Maya prophecy proponents respond by suggesting that either the Maya forgot their ancient knowledge with the collapse of the Classic Era civilization or today's Maya people are actually an inferior race that served the "true" Maya, a now-vanished priestly class who may have come from Egypt, Atlantis, or even a faraway galaxy. Maya shamans have often encouraged the perception that they are ignorant of ancient metaphysical practices by refusing to discuss them with anthropologists and other outsiders.

Recently, spiritual leaders representing the various Maya groups and most other traditional Native American tribes have been presenting their own more optimistic version of the ancient prophecy. The Confederation of Indigenous Elders of America, an assembly of more than 200 tribal healers and visionaries formed at the invitation of the Maya High Council "to unite the Eagle of the North and the Condor of the South," first met in Guatemala in 1995 to share their ancestral wisdom, medicine and prophecies. Subsequent gatherings have been held in Colombia in 1997 and New Mexico in 1999.

Confederation spokesperson Patricio Dominguez explains that a council of Maya leaders in A.D. 1490 (two years before Columbus arrived in the Caribbean) prophesied that the year 1517 (the same year that Spanish explorers first discovered the land of the Maya) would mark the start of the"Nine Cycles of Hell"—a 468-year period during which time, indigenous Americans would lose their culture, religion, sciences and languages. This dark age ended in 1985, according to the tribal elders, and humankind is now witnessing the dawn of a new golden age in which ancient knowledge and native thought will become central to mainstream American spiritual life. The world as we knew it, they say, has already ended—and not a minute too soon!

If you're serious about learning to speak Spanish well, consider spending some extra time in Guatemala, where language schools are now a booming industry. Many American college students come to Guatemala to gain practical experience in speaking Spanish, and long-term travelers come to brush up on their language skills before proceeding to other parts of Latin America. These schools arrange for you to live with the family of one of their teachers. The total cost for a week's lodging, meals and 20 hours a week of Spanish instruction ranges from US$100 to $150 a week. There are over 80 language schools in Antigua Guatemala and others in Panajachel, Xela (Quetzaltenango), Huehuetenango and elsewhere.

Prospective language students will want to meet their instructors and look at the homestay household before making their choice of schools and signing up, but may wish to contact schools in advance to ask about availability. Among the most reputable language schools in Antigua Guatemala are **Monja Blanca** (6 Avenida Norte No. 41; 8-322-548), **Nahual Academia de Español** (6 Avenida Norte No. 9; 8-322-548), **Centro de Español Don Pedro de Alvarado** (1 Calle Poniente No. 24), **Centro Lingüístico Maya** (5 Calle Poniente No. 20; 8-320-656), **Tecún Umán School of Spanish** (6 Calle Poniente No. 34), **La Alianza Spanish School** (1 Avenida Sur No. 20) and **Instituto Antigüeño de Español** (1a Calle Poniente No. 33, Antigua; phone/fax 8-322-682).

Ironically, language schools here have grown so popular with American students that Antigua has taken on many of the trappings of a small college town in the United States. English is so widely spoken that if you wish, you can spend quite a bit of time in Antigua without ever finding it necessary to utter a word of Spanish. For this reason, many serious students have begun exploring other language school options, particularly in Quetzaltenango and also in more remote areas such as Huehuetenango, Santa Cruz del Quiché and even Flores in the Petén.

In Panajachel, there's **PanAtitlán Spanish School**. ~ Callejón de Don Armando, Zona 1, Panajachel, phone/fax 9-621-196; or contact Amerispan Unlimited, 56 North Front Street #501, Philadelphia, PA 19106, 215-829-0996, 800-879-6640, fax 215-828-0418.

In Quetzaltenango, classes are offered by the nonprofit cooperative **Proyecto Lingüístico Quetzalteco de Español** (5 Calle No. 2-40, Zona 1, Quetzaltenango; 9-063-1061), and at **Escuela de Español I.C.A.** (1 Calle No. 16-93, Zona 1, Quetzaltenango; 9-063-1871 or 9-616-786).

In the Petén, a combined language and rainforest ecology curriculum is offered by **ProPetén Eco-Escuela**. ~ Avenida Barrios y Calle Central, Flores, Petén; fax 9-501-370.

Some language schools offer classes for children as young as age six as well as adult classes. A number of schools both in Antigua and in other highland towns also offer instruction and homestay experiences in various Maya languages.

Remember, in the Indian areas of Guatemala at least half the people cannot speak Spanish. Also, in many small towns and villages, hardly anybody knows how to read either words or numbers, so there are no signs on stores or streets. Communication in these parts calls for extra portions of body language and enthusiasm. Maya peasants speak any of 22 mutually unintelligible languages and are often adept at communicating despite the lack of a common language.

FOUR

Guatemala City

The jetliner descends into the black pall that hangs over the capital. Wood is burned for cooking and heat by more than half the city's residents, creating a thick smog. The city sprawls along a plateau sliced by a series of deep canyons. Its two-and-a-half million inhabitants dispose of their trash by dumping it into the canyons and setting it on fire after dark. The air quality ranks among the worst in the Western Hemisphere. Through the murk, the airport comes into view flanked by huge, haphazard heaps of makeshift slum houses. Industrial debris lines the runway, which commercial jetliners share with olive-drab military aircraft. It's hard to see why I don't recommend spending your vacation in Guatemala City.

About the same size as Chicago, Guatemala City (which Guatemalans call simply Guatemala or, informally, "Guate") is the largest city between Mexico City and Medellín, Colombia. Contrasting completely with the rest of the country, the capital city is a low-budget, landlocked version of Los Angeles, full of cheap concrete-block buildings, traffic snarls, smog and street crime. In planning your travel itinerary, it is best to minimize your time in the capital in favor of gentler destinations. Travelers arriving at La Aurora International Airport in the southern part of Guatemala City, take my advice: as soon as you clear immigration and customs, look for the next shuttle van going to Antigua, a 45-minute drive away on the other side of a nearby mountain, and take it. Leave the big city behind until the time comes to fly back to the rest of the world.

Don't get me wrong. Guatemala City does have a few good sightseeing attractions, which are the subject matter of this chapter. Its museums are the finest in Central America, and the giant relief map of the country in Parque Minerva offers an overview that enhances any traveler's perception of the country. Yet, with all this, Guatemala City is a stressful place to visit.

Unfortunately, there is no practical way to avoid the place—inevitably, you will visit Guatemala City at least once on any trip to Guatemala. The international airport is there. Bus travelers arriving from the western highlands must change buses in Guatemala City to continue into the eastern or northern part of the country.

As for driving, all roads in Guatemala lead to the capital, and en route from the western highlands to any other part of the country there is no way to avoid a hair-raising spin on the *periféricos* (freeways) that wander crazily through the city. And if you opt to stay in the country for longer than 30 days, a personal visit to the immigration office in downtown Guatemala City is mandatory to obtain a visa extension.

One might expect Guatemala City, founded in 1776 after the abandonment of the ruined capital at Antigua Guatemala, to have fine old colonial buildings. Such 19th-century literary travelers as John Lloyd Stephens and Anthony Trollope sang the city's praises. In the early 20th century, Aldous Huxley described Guatemala City in glowing phrases, holding it up as the most magnificent city in Central America, in many ways the equal to any European capital. (Of course, when he came to Guatemala, Huxley was almost blind.)

Sadly, the last vestiges of colonial architecture were smashed by a violent earthquake that struck Guatemala City in its bicentennial year, 1976. It was the third major quake to wreak havoc on the city, surpassing others that had struck in 1830 and 1917–18, and this time shattered neighborhoods were apparently rebuilt as plainly and cheaply as possible, abandoning the delusion that any structure could be permanent here. Complementing the city's concrete block architecture is an almost complete absence of trees; saplings are only now being planted along the capital's boulevards.

An exploding population has also tarnished the capital's former charm. As Guatemala City has grown to over two million people, the former farmland at the city's outskirts has become a boundless sprawl of slum housing that scrambles up mountainsides and spills off into deep gorges. In the poor neighborhoods, modern urban life is uneasily married to ancient village ways. It is not unusual to see men on bicycles herding flocks of goats down the freeway.

Besides standard urban nightmares such as poverty and pollution, Guatemala City has a peculiar problem that contributes to the crime risk for travelers. Since Guatemala's government provides very little law enforcement in rural towns and villages, it is common practice in the countryside for local vigilante groups to banish criminals from the community with a beating or worse. The city is the only place these outcasts can go to survive, and their most likely means of survival is crime. There is not much effective law enforcement in Guatemala City, either, and there's a lot more room for anonymity.

The risk of physical violence is not serious during daylight hours, but no Guatemala City neighborhood is a good neighborhood to walk around in after dark. Theft of property is epidemic, though, at any hour. Every street has its pickpockets, and crowds are the hunting grounds of thieves who stand behind you and slice open your backpack, purse, suitcase or even hip pocket with a knife and help themselves to whatever is inside. The theft situation is notoriously bad at the Zona 4 bus terminal and adjacent market; I know people who claim to have been ripped off several times while trying to catch a bus here. The main rules for theft prevention are to be aware at all times, to be on guard when someone touches or distracts you, and above all, to avoid crowds. The best plan is to travel with at least one companion and watch each other's backs.

If, after all these cautionary words, you still find yourself with time on your hands in Guatemala City, here's how to see the sights.

▼▼▼▼▼▼▼▼▼▼▼▼▼▼▼▼
Old Guatemala City (Zona 1)

The last hints of the old, pre-earthquake Guatemala City are to be found in the city center, around the *parque central*. Situated in Zona 1 between 6 Calle and 8 Calle, the plaza consists of two adjoining parks—the Parque de Centenario on the west side of 6 Avenida and the Plaza de Armas (also called the Plaza Mayor) on the east side.

From the Trébol ("cloverleaf") freeway interchange, follow Avenida Bolivar northeast to the heart of the old city. From the Zona Viva (Zonas 9 and 10), take 7 Avenida north. Better yet, catch a taxi or public bus downtown. Parking there is nearly impossible.

SIGHTS

The **Plaza de Armas**, which had been left in ruins through most of the 20th century after the 1917 earthquake, was excavated after the 1976 earthquake to make an underground parking garage. Today, the park is a bare expanse of concrete providing plenty of open space but not much in the way of beauty. The **Parque de Centenario**, however, remains a small gem of a park with shade trees, a big old-fashioned bandshell and benches where a full array of Guatemala City's people can be found chatting, reading newspapers or otherwise whiling away the day.

The huge **Palacio Nacional** (National Palace) was built between 1939 and 1943 in neoclassical style with a huge portico supported by many pillars. It is the "White House" of Guatemala, where the president of the country and his executive staff have their offices. The atmosphere of the National Palace seems to have a sinister and oppressive edge, echoing ruthless dictators who have held court here. Partly it is the large, heavily armed military guard. Partly, too, it is the architectural resemblance to government structures built during the same period in Nazi Germany. Two of the palace's 350 rooms—the reception room and the banquet room—are open to the general public. Don't be intimidated by all the soldiers. Just say *"Estamos turistas"* and walk into the central courtyard to see the murals by Guatemalan artist Alfredo Galvez Suárez re-creating the nation's history from ancient Maya times through Central American independence in 1821. On the second floor, historical scenes are also the subjects of elaborate stained-glass windows in the vast *sala de recepción* where presidential receptions are held. Notice the stuffed quetzal, the national bird, an official example of the Guatemalan enthusiasm for wildlife taxidermy, in the coat of arms behind the row of flags at the end of the room. The stained glass windows were destroyed by a terrorist bomb in

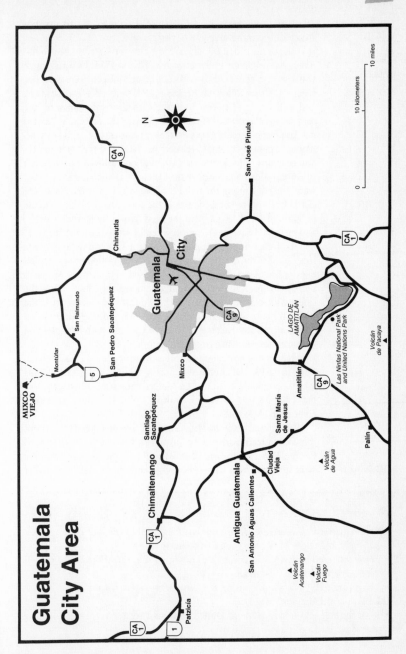

Guatemala City Area

1980, and two decades later some of them are still being reconstructed. ~ On the east side of the plaza.

One of the oldest buildings in the city, the **Catedral Metropolitana,** was originally built between 1782 and 1815. Its squat, thick
walls were engineered to withstand earthquakes. Extensive restoration efforts followed the 1830, 1917 and 1976 earthquakes,
and today, two centuries later, the cathedral still stands on the
east side of the central square. Along with the adjoining **Palacio
del Arzobispo** (Archbishop's Palace), it is the capital city's last remnant of Spanish colonial architecture. Many of the saint figures
and religious relics inside the cathedral once graced the churches
of Antigua Guatemala before the old city was abandoned and they
were moved. Among them are the Virgen del Socorro, one of the
oldest Catholic religious figures in the Americas, which was made
in Spain in 1475, brought to the New World by Hernán Cortés,
and given to Pedro de Alvarado when he set out to conquer Guatemala. Other impressive pieces include a 780-pound lamp made
from solid silver during the colonial era and 14 paintings depicting the life of the Virgin Mary by famed 17th-century Mexican
painter Pedro Ramírez. Although some of the altars along the
sides of the cathedral radiate with gold leaf and fine artwork, the
main church is surprisingly austere, evidence of the Guatemalan
government's ambivalence toward the Catholic faith from the first
years of independence to the present day.

Five blocks east stands another historic church, **La Merced.**
Built in 1813, the church contains a treasure trove of religious
art that originally decorated La Merced church in Antigua, the former capital's first cathedral, built in 1549. ~ At the corner of 5
Calle and 11 Avenida.

Returning to the *parque central,* drive or take a taxi about
three kilometers north along 6 Avenida, beyond the *periférico,* to
Parque Minerva in Zona 2 and you'll find the most remarkable
HIDDEN ▶ sight in Guatemala City—the **Mapa en Relieve.** This huge relief

✔ **CHECK THESE OUT**

- View Guatemala's dramatic terrain miniaturized to the size of a foot-
  ball field at Parque Minerva's **Mapa en Relieve.** *page 106*
- Enjoy vintage luxury at affordable rates downtown in the 1930s art
  deco–style **Hotel Pan American.** *page 107*
- Savor candlelit Continental cuisine at Guatemala's finest restaurant,
  La Fonda del Camino. *page 115*
- Scale the steep mountain slope to **United Nations Park** for spectac-
  ular views of Lago de Amatitlán. *page 119*

map of the country was sculpted from concrete in 1905 and is repainted annually. It fills an area of 130 feet by 265 feet—nearly the size of a football field! Water runs in the rivers, and major roads and towns are shown. Viewing the vast map from an observation tower, visitors sense the complexity of Guatemala's mountain ranges and understand how, in such a small country, large areas—the western highlands, the Petén jungle—can be so completely isolated from the mainstream of society as represented by Guatemala City. Trace your travel route around the country and let your imagination take wing.

For a different kind of bird's-eye view, head 12 blocks south of the central plaza on 6 Avenida or 7 Avenida, the main downtown thoroughfares, to a cool, nicely landscaped park that is the setting for the strangely shaped blue-and-white **Centro Cultural Miguel Angel Asturias**, a complex of three theaters looming among the battlements of an old hilltop fortress. It is named for Guatemala's first Nobel Prize-winning novelist. The theater building is usually open to the public, and its round windows provide the best views of the city's downtown area. The building also houses the bizarre, self-congratulatory **Museo Militar** (Military Museum). ~ 24 Calle 3-81, Zona 1; 2-24-041.

The theater overlooks the **Centro Cívico**, a group of buildings that contain municipal and national government offices, including the headquarters of INGUAT, the Guatemalan government tourist office, which has maps and tourist information galore. ~ 7 Avenida 1-17; 2-311-333. From the hilltop, you can also see the new downtown commercial district and the **Ciudad Olímpico** (Olympic City), a sports complex that includes the national soccer stadium, an indoor arena, a gymnasium, tennis courts and a swimming pool.

Zona 1 offers a wide selection of accommodations right in the noisy, congested heart of downtown Guatemala City. The city's original luxury hotel, the **Hotel Ritz Continental** was the height of luxury in old-fashioned grand hotels around 1950. The 202 guest rooms have wood floors, ornate hand-carved moldings and furnishings and marble bathroom fittings. All rooms have private baths, air conditioning, phones, TVs and balconies overlooking the downtown streets; there's also a pool. Just like the National Palace a few blocks away, the lobby has a stuffed quetzal. ~ 6 Calle A No. 10-13, Zona 1; 2-381-671; fax 2-328-431. DELUXE.

LODGING

A much smaller hotel than the Ritz Continental, the **Hotel Pan American** offers a touch of art deco class at affordable rates in the middle of downtown. The 60 guest rooms are high-ceilinged, old-fashioned and still elegant. The rooms are clean and well kept, and the original 1930s-vintage furnishings have been in use for so long that the rooms now qualify as "antique-furnished." In addition, rooms have private baths, phones and TVs; some rooms have balconies overlooking the stately interior courtyard with its soothing fountain. The lobby decor features fine examples of Maya weaving, and some staff members wear colorful village *traje*. ~ 9 Calle No. 5-63, Zona 1; 2-326-807; fax 2-326-402. MODERATE.

Most of the 43 rooms in the two-story **Hotel Spring** open onto a sunny interior courtyard with potted plants and sitting areas secluded from the busy avenue outside. The rooms are spacious and Spanish-colonial style, with high ceilings and carpeting; some have private baths. Nineteen of the 42 rooms are older and a little run-down, with shared baths. The other 23 rooms have private baths and televisions. ~ 8 Avenida No. 12-65, Zona 1; 2-26-637, fax 2-20-107. BUDGET.

HIDDEN ►

On a quiet side street toward the southeast corner of downtown, the **Posada Belén** is a homey ten-room *pensión*—like an English or American bed and breakfast—decorated with native handicrafts and houseplants. The clean, simple rooms with private baths surround a courtyard brightened by parrots and lots of tropical flowers. Although the Posada Belén is far enough from most of Guatemala's tourist attractions that you might want to take a taxi, the peaceful location in a nice older residential neighborhood is worth it. Reservations are essential. ~ 13 Calle A No. 10-30, Zona 1; 2-29-226, fax 2-513-478; e-mail pbelen@guatemalaweb. com. MODERATE.

You'll also need to call ahead if you want to stay at the **Hotel Chalet Suizo,** a low-priced place that has enjoyed a near-legendary reputation among international backpack travelers for decades. Some of the 25 rooms have private baths, and all are budget-basic. Some are more comfortable than others. Be sure to ask for one on the side of the building away from the noise of the street. The decor in the common areas consists of a veritable jungle of potted plants and some travel posters of Switzerland, but the real ambience of the place comes from its guests—as youthful, sociable and energetic a crowd of foreign visitors as any you'll find in Guatemala. ~ 14 Calle 6-82, Zona 1; 2-513-786. BUDGET.

DINING

The dining room in the grand old **Hotel Pan American** is a special place to eat. Its decor features arts and crafts from the Maya highlands, and the waiters wear *traje* from Chichicastenango. The menu, which changes daily, features Guatemalan regional dishes, as well as American-style sandwiches, generous fixed-price luncheons and full dinners. ~ 9 Calle No. 5-63, Zona 1; 2-326-807. BUDGET TO MODERATE.

You can watch tortillas being made by hand while you eat at **Los Antojitos,** a casual, very popular downtown restaurant specializing in native Guatemalan and southern Mexican food. Big picture windows let you watch the throngs of people who pack the sidewalks outside as you listen to marimba music and savor a variety of light dishes (*antojitos* means "appetizers") or a full meal of grilled meat with fried plantains, black beans and tortillas. ~ 15 Calle 6-28, Zona 1; 2-511-167. BUDGET.

Spanish cuisine is featured at **Altuna**, a large restaurant lush with potted plants and full of Old World charm, from its massive, hand-carved, dark-finished wooden tables and chairs to the cool, dignified serving staff. The restaurant is known for its numerous shrimp dishes. It also offers an array of Iberian dishes from paella to roast dove. ~ 5 Avenida No. 12-31, Zona 1; 2-517-185. MODERATE.

El Gran Pavo is Guatemala City's best Mexican restaurant—not the sort of piñata-festooned tacos-and-tostadas place that most Americans think of as a Mexican restaurant, but a huge complex of plain, bright dining halls in an old house. Designed with Mexican visitors in mind, the menu features specialties from every region of Guatemala's big neighbor to the north—*poc-chuc, pescado veracruzano, enchiladas suizas, pollo en mole* and lots more. ~ 13 Calle No. 4-41, Zona 1; 2-510-933. BUDGET. There is a second location near the Zona Viva district at 12 Calle No. 6-54, Zona 9, 2-325-693.

SHOPPING

A block from the central plaza and directly behind the cathedral, the **Mercado Central** was Guatemala City's main public market before the 1976 earthquake destroyed it. Rebuilt underground beneath a parking lot, the market has vendors' stalls filling two floors that each span a full city block in area. The bottom level has food and the level above it has textiles, leather goods, pottery, incense, and other handmade items. Prices at the Mercado Central

◆◆

THE LAST STAND

Driving in Guatemala City is best avoided, since innumerable dead ends and unmarked turnoffs make it easy to get lost in a world of wrong-way streets and hungry-looking traffic cops. If you must drive here, remember that almost all the highways through Guatemala City come together in a single complex cloverleaf interchange called the Trébol west of the old and new downtown districts. The only main highway that does not intersect at the Trébol is Route 9 to the Caribbean coast. To reach it, take the Anillo Periférico, a ring road that skirts the west and north sides of the city before heading east. The main trick in traversing between the western and eastern halves of the country is to make the inconspicuous turn between Route 1 (Calzada Roosevelt) and Route 9 (Anillo Periférico).

run somewhat lower than at the more touristy markets in Antigua, Panajachel and Chichicastenango, and you may find very good buys on handwoven cloth. Be alert. Pickpockets and pack slashers abound in Guatemala City's public markets, and foreign visitors are their favorite targets.

Today, the Mercado Central has been eclipsed as an everyday shopping place for locals by the **public market** adjoining the second-class bus "terminal" in Zona 4, which is easier for most city residents to reach. This huge market overloads the senses with its noise, smells and crowds. Most vendors sell fresh produce, meats and household goods. You won't find much in the way of souvenir or gift items here—or many tourists—but if you want to immerse yourself in one of the biggest, brashest and most raucous marketplaces in Latin America, this is the place. This market is also where a good percentage the city's pickpockets, pack slashers and petty thieves ply their trade, so if the spirit of adventure draws you into this labyrinth, leave all your valuables and most of your cash back at the hotel. ~ Bounded by 1 Avenida, 1 Calle, 4 Avenida and 7 Calle.

NIGHTLIFE   Downtown in the Hotel Ritz Continental, you'll find **Brasilia**, a glitzy salsa club that seems to be right out of the 1950s. Sip a drink with fruit floating in it in a hotel bar version of tropical ambience and join suave men and glamorous women as they rhumba across the tiny dancefloor. In the basement of the same hotel is the more tranquil **La Taberna**. ~ 6 Calle A No. 10-13, Zona 1; 2-80-899. Look for a more unusual scene at **La Bodeguita del Centro**, a dark, intellectual hangout full of poetry, political folk music and Guatemalan neo-beatniks. Classic American and international films dubbed in Spanish are shown here on Wednesday evenings. ~ 12 Calle No. 3-55, Zona 1.

The city also hosts virtually all the cultural events staged in Guatemala. The **Instituto Guatemalteco-Americano**, where Guatemalan students go to learn English, often presents live theater performances and films in English. The theater is also used for dance performances. ~ Ruta 1 and Via 4, Zona 4; 2-310-022. Guatemala's national theater, the **Centro Cultural Miguel Angel Asturias**, in a park at the south end of the old downtown area along 6 Avenida, presents a wide variety of live performances. It actually consists of three theaters—an outdoor concert stage, a 2000-seat indoor playhouse and a small, intimate theater designed for chamber music concerts. ~ 24 Calle 3-81, Zona 1; 2-324-041. You'll find a calendar of upcoming events for both theaters in the *Guatemala News*, a free English-language weekly distributed at many hotels and restaurants.

Guatemala City's oddly old-fashioned **red light district**, one of the most notorious in Central America, is a dangerous place to

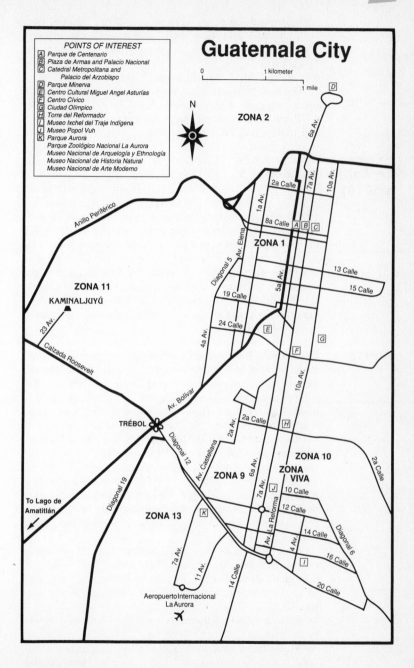

Guatemala City

POINTS OF INTEREST

- [A] Parque de Centenario
- [B] Plaza de Armas and Palacio Nacional
- [C] Catedral Metropolitana and
       Palacio del Arzobispo
- [D] Parque Minerva
- [E] Centro Cultural Miguel Angel Asturías
- [F] Centro Cívico
- [G] Ciudad Olímpico
- [H] Torre del Reformador
- [I] Museo Ixchel del Traje Indígena
- [J] Museo Popol Vuh
- [K] Parque Aurora
       Parque Zoológico Nacional La Aurora
       Museo Nacional de Arqueología y Ethnología
       Museo Nacional de Historia Natural
       Museo Nacional de Arte Moderno

0   1 kilometer

                     1 mile

N

ZONA 2

ZONA 1

Anillo Periférico

ZONA 11

KAMINALJUYÚ

23 Av.

Calzada Roosevelt

Av. Bolívar

TRÉBOL

To Lago de
Amatitlán

ZONA 13

ZONA 9

ZONA 10

ZONA
VIVA

Aeropuerto Internacional
La Aurora

2a Calle
1a Av.
7a Av.
10a Av.
8a Calle
Av. Elena
Diagonal 5
13 Calle
15 Calle
5a Av.
19 Calle
24 Calle
4a Av.
10a Av.
2a Calle
2a Av.
Diagonal 12
Av. Castellana
6a Av.
7a Av.
Av. La Reforma
10 Calle
12 Calle
14 Calle
4a Av.
16 Calle
20 Calle
Diagonal 6
2a Calle
Diagonal 19
7a Av.
11 Av.
14 Calle

walk around after dark—as is everyplace in Zona 1. And yes, there is AIDS (called *SIDA*) in Guatemala City. But anyone curious about Third World sleaze can lock the car doors and cruise past to see how sex is sold in this rather prudish country. ~ The action is along 18 Calle in Zona 1, centered around 9 Avenida.

Gay nightlife is in its infancy in Guatemala City. Two recently opened gay clubs, both downtown, are **Eclipse** (11 Calle No. 4-53, Zona 1; cover) and the **Happy Rooster** (3 Calle A between 9 and 10 Avenidas, Zona 1).

▼▼▼▼▼▼▼▼▼▼▼▼▼▼▼▼▼
La Zona Viva (Zonas 9 and 10)

La Zona Viva is located directly south of the Old City (Zona 1). Also called the Ciudad Nuevo (New City), where most of the city's skyscrapers have sprouted since the 1976 earthquake and briefcase-carrying people in business suits bustle along the boulevard talking about financial matters, it flanks broad and (by Guatemala City standards) beautiful Avenida La Reforma, which marks the boundary between Zona 9 on the west side of the street and Zona 10 on the east. The city's best hotels, restaurants and museums are in this area. Driving from Zona 1, take 6 Avenida south. Turn right on any street past 2 Calle and drive two blocks east to reach Avenida La Reforma, the main street of La Zona Viva.

SIGHTS

The **Torre del Reformador** (Tower of the Reformer) is dedicated to the memory of President Justo Rufino Barrios, the "liberal" dictator who, during his 1873-to-1885 reign, revolutionized the nation's caste system by including both elite *creolos* (of Spanish heritage) and Hispanicized *mestizos* (people of mixed Spanish and Indian blood) in a new social caste known as ladinos, allied to repress, exploit and pity the Maya people. This two-tiered caste system remains strong today, and Barrios is remembered—by ladinos, anyway—as one of the nation's greatest leaders. The tower, a downscaled replica of the Eiffel Tower in Paris, is visible from most parts of the city. The bell at the top is rung just once a year, on the June 30 anniversary of the revolution that brought President Barrios to power. ~ At the corner of 7 Avenida and 2 Calle in Zona 9.

From the Torre del Reformador, sightseers can jog two blocks east to Avenida La Reforma and head south along the avenue through the **Zona Viva**, the city's chic international district, with its upscale restaurants, nightclubs, hotels and high-fashion boutiques.

From Avenida La Reforma, take 6 Calle east for three blocks to the spacious quarters of Guatemala City's premier museum, the **Museo Ixchel del Traje Indígena**, on the campus of the Universidad Francisco Marroquín. Ixchel was the only female among the pantheon of ancient Maya gods. The goddess Ixchel represented the moon and is still revered throughout the Maya world in the form of the Virgin of Guadalupe (thus the crescent moon on which Latin America's dark-skinned Virgin Mary stands). According to legend, Ixchel originated the art of weaving, so hers is a fitting name for a museum exhibiting the best collection on earth of traditional Maya clothing and textiles. Mannequins model *traje* from what seems like every Maya village in Guatemala. The museum shows in great detail the methods and meanings of native dress, with examples of the evolution of village *traje* over the centuries to that seen in markets and villages today. In front of the museum, Maya women offer handmade apparel for sale. Interpretive plaques at this museum are in English, as well as Spanish. Admission. ~ 6 Calle Final, Zona 10; 3-313-638.

Back on Avenida La Reforma and a few blocks farther south is another of Guatemala City's finest museums, the **Museo Popol Vuh**. Located on the top floor of an office building, the museum is operated by a private college, the Universidad Francisco Marroquín, which received the outstanding collection of pre-Hispanic Maya artifacts it contains from a wealthy benefactor in 1977. The Popol Vuh Museum, named for the mythic history of the Quiché Maya (the manuscript is *not* in this museum), exhibits Maya artworks from all parts of Guatemala—Kaminaljuyú in suburban Guatemala City, the great Quiché, Cakchiquel and Mam cities of the western highlands, Quiriguá in the east, and Tikal and the other great centers in the Petén far to the north. While the collection of Maya pottery is said to be the best on earth, the most striking exhibit is a display of mannequins representing masked and costumed dancers in a Quiché reenactment of the Spanish conquest. Admission. ~ Avenida La Reforma No. 8-16, Zona 9; 2-347-121.

A few blocks west of Avenida La Reforma (take 14 Calle), near the airport, is the city's largest park, **Parque Aurora**, which contains the zoo and most of Guatemala's government-run museums. The **Parque Zoológico Nacional La Aurora**, like most in Latin America, is cramped and a little sad, but it does have an interesting newer exhibit area featuring the animals of the Petén rainforest—armadillos, coatimundis, tepescuintles, jaguarundis, spider monkeys and even endangered Petén crocodiles. Admission. ~ 7 Avenida, Zona 13; 2-720-507.

The most respected of the museums is the **Museo Nacional de Arqueología y Etnología**, which houses the largest collection in the world of Guatemalan Maya sculpture, together with ancient pottery, jewelry and masks. Here you'll find stelae from the ruins of Kaminaljuyú and a massive throne from the hard-to-reach site of Piedras Negras, north of Yaxchilán on the Guatemalan side of the border with Chiapas. Besides antiquities, the museum has an ethnology hall with 150 fine examples of village *traje* and displays on traditional ways of life among the highland Maya. Admission. ~ La Aurora, Zona 13 Salón 5; 2-720-489.

Also in the park is the modest **Museo Nacional de Historia Natural**, where stuffed bird and beast specimens are displayed in dioramas that simulate natural habitats in various regions of the country—good preparation for a journey to Tikal National Park and other areas in the Petén where wildlife abounds. ~ La Aurora, Zona 13 Salón 4; 2-720-468. The third museum, the **Museo Nacional de Arte Moderno**, features a well-focused selection of Guatemalan "modern" art spanning two centuries, from the end of the Spanish colonial era to the present day, and including works by the country's best-known painters, Carlos Mérida and Humberto Garavito. ~ La Aurora, Zona 13 Salón 6; 2-720-467.

LODGING   Guatemala City's most sophisticated (and expensive) hotels are located in and around the Zona Viva. This is the most convenient hotel area to the airport. The big Zona Viva hotels are flawlessly designed for business travelers, but may prove a bit of a bore for more adventuresome or romantic souls.

Most Zona Viva hotels are huge highrises with hundreds of rooms. The top of the line is the **Camino Real Westin**, a ten-story, 400-room megastructure that offers every conceivable amenity including a fully equipped gym and health spa, tennis courts and swimming pools, a beauty shop, 24-hour room service and same-day dry cleaning. The guest rooms are large and tastefully decorated, though with no hint of distinctively Guatemalan character. All feature private baths, air conditioning, phones and cable TV. The rates are about the same as for comparable accommodations in most United States cities, and give the Camino Real and other hotels of its ilk a certain air of privilege and elitism. A night's stay here costs more than the average Guatemalan citizen earns in two months. ~ Avenida La Reforma at 14 Calle, Zona 10; 4-484-633, fax 3-374-313. ULTRA-DELUXE.

Hotel Cortijo Reforma, an almost modern high-rise, has 150 bright, spacious, air-conditioned suites, each with a private balcony overlooking the Zona Viva. Each suite consists of a bedroom and separate living room with a couch that folds out into a spare bed. The suites have phones, cable TV and refrigerators but no cooking facilities. The hotel has an underground parking garage. ~ Avenida La Reforma No. 2-18, Zona 9; 3-318-876. DELUXE.

Also in the Zona Viva area, the **Hotel Guatemala Fiesta** has 240 air-conditioned rooms and suites (each with a private bath, phone and cable TV) in a 16-story building. We mention this place because it is where the airlines put up passengers stranded for the night by flight cancellations or reroutings, which are quite common in Central America. The hotel's kitchen also prepares the in-flight meals for all commercial planes departing from La Aurora International Airport. Rooms cost nearly as much as at the Camino Real, but the rooms seem a little frayed around the edges, and the loud orange color scheme makes this a place where you wouldn't want to wake up with a hangover. The hotel's best feature is its extensive array of indoor and rooftop sports facilities, including swimming, tennis, racquetball, squash, volleyball, soccer and a complete gym and spa. ~ 1 Avenida 13-22, Zona 9; 3-322-555, fax 3-322-569. DELUXE.

One attractive alternative to the plethora of high-rise hotels designed with politicians and businessmen in mind is the **Residencial Reforma**. Also known as La Casa Grande, this turn-of-the-century mansion near the U.S. Embassy contains 28 spacious guest rooms with tile floors, private baths and period reproduction furnishings. Some rooms have balconies. Common areas include a sitting room with a fireplace and beautifully landscaped gardens. ~ Avenida La Reforma No. 7-67, Zona 10; 3-320-914, fax 3-367-911. MODERATE TO DELUXE.

Lower-priced hotels are few and far between in the Zona Viva. A good compromise between budget and convenient location is the **Villa Española**. Located midway between the Old City and the Zona Viva, this three-story motel with its ersatz Spanish colonial architectural gingerbread and its 63 hauntingly familiar motel rooms (with private bath, ceiling fans, phone and cable TV) would seem right at home near an interstate off-ramp back in the United States. By Zona 9 standards, this place certainly qualifies as a bargain, even though its room rates are higher than you would expect to pay for a similar room in the United States. ~ 2 Calle No. 7-51, Zona 9; 3-318-503, fax 3-332-515. MODERATE TO DELUXE.

La Fonda del Camino, in the Hotel Camino Real Guatemala, is the city's most elegant French restaurant. This is the place where Guatemala's privileged class goes to savor haute cuisine in an atmosphere of candlelit underground intimacy. The prices offer wonderful bargains compared with similar restaurants in the United States or Europe. ~ Avenida La Reforma at 14 Calle, Zona 10; 4-484-633. MODERATE TO DELUXE.

DINING

Sophisticated versions of local dishes such as *chile rellenos* (chile peppers stuffed with cheese), homemade sausage and *carne adovada* (beef marinated in a tangy sauce before cooking) are served at the popular **El Parador**. The one on 12 Calle offers a more exotic ambience, with a lofty *palapa* roof and women making tortillas by hand near the entrance. ~ 12 Calle No. 4-09, Zona 9, with a second location at Avenida La Reforma No. 6-70, Zona 9; 2-320-062. MODERATE.

One of the classiest Mexican restaurants you're likely to find this side of Mexico City, **El Pedregal** has intimate dining areas clustered around a landscaped courtyard with a fountain and a fig tree. If that's not romantic enough, there are even mariachi musicians to serenade you. Menu choices range from shrimp sizzled in cognac to chicken *mole,* the Aztec "food of the gods." ~ 1 Avenida 13-42, Zona 10; 2-680-663. MODERATE TO DELUXE.

HIDDEN ►   Just north of the Zona Viva, **Nim-Guaa** is a favorite restaurant for regional cuisine served in an honest atmosphere of rough-hewn wood paneling and handwoven tablecloths. Short but savory, the menu features *carne a la parrilla,* enchiladas and Guatemalan-style tamales. Service is leisurely but enthusiastic. ~ Avenida La Reforma at 8 Calle, Zona 10. BUDGET.

One of the most offbeat and fun places among the international eateries in the Zona Viva is the **Sushi Rock Café**. Here you'll find a complete, authentic sushi bar along with tempura and teriyaki options in an East-meets-West rock music environment complete with big-screen TVs showing rock videos from the United States. If, in the throes of culture shock, you need a place where you can convince yourself that you're not *really* in Guatemala City, this is a better place than most. ~ 2 Avenida No. 14-63, Zona 10; 2-334-740. MODERATE.

You'll find wood-paneled walls, rustic tables and good beefsteaks grilled over an open fire as you watch at **El Rodeo**. The meals are served American-steakhouse style, with baked potatoes, salad and garlic bread on the side. Service here is prompt and portions are immense. In the evening, you can catch the marimba band while you eat. ~ 7 Avenida No. 14-84, Zona 9; 2-314-928. MODERATE.

SHOPPING   The **Zona Viva** section of Paseo La Reforma is lined with stylish boutiques and jewelry shops, but it's not exactly a world-class shopping district. In fact, most wealthy Guatemalans fly to Miami for their serious spending sprees. But a little browsing along this street will give you a good idea of what Central America's high-fashion designers are up to these days—often surprising bursts of creativity.

At the **Mercado Artesanía** in Parque Aurora, you'll find a good selection of *típica* clothing, leather goods, and other handicraft items. Prices tend to run higher than at the Mercado Central downtown, and much higher than at village markets in the highlands.

NIGHTLIFE   In case your travels in other parts of the country have led you to the conclusion that there is no life after dark in Guatemala, an evening in the Zona Viva will dispel that notion once and for all. Here, you'll find real nightclubs with a touch of glitz and "beautiful" people in evening dress.

Dash Disco used to be the hottest dance club in Guatemala City. Though now considered a bit déclassé by local trendsetters, it still has one of the best sound systems and light shows in town and a big library of international disco tunes. ~ 12 Calle No. 1-25, Zona 10; 2-352-712.

A classic Guatemala City hangout frequented by gringos and those who wish to hang out with gringos, the **William Shakespeare Pub** is a conversation bar with live music on some weekend evenings. ~ 13 Calle No. 1-51, Zona 10; 3-321-550.

Homesick in Guate? Try **Cheers Sports Bar**, where a mostly Guatemalan crowd gathers to watch American basketball on the big-screen TV and play foosball. ~ 12 Calle No. 0-60, Zona 10; 2-314-125.

Among the chic spots in the Zona Viva is **El Jaguar Discotheque** in the Hotel Camino Real Guatemala. Small but completely paneled with mirrors that make it seem vast, this place draws a fashionable clientele and can be hard to get into on weekends. ~ Avenida La Reforma at 14 Calle, Zona 10; 2-681-471.

For live music, one of the top Zona Viva clubs is **Kahlua**, which features Guatemalan rock-and-roll and a reggae-like Caribbean style of dance music known as *punta* that comes from the east coast. ~ 1 Avenida No. 13-29, Zona 10.

Kaminaljuyú (Zona 11)

From Parque Aurora, it is relatively easy to visit the ancient ruins of Kaminaljuyú in the city's northwestern suburbs. Buses go there, and drivers can simply head west on Diagonal 12, which becomes Calzada Roosevelt, to 23 Avenida, which runs north to the site. Kaminaljuyú was originally built in the Preclassic area, about 700 B.C., by early proto-Maya farming people known as the Miraflores. It became the largest center for jade mining and carving in the ancient Maya world. Unlike later highland Maya cities, Kaminaljuyú was built on an open plain without defensive fortifications. The city existed in peace for a thousand years before it was conquered by Toltec invaders from the central Mexican capital of Teotíhuacan around A.D. 300. The synthesis of Toltec and Maya influences seen in the art of Kaminaljuyú's Classic Period, which is on display in both the Popol Vuh Museum and the Museo Nacional de Arqueología y Etnología, is hauntingly similar to that of Chichén Itzá in the Yucatán several centuries later, and stelae found here rank as the oldest-known Maya glyph carvings. Kaminaljuyú continued to reign as the greatest city of the Guatemalan highlands throughout the Classic Maya period, enjoying trade relations with Tikal and other cities of the Petén, as well as with Copán, until it was destroyed in a war around A.D. 900 at the same time that Tikal, Copán and other cities all over the Maya world collapsed.

SIGHTS

HIDDEN ►

Kaminaljuyú, one of the oldest major ruins in the Maya world, is a simple trip from Parque Aurora. (Before going there, though, it's essential to check in with the **Instituto Guatemalteco de Antropología e Historia**. ~ 12 Avenida No. 11-65, Zona 1; 2-531-570.) After many years of neglect, the current renewal of interest in ancient Maya culture has inspired new, ongoing excavations at Kaminaljuyú, and the site is intermittently closed to the public. If you can convince the bureaucrats at the institute that you have a sincere interest in Maya archaeology, they're likely to give you a permit to enter. If there are workers at the site, you may even be allowed to enter the underground maze that is the true glory of this site. (If not, the barely recognizable surface structures are not really worth the trouble.)

Although Kaminaljuyú was one of the largest Maya cities, with 50,000 people, few traces of its architecture remain today. The temple and palace walls were made from light volcanic pumice mortared and stuccoed with adobe, materials that eroded back into earth soon after the buildings were abandoned, leaving the bare fields and grassy mounds seen at Kaminaljuyú today. Much of the area covered by the original city has been bulldozed for residential development, and much of the site has been dug up over the years by looters in search of pre-Columbian pots and jade jewelry.

Archaeologists are studying the sadly neglected site with new interest, exploring the city's foundations through underground tunnels. It is here, beneath the sad, dusty surface of the site, that the secrets of Kaminaljuyú lie: tombs, altars, hieroglyphic inscriptions and even a skeleton or two. The Guatemalan government is slowly restoring Kaminaljuyú in hopes of enhancing tourist interest. Admission. ~ Kaminaljuyú, Zona1.

Kaminaljuyú is located in a residential *colonia* of the same name with no tourist lodgings and no restaurants where it would be advisable to eat.

▼▼▼▼▼▼▼▼▼▼
Mixco Viejo

A better-preserved Maya ruin than Kaminaljuyú, Mixco Viejo can be visited on a day trip from either Guatemala City or Antigua. The route passes through verdant hill country and the colorful, infrequently visited Cakchiquel Maya villages of San Pedro Sacatepéquez and San Juan Sacatepéquez, where cut flowers are the main cash crop. Mixco Viejo is one of the most remote Postclassic Maya sites, and if you make it there you can pretty much expect to have the ruins to yourself.

The descendants of the Pokomam Maya people who inhabited Mixco Viejo now live in the modern suburban village of Mixco, on Route 1 between Guatemala City and Antigua; this village is the starting point for a trip to the ruins. From Mixco, take paved Route 5 north for 25 kilometers (15 miles) to the tiny village of Montúfar, where a marked turnoff to the left takes you for an-

The Lake and the Volcano

Lago de Amatitlán, a long, narrow lake at the foot of fuming, rumbling **Volcán Pacaya**, used to be an ultra-exclusive recreation area for the elite few who could afford vacation homes along the privately owned lakefront. Air and water pollution, as well as litter, have now made the lake less attractive up close than at a distance. The wealthy have abandoned the spot, and plummeting real estate prices have opened up the lakefront to construction of large numbers of small, shacklike cabañas. On the lake's western tip, the Cakchiquel Maya town of Amatitlán has a public beach and docks where boatmen offer cruises on the lake, and there are hot springs at several small *balnearios* (bathing resorts) along the lakeshore; neither the lake nor the hot springs are for bathers who are squeamish about polluted water. Perhaps the most pleasant option is a drive around the perimeter of the lake, among pine-covered foothills along the base of the volcano.

A bubble-shaped gondola supposedly runs from **Las Ninfas National Park** on the south shore of the lake 2000 feet up a steep mountainside to **United Nations Park** (admission), where there are scale models of Tikal's Great Plaza and other renowned structures as well as a full-size Maya hut, plus magnificent views of the lake and hiking trails through the forest. However, the gondola has been closed for repairs for two years. When it was operating, it ran on weekends only, and at those times the park at the top was mobbed with picnickers from the city. As long as the gondola stays closed, hikers who tackle the steep 2-kilometer trail to the United Nations Park are likely to find that they have the whole park to themselves. (Hike in groups only. Lago de Amatitlán is close enough to Guatemala City to attract the occasional armed robber.)

The well-marked Lago de Amatitlán road turns off Route 9 beyond the southern outskirts of Guatemala City. The turnoff is about 25 kilometers (15 miles) south of the Trébol freeway interchange and the central part of the city. Buses run to Lago de Amatitlán from 20 Calle at 3 Avenida in Zona 1. By car or bus, the trip from the city takes about half an hour.

other 16 kilometers (10 miles) on a rocky, unpaved mountain road to the ruins of Mixco Viejo.

SIGHTS   **Mixco Viejo** was the stronghold of the Pokomam people, a fiercely independent minority tribe living within the boundaries of the Quiché empire in the 13th and 14th centuries A.D. They built their fortress-city on the top of a mesa surrounded by cliffs so steep that invasion by Quiché armies was impossible. They fortified the cliffs with massive stone walls to create a great walled city as unassailable with its panoramic 360-degree view of the surrounding countryside as any medieval European castle. They even engineered an escape tunnel through which they could escape if the city was ever overrun by their enemies. It never was. The city seems to have grown remarkably fast. The earliest buildings on the site were built sometime after A.D. 1400, but by the time conquistador Pedro de Alvarado laid siege to the city and destroyed it in 1525, it had grown to between 8000 and 9000 people, making it one of the largest highland Maya strongholds. One of the largest pyramids on the main plaza is built on top of an earlier temple pyramid that contained another temple inside—three phases of construction within the span of a century, also indicating explosive growth.

Mixco Viejo has been more extensively restored than any other Postclassic highland Maya ruin, thanks to the efforts of the French-Guatemalan Archaeology Mission from 1954 through 1967. Almost all the main structures—pyramids, platforms, temples, ball courts, altars—were entirely restored. Unfortunately, the earthquake that tumbled Guatemala City in 1976 hit these ruins so hard that in places it's now hard to tell what was restored and what was not. In its spectacular setting, the ruins pose a challenge to the imagination. The structures, most of which take the form of long platforms or steep, truncated pyramids, supported buildings made of thatch and wood. Only one piece of architectural sculpture—a serpent head with a human face emerging from between the jaws—has ever been found here. Otherwise, the stonework was smooth and covered with stucco. Many fragments of colored stucco at the site show that the walls were painted in various bright hues and may have contained murals. The most striking features of Mixco Viejo, besides its magnificent location, are its two large ball courts.

LODGING   **Camping** is permitted; a few thatch shelters are provided. Food can be found en route to the site in the town of San Pedro Sacatepéquez on Friday market days and four miles farther along in San Juan Sacatepéquez on Fridays and Sundays. At other times, it's best to pack a picnic lunch before leaving the city.

SHOPPING   **San Pedro Sacatepéquez**, en route to Mixco Viejo on Route 5, is home to the largest T-shirt manufacturing industry in Guatemala.

And if you were wondering where all those fireworks that explode on the slightest pretext in the streets of every Guatemalan town come from, they're handmade by the villagers of **San Raimundo**, a few kilometers east of Route 5 shortly before you come to the Mixco Viejo turnoff on the other side of the road.

Outdoor Adventures

Volcano climbing is a favorite sport in the Guatemalan highlands. **Volcán de Pacaya**, near Guatemala City, is the most popular of all volcano climbs because it is a relatively short distance to the 8500-foot summit and because the mountain erupts almost constantly. The bursts of lava can be observed from the summit of an inactive cone nearby. For years, U.S. State Department advisories have warned of robberies by bandit gangs on the trail up Pacaya, so it is better to sign on with a group tour, offered almost daily through travel agencies in Antigua and costing around Q70.

HIKING

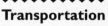

Transportation

For most travelers, the best way to get from the United States to Guatemala is to fly. Various commercial airlines operate daily (or in a few cases every other day) international flights to Guatemala City from Miami, New Orleans, Houston, Dallas and Los Angeles.

AIR

La Aurora International Airport, in the southern part of Guatemala City, on the boundary between Zona 9 and Zona 13, is one of only two commercial airports in the country. (The other is at Santa Elena near Tikal National Park.) It is served by American, Air France, British Airways, Continental, Iberia, Japan Air Lines, KLM Royal Dutch Airlines and Lufthansa, as well as Guatemala's national airline, Aviateca, Aeroquetzal (Guatemalan), Aerocaribe and Mexicana (Mexican), Aeronica (Nicaraguan), COPA (Panamanian), LACSA and TACA (Costa Rican), and SAHSA (Honduran).

I strongly advise travelers to leave Guatemala City by shuttle van and rent a car in tourist-friendly Antigua. Traffic in the capital is crazy at best and sometimes downright deadly, and rental car plates identify you as easy pray for traffic cops seeking bribes.

CAR

If you must drive in Guatemala City, the most important thing to remember is **the Trébol**, a tangled cloverleaf that connects most of the highways that go through the city. Route 9 to the Caribbean coast is only main highway that avoids the Trébol. To reach it, take the Anillo Periférico, a ring road that skirts the west and north sides of the city before heading east.

If you must drive in the city, the major international car-rental agencies with booths at La Aurora International Airport in Guatemala City include **Avis Rent A Car** (2-310-017; also at 12 Calle No. 2-73, Zona 9, 2-316-990), **Budget Rent A Car** (2-310-273; also at

CAR RENTALS

Avenida La Reforma No. 15-00, Zona 9, 2-316-546), **Dollar Rent A Car** (2-317-185; also at Avenida La Reforma No. 6-14, Zona 9, 2-348-285), **Hertz Rent A Car** (2-311-711; also at 7 Avenida No. 14-76, Zona 9, 2-322-242) and **National Interrent** (2-318-365; also at 4 Calle 1-42, Zona 10, 2-680-175). Guatemala's largest car-rental agency is **Tabarini Renta Autos** (La Aurora International Airport, 2-314-755; also at 2 Calle A No. 7-30, Zona 10, 2-316-108). Motorcycles, as well as cars, are for rent in Guatemala City at **Rental Moto-Car** (11 Calle 2-18, Zona 9; 2-341-416).

BUS

Buses run back and forth between the Old City and La Zona Viva constantly. They also go to every other part of the city, since many residents are too poor to own cars and depend on public buses as their sole mode of transportation. The buses are crowded and uncomfortable, however, and after giving them a try you may conclude that taxis are well worth the few dollars extra.

You can catch a bus to Kaminaljuyú from the corner of 6 Calle and 6 Avenida in Zona 1, several blocks' walk from the Instituto de Antropología e Historia office. It's a 20-minute bus trip from downtown.

By bus, the trip to Mixco Viejo is difficult. You can catch a slow midday bus to Pachalum from the Zona 4 terminal in Guatemala City, but getting back is a problem—the return bus passes the ruins in the middle of the night. Travelers who wish to visit Mixco Viejo by bus are better off taking a tour van from Antigua.

PUBLIC TRANSIT

Taxis in Guatemala City are relatively inexpensive in the daytime, though they become fewer and pricier after dark. Look for them at cab stands called *sitios* near most hotels and downtown plazas. For longer trips, especially the drive over the mountain to Antigua, your best bet is one of the many shuttle vans that wait at the airport. Van transportation can also be arranged at the travel desk of any large Guatemala City hotel or through the manager of most smaller hotels.

▼▼▼▼▼▼▼▼▼▼▼▼▼▼▼▼▼▼▼▼▼▼

Addresses & Phone Numbers

U.S. Embassy ~ Avenida de la Reforma No. 7-01, Zona 10; 3-311-541

Canadian Embassy ~ Edyma Plaza Building, 13 Calle No. 8-44, Niv. 8, Zona 10; 3-333-6102

British Embassy ~ 7 Avenida No. 5-10, Zona 4; 3-321-601

Immigration office ~ 41 Calle No. 17-36, Zona 8; 4-714-864

Post office ~ 7 Avenida No. 11-67, Zona 1; 2-326-101

Police headquarters ~ 6 Avenida No. 13-71, Zona 1; dial 120

Ambulance ~ dial 128

Cruz Rojo (Red Cross) ~ 3 Calle No. 8-40, Zona 1; dial 125

FIVE

La Antigua Guatemala

Okay, let's put Guatemala City behind us until the time comes to return to the real world. Let's take a 45-minute shuttle ride to the other side of the mountain. The small, history-packed city of La Antigua Guatemala (pop. 50,000), referred to simply as Antigua, is the preferred starting point for travelers arriving in Guatemala by air, who can avoid the harsh realities of Guatemala City by catching a shuttle directly from the airport to this fairytale town. In fact, a stay in Antigua provides the gentlest and friendliest possible introduction to Guatemala.

While in Antigua, pause a moment to imagine the sound the towering brick-and-mortar archways and colonnades, the four-foot-thick walls and ornately detailed church facades, all the proudest architecture of one of the greatest Spanish colonial capitals, must have made as they came crashing down in 1773. That the wreckage lay in its stately and haunted quietude for more than two centuries after the final earthquake is remarkable enough, when you consider that even the great pre-Columbian Maya cities in the region have been scavenged for building materials until nothing remains but dirt mounds. It may be that these old churches and mansions inspired such awe as to repel looters, or it may simply be that the architecture was so massive as to defy attempts to dismantle it and carry it off. Whatever the explanation, the sources of Antigua's special ambience were that sudden crash and the long silence that followed.

UNESCO has designated Antigua both a World Heritage Site—a sort of international historic district that qualifies the town's buildings for preservation funding from international sources—and a Monument of the Americas. Some of the world's toughest architectural style laws now will keep this fragment of the old Spanish empire, like a citywide open-air museum, basically unchanged for centuries.

The city lies sheltered within the natural fortress formed by the three massive volcanoes that surround it: Volcán de Fuego, which still smolders with sulfurous fumes; solitary Volcán de Agua, which once destroyed an older Spanish city; and the highest, 13,250-foot Volcán Acatenango. Antigua's stately old buildings, chic shops, colorful native markets and nearly constant celebrations and processions makes it a world apart from nearby Guatemala City.

In contrast to other Latin American countries like Mexico, which has been ruled from a single capital since long before the Spanish conquest, Guatemala's capital has changed again and again. Antigua was the capital city through most of the Spanish colonial era, from 1543 to 1773—longer than Washington has been the capital of the United States. Known then as Santiago de los Caballeros de Guatemala, it was one of the most elegant cities of the Spanish empire, rivaling Mexico City or Lima. With a population of 70,000—nearly twice its present-day population—it had 38 Catholic churches, one of the first universities in the Western Hemisphere and one of the first newspapers. Noble families born to wealth and power, as well as those who had grown rich exploiting the people and resources of the Americas, held court in private palaces impressive in their grandeur.

Little architecture remains from the 16th and 17th centuries because the capital was ruined by an earthquake in 1717. Following the earthquake, Antigua's residents immediately began to rebuild it, using the architecture we see in Antigua today: low baroque-style structures of massive adobe walls and arches reinforced with thick, squat pillars, designed to survive any conceivable earthquake. But then, 56 years later, following a year-long series of warning shocks, a mammoth quake rolled through the capital in 1773, laying waste to its great churches and palaces. Disaster relief to Guatemala became a hotly contested issue between the pope in Rome, who wanted to see the capital restored, and the king of Spain, who wanted to move it elsewhere. The people of the city huddled among the crumbling walls and collapsed roofs for three years before the dispute was settled and the king ordered Santiago de los Caballeros de Guatemala (thereafter called Antigua Guatemala) abandoned. All the building materials and works of art that could be salvaged from the ruins were to be carried 28 miles over a mountain range to the new capital, Nueva Guatemala de la Asunción (now Guatemala City).

Despite miserable living conditions and the ravages of epidemic diseases, and in defiance of the king's commands, residents refused to leave the bleak remains of what had been Central America's grandest and most beautiful city. Antigua was never entirely abandoned, though it remained in a woeful state of decay and disrepair for nearly two centuries as coffee plantations took over the surrounding countryside.

British author Aldous Huxley visited in 1934 and reported to his English-speaking readership, "There is nothing grand at Antigua; but there is much that is charming; much that is surprising and queer; much—indeed everything—that is picturesque and romantic in the most extravagantly 18th century style." His description turned Antigua into a tourist destination and attracted the founders of Antigua's expatriate community. Today, hundreds of American, Canadian, British and South African retirees and expatriates make their permanent homes in Antigua. Hundreds and sometimes thousands of other, mostly young, gringos come to town for weeks or even months at a time to study Spanish, sometimes in such overwhelming numbers as to make the city feel something like an American college town.

The sizable English-speaking presence helps make Antigua a major travelers' destination. Just an hour-long drive from Guatemala City and within easy day-trip distance of other key tourist spots like Chichicastenango and Lago de Atitlán,

Antigua is perhaps the most comfortable and gringo-friendly place in Guatemala to use as a base camp for explorations to other parts of the country. From the Trébol in Guatemala City, take Route 1, also marked as Calzada Roosevelt, west to San Lucas Sacatepéquez and follow the big green signs onto the wide, paved road to Antigua. Here, you'll find colorful markets where Indians in village *traje* sell beautiful textiles and handicrafts. You'll find time-honored folk rituals and echoes of grandeur from the Spanish empire. But you'll also find televisions featuring CNN and HBO in English, almost-current editions of the *Miami Herald* and sympathetic Americans knowledgeable in the ways of Guatemala who are happy to share words of caution and encouragement with anyone who is truly interested in understanding this small and surpassingly strange country.

In the past decade, as Guatemala City's crime and congestion problems have made the capital a more and more unpleasant place to live, wealthy Guatemalans have also begun to move to Antigua. The result is that the town has become the most chic neighborhood in Guatemala, with a growing number of residents commuting to the city in long black chauffeur-driven limousines. Since historic preservation laws prohibit commercialization of colonial buildings, which comprise most of the city, excess demand has pushed real estate prices in Antigua to levels that are exhorbitant even by U.S. standards, and the brisk real estate trade is in buying and selling leases, not deeds. Yet a feeling lingers that the prosperous Guatemalans are somehow outsiders in a solid community of artists and poets, gringo expatriates and Indians, an accidental community that has no economy except tourism and no reason for its existence except an ideal climate and an eccentric sort of charm.

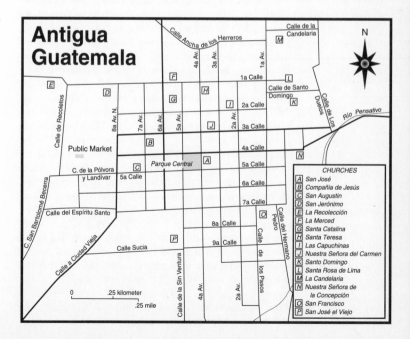

Nothing in the city is more than 2 kilometers from anything else or about eight blocks from the central plaza. All over Antigua are many crumbling remains of grandiose structures, most of them stabilized and propped up with reinforcing buttresses since the most recent major earthquake in 1976. There are narrow, stone-cobbled streets that feel very much like the 18th century, and the unexpected can lie around any corner, as Antiguans love public celebrations of all kinds. Almost every late afternoon sees a school marching band parade, a birthday party erupting with fireworks in the streets or a religious procession of the faithful walking beside a pickup truck that carries a life-sized statue of a saint.

Antigua is laid out on a square grid. All streets have both a number and a long name left over from the colonial era; an intersection may be marked with one or the other, neither or both. For example, the Parque Central is located in the exact center of the city between 4 and 5 Calles and 4 and 5 Avenidas, or to put it another way, between Calle del Ayuntamiento/Calle de la Concepción, Calle de la Polvora y Landivar/Calle de la Universidad, Calle del Obispo Marroquín/Calle del Conquistador, and Calle de Santa Catalina/Calle de la Sin Ventura. The number system is much simpler. Just remember that numbered *calles* run east and west, the numbers go up as you go south—toward the Volcán de Agua—and the word *poniente* (west) or *oriente* (east) tells which direction you are from the central plaza; *avenidas* run north and south, the numbers increasing as you go west—toward the Volcán Acatenango and its steamy, nearly hidden companion, Volcán de Fuego—and the word *norte* (north) or *sur* (south) tells which way you are from the plaza.

SIGHTS

It is easy to get lost in Antigua, since every block in the city looks pretty much the same as the others with its bumpy cobblestone streets lined by similar-looking buildings with red tile roofs, stucco walls and inconspicuous doorways. Fortunately, since the city covers an area of just over one square mile, it's hard to stay lost for very long. Store signs are small by law and too inconspicuous to serve as landmarks, and it takes a while to learn the various churches and old ruins well enough to locate them on a map. For the first couple of days in Antigua, a good navigational strategy is to always start your explorations at the **Parque Central**, the graceful and busy town plaza also known by its colonial name, the Plaza de Armas. Ask your hotel manager to point you in the right direction the first time, and make mental notes of the return route. In the Parque Central, benches set amid flower gardens and shaded by trees trimmed to circular perfection surround a fountain (c. 1936, reconstructed after the 1738 original) adorned by a bevy of female statues gushing water. The central plaza is one of the great spots of the world for people, watching, offering a daily kaleidoscope of beggars and vendors, village peasants and wealthy businessmen, soldiers and nuns, elderly people and little children, not to mention travelers from all parts of the globe.

Historic buildings face the Parque Central. On the east side of the plaza, the **Church of San José** was built around two chapels, all that remained after the 1773 earthquake of the Cathedral de

Santiago (c. 1669), which had been the largest cathedral in Central America. Ruins of the rest of the cathedral can still be seen behind the present-day church. Conquistador Pedro de Alvarado and his wife, Doña Beatriz, lie buried beneath the floor of the old cathedral.

Along the plaza's south side, the **Palace of the Captain-Generals** was originally built in 1558 and extensively renovated in 1764. It served as the nation's capitol building for less than ten years before the earthquake ruined it. Recently restored, the palace once again houses government offices, including an INGUAT tourism office and a police barracks.

On the north side of the plaza, the **Ayuntamiento** (c. 1740) still serves as Antigua's city hall after more than 250 years. It also contains two small museums, the **Museo de Santiago**, which exhibits antiques from the colonial era, and the **Museo del Libro Antiguo**, where old books and historical documents are on display, including such rarities as a 17th-century edition of *Don Quixote,* a colonial-era Maya-Spanish dictionary and a woodcut map of Lake Atitlán made in 1800, as well as exhibits on 18th-century bookmaking and binding methods. Admission.

From the Parque Central, the first place to explore should be the **public market**. Many travelers make their arrival there, as all buses pick up and let off passengers at the row of stores directly in front of the market. The covered market sprawls over an area of about six square blocks and operates every day. Saturday is the busiest market day. You'll find a wonderful maze of stalls both mundane and exotic in Antigua's market—everything from shoe repairers and onion vendors to medicine women who sell herbs to heal every ailment. Cardamom and other spices, which have recently become major cash crops in this part of Guatemala, are also displayed in abundance. Unusual souvenir and gift possibilities here include incense, green (unroasted) coffee beans and many kinds of dried spices. (Although you cannot bring fresh produce

✔ **CHECK THESE OUT**

- Become an instant expert on the subject on Mayan textile art by browsing through the **Centro de Textiles Tradicionales Nim Po't.** *page 138*

- Sleep soundly after a sauna, jacuzzi and massage in a suite at the **Antigua Spa Resort.** *page 135*

- Sample traditional Guatemalan cuisine at one of the few restaurants in Antigua that serves it, the **Café Panchoy.** *page 136*

- Make the strenuous 14-hour round-trip climb to the crater of an active volcano, the 12,350-foot **Volcán Fuego.** *page 142* back to the United States, dried plant products pose no problem.) To get to the public market, follow either 4 Calle Poniente or 5 Calle Poniente westward for three blocks.

Along the way, 4 Calle Poniente takes you past the ruins of the **Church and Convent of Compañía de Jesús** (c. 1626), also the site of an early Jesuit college. The king of Spain expelled the Jesuits from his empire 150 years later, and shortly after that the massive church was completely ruined by the great earthquake, leaving only a crumbled facade and some broken statues to hint at its former glory. Today, it is filled with stalls of *típica* clothing and jewelry vendors. The Jesuit college was the home of Rafael Landívar, whom scholars consider to be the finest poet in Spanish colonial literature. Notwithstanding that he wrote his poetry in Italy after being expelled from Guatemala along with the other Jesuits, he is commemorated in the **Monumento a Landívar,** a little park with a series of five arches on the south side of the main public market. ~ 4 Calle Poniente. Nearby, the ruin of the **Church of San Augustín** dates back to 1615, making it one of the oldest structures in Antigua. ~ 5 Calle Poniente.

Immediately south of the public market, behind the Pollo Campero fast-food fried chicken place, the **Mercado de Artesanías** was built by the local government and opened in 1999 to provide a more tourist-friendly atmosphere for folk art vendors who had previously displayed their wares in the main market. The 108 stalls in two cool, shady terrazas surrounding green lawns provide clean, attractive display space for an exceptionally high quality array of products. The prices are right. The only trouble is, few shoppers go there. Tour guides shun the place because vendors don't pay them commissions, and many tourists steer clear of both the public market and the artesans' market because of the din of trucks, buses, and crowds surrounding them. Don't miss this place—it's one of the best shopping bets in town.

HIDDEN ►   While in the market area, check out the fascinating **Casa K'ojom,** a museum dedicated to Mayan music and dance. The high points of a visit here are the hourly live music demonstrations and slide shows of indigenous ceremonies. Cassette tapes and replicas of Maya musical instruments are for sale in the gift shop. Admission. ~ Avenida de Recoletos No. 55; 8-323-087.

A walk through the northwest side of town on 1 Calle Poniente will take you past the walls of the abandoned **Church of San Jerónimo** (c. 1757) to the ruins of **La Recolección** (c. 1708), formerly a monastery where colonial Central America's largest church library was housed along with a collection of oil paintings on sacred themes. Today, La Recolección has been reduced to a few still-standing columns and arches that invite comparison to ruins of ancient Rome. ~ 1 Calle Poniente.

Farther east, **La Merced Church** (c. 1552) may be the most striking example of colonial architecture in Antigua. The church was spared any serious damage in the great earthquake, a fact that was briefly seen as a miracle until the church was damaged by a smaller quake a few months later. Churrigueresque ornamentation—complex patterns of stucco vines, birds and flowers—covers the entire pink church facade, whose massive columns and niches hold brightly painted saints. The church has been mostly restored and is now used for regular services. The four-ton statue of the Black Christ in the church is carried through the streets annually as a centerpiece of Antigua's lavish Semana Santa observances. Adjoining La Merced, the **Convent of Santa Clara** contains what must have been a beautiful fountain before the statuary was removed to Guatemala City. ~ On 1 Calle Poniente, between 6 Avenida Norte and 5 Avenida Norte.

Other historic ruins in this part of town include the **Church and Convent of Santa Catalina** (c. 1606), a half-block south on 5 Avenida Norte, and the **Church and Convent of Santa Teresa** (c. 1675), two blocks east on 1 Calle Oriente.

Farther east is the **Church and Convent of Las Capuchinas** (c. 1736), one of the city's most interesting ruins. Of the many convents in Antigua, where young women retreated after failures in love or were sent by irate parents after becoming pregnant, this was the most luxurious. Although the convent cells in the unique, circular *torre de retiro* (tower of retreat) are tiny, just four feet by eight feet, each had its own private bathroom with running water, an extravagance practically unheard of in those days. Below ground level, a huge round vault with a single massive column flaring from the center to form a continuous arch with the outer walls is considered one of the architectural wonders of the Spanish empire. It was probably used as a cooling cellar for perishable foods, though tour guides like to suggest that it was a torture chamber. ~ On 2 Calle Poniente at 2 Avenida Norte.

Between the central plaza and Las Capuchinas is the small, charming **Church of Nuestra Señora del Carmen** (c. 1686, mostly rebuilt in 1728). ~ On 3 Avenida Norte near 3 Calle Oriente. In the extreme northeast corner of the city, are several colonial churches including the pretty little **Church of Santa Rosa de Lima** (c. 1570) at the end of 1 Calle Oriente and, two blocks farther north on 1 Avenida Norte, the hopelessly ruined **Church of La Candelaria** (c. 1550).

A stroll east from the Parque Central along 5 Calle Oriente first takes you past the sole remaining building of the **Royal University of San Carlos de Borromeo**, which has suffered very little earthquake damage since its construction in 1760. In colonial times, teaching prelates from the Jesuit, Dominican and Franciscan orders held classes here in law, theology and medicine, as well as such unusual subjects as the Cakchiquel language. The university building now houses the **Museo Colonial**, where exhibits depict everyday life and learning in 18th-century Guatemala. Especially good are the collection of religious oil paintings and saints carved from wood and the restorations of colonial classrooms. ~ 5 Calle Oriente.

Two blocks farther east, the **Díaz del Castillo House** is open to the public. Far from elegant, this old house is historically note-worthy because its original owner, Bernal Díaz, a retired Spanish foot soldier who became a founding father of the town and a city councilman of Santiago de los Caballeros de Guatemala (now An-tigua), wrote the classic *History of the Conquest of New Spain* while living here. This definitive eyewitness account of Cortés' victories in Mexico is still in print in ten languages after nearly 450 years.

Up the block and across the street at the corner of 1 Avenida—known in Spanish colonial times as Calle de la Nobleza, which means Street of the Nobility—the more imposing **Casa Popenoe** was the finest mansion in the city when it was built in 1636. It was reduced to rubble by the 1773 earthquake. In 1931, U.S. agri-cultural advisor Dr. William Popenoe bought the wreckage and spent a fortune restoring it to its former glory with careful atten-tion to detail and 17th-century authenticity. Fully furnished with the finest in Spanish colonial antiques, the mansion is open for mid-afternoon tours daily except Sunday. Admission. ~ 1 Avenida.

A block north and a block east of the mansion are the ruins of the **Temple and Convent of Nuestra Señora de la Concepción** (c. 1578), the oldest convent in the city. Although little remains except fragments of collapsed walls, the convent holds a special

◆◆

CREATIVE ADVENTURES IN ANTIGUA

For a memorable foreign study experience, check out **Art Workshops in Antigua Guatemala**. This group organizes week-long classes led by world-class teachers, mostly from the U.S. More than two dozen workshops a year include photography, painting, textile work, travel writing, sculpture, dance, shamanism, and the making of *alfombras*, the flower petal carpets that cover Antigua's streets during Semana Santa. Local Maya women are available to instruct workshop members in traditional backstrap weaving. ~ Information: Liza Fourre, Director, Callejon Lopez No. 22, 8-326-403, fax 8-326-925 in Antigua, or 4758 Lyndale Avenue South, Minneapolis, MN 55409, 612-825-0747, fax 612-825-6637; www.artguat.org, e-mail fourre@artguat.org.

place in Antigua history. Sor Juana de Maldonado, the daughter
of one of Guatemala's wealthiest families, retreated here after an
unhappy love affair to live, despite a vow of poverty, in a huge private apartment lavishly decorated with Spanish artwork, lace, gold
and jewels. Thanks to her father's influence, she was made abbess
of the convent in disregard of older and more devout nuns. Public
anger over the appointment embroiled the whole city in turmoil
and sporadic violence. In later years, however, Sor Juana distinguished herself as one of Guatemala's greatest poets. ~ 4 Calle
Oriente.

Two blocks south of Casa Popenoe, the **Church of San Francisco el Grande** (c. 1543) is one of the largest and most beautiful
colonial churches in Antigua. Although some buildings on the
church grounds remain in ruins, the main church has been under-
going a long, loving restoration since the 1960s and now is once
again used for services. ~ 1 Avenida Sur and 7 Calle Oriente.

Midway between the parque central and the Church of San
Francisco, adjacent to San Jose el Viejo, is a narrow, palm-lined
park where Indian women sell *huipiles*, embroidery and weavings
of variable quality. At the east end of the park you'll find the
Pilas de la Union. *Pilas* are wash basins used to wash clothes, and
Maya women—many of whom live in houses without running
water—have been coming here to do their laundry since the public pilas were built in 1853. The water comes from a spring that
was Antigua's original water supply and the reason the town was
located here. Thanks to colorful *traje*, what seems mundane to the
locals is exotic and picturesque to camera-toting visitors. ~ 2 Avenida Sur between 6 and 7 Calles Oriente.

At the other end of the park from the *pilas*, **San José el Viejo**
was built by a crew of devout volunteers without permission from
the king of Spain, who ordered the church demolished. Local residents refused, resulting in a 25-year standoff before the church
was finally allowed to open its doors. From here, the Parque Central is three blocks north along 5 Avenida Sur. ~ 8 Calle Oriente.

Just past the northwest edge of town near the Jocotenango
cemetery is the recently opened **Mariposario Antigua**, a lovely
mesh-enclosed garden filled with live native and exotic butterflies. Guides are available to point out the many different species.
If you're not planning to visit Panajachel, which has a longer-
established and lusher butterfly park, then don't miss this one.
Also on the grounds of this old coffee *finca* is a serpentarium displaying snakes native to Guatemala. Admission. ~ Finca Gravi-
leas de San Isidro, off Calle Ancha; 2-033-190.

◄ HIDDEN

Antigua's lodging scene offers an extraordinarily wide range in
terms of price and class. Though there are a number of very inexpensive hotels that host mainly students, several of the better ac-

LODGING

commodations rank among the most luxurious in Central America. Rates vary greatly depending on the season, peaking during Semana Santa. At other times of the year, room prices are often a small fraction of the maximum authorized rate, which the government requires be posted (in dollars!) on room doors. Antigua has many hotels, and except during Semana Santa, advance reservations are needed only at the most exclusive ones. The drivers of shuttles from the Guatemala City airport are happy to help you locate a hotel to suit your budget. Although the drivers receive a commission from the hotel for steering you there, the rate you pay is no higher than it would be if you came there on your own.

Look for quality lodgings on Antigua's chic shopping and restaurant street at the **Posada de Don Rodrigo**. This inn, originally a colonial mansion known as Casa de los Leones, has been so beautifully restored that it is worth visiting as a sightseeing highlight even if you're not staying there. It fills an entire city block near La Merced church and an ornate old city gate that arches over 5 Avenida. The 34 guest rooms are set around two open courtyards, each with gardens. The rear courtyard has a large fountain surrounded by restaurant tables, where musicians play the marimba in the afternoons. Each room is individually decorated and furnished with Spanish colonial antiques. While all rooms have private baths and phones, other amenities vary tremendously, so be sure to look at the room before renting it. Some have fireplaces or views of the volcanoes. ~ 5 Avenida Norte No. 17; phone/fax 8-320-291. DELUXE.

If money is no object, the ultimate place to stay in Antigua is the **Casa Santo Domingo**, built among the ruins of the former Santo Domingo Monastery. This hotel recaptures the atmosphere of colonial Antigua in its lobby accented with dark wood, wrought iron and fine Spanish antiques. Lush courtyard gardens set the ambience with colorful flowers, fountains and live parrots. The 26 contemporary-style guest rooms and suites, luxurious enough to satisfy even the most sophisticated world traveler, feature jacuzzi tubs and fireplaces along with private baths, cable TV and phones. ~ 3 Calle Oriente No. 28 8-320-140, fax 8-320-102. ULTRA-DELUXE.

A smaller, less expensive but still very comfortable downtown lodging that also offers wonderful colonial charm is the **Hotel Aurora**, just east of Doña Luisa's Restaurant and several blocks east of the central plaza. The oldest hotel in Antigua, it has been operating continuously since 1923. The 16 large rooms, which have private baths, very high ceilings and heavy, rustic wood furnishings, are situated around a courtyard with a carefully tended lawn and flowering trees and shrubbery. There is a gracious sitting room

Holy Week in Antigua

Antigua's greatest claim to fame is Semana Santa. While the week before Easter is the biggest holiday of the year throughout Guatemala, no place—not even Guatemala City—rivals the magnificent processions held in Antigua. The largest Easter week observance in the Western Hemisphere, Semana Santa in Antigua continues to draw more spectators each year from all parts of the world.

Annual Semana Santa processions took place in Antigua as early as the 1590s. But when the government ordered the capital moved from Antigua to Guatemala City following the 1773 earthquake, the order included moving all religious art and relics from the churches of Antigua to those of the new capital. To prevent important religious statues from being taken away, local *cofradías* (religious brotherhoods, usually devoted to specific saints) looted their statues from the ruined churches and worshiped them in secret for generations. The *cofradías*, most of which disassociated themselves from the Catholic clergy to become lay brother-hoods called *hermandades*, grew in power and influence throughout the 19th century despite an 1872 presidential decree outlawing them. In the early 20th century, when the ban on *cofradías* and *hermandades* was lifted, the custom of showing the long-hidden saint statues in Holy Week religious processions was revived.

Semana Santa processions center around huge floats called *andas* on which religious statues are mounted. The floats are carried by as many as 60 to 80 men in biblical clothing. The entire procession route is covered with elaborate *alfombras* (carpets) made of pine needles, flower petals and sawdust. Although the *alfombra* custom is practiced throughout Guatemala and can be seen during Holy Week even along back roads to remote Indian villages, none are as magnificent as those that decorate the streets of Antigua. Hundreds of people work all night long to create an *alfombra*, often several blocks long with dozens of detailed, colorful pic-torial panels, in front of a church where a holy vigil or procession will take place. In addition, people who live along a procession route create their own *alfombras* on the street in front of their homes. After the floats and processioners walk over the carpets, many people take the flower petals and pine needles, which are believed to possess miraculous healing power. Then the magnificent carpets are swept away during the night without a trace.

with a fireplace and a television. Breakfast is included. ~ 4 Calle Oriente No. 16; phone/fax 8-320-217. MODERATE.

The exclusive 60-room **Hotel Antigua**, located on the south side of the city near the historic Church of San José and just four blocks from the Parque Central, caters to Guatemala's wealthy class, offering every imaginable amenity, such as a fireplace, cable TV, a bar and two double beds (a rarity in Guatemala hotels) in each guest room. Accommodations are in a series of low buildings with furnished porticoes around lovely courtyard gardens. The hotel also has a heated swimming pool and off-street parking. Non-guests who eat breakfast or lunch at the hotel are invited to use the pool free. ~ 8 Calle Poniente No. 1; 8-320-288, fax 8-320-807. ULTRA-DELUXE.

Two blocks south of the Hotel Antigua, colonial charm comes with a much lower price tag at **El Rosario Lodge**. At the pavement's end, surrounded by shade trees, the lodge is the former main house of a coffee plantation. It offers bargain room rates and more in the way of peace and quiet than any other hotel in Antigua. Though the ten guest rooms are spare and functional with private baths, they are brightened by colorful locally woven textiles. El Rosario is only a 15-minute walk from the center of town, but guests are advised not to stroll after dark in this isolated neighborhood. ~ 5 Avenida Sur No. 36; 8-320-366. BUDGET TO MODERATE.

You'll find good value for the money at the **Posada San Sebastián** located near the church of San Francisco on 2 Avenida Sur. The 12 dark, cool rooms with heavy wood furniture open onto a grassy courtyard with a small swimming pool, a display of *huipiles* for sale, several tables where breakfast is served, and a cage of parrots. ~ 2 Avenida Sur No. 36A; 8-323-282. MODERATE.

Actually, there are two hotels in town named **Posada San Sebastián**, and they're under different ownership. The other is a little more modest, a little lower in price, and also worth checking out. ~ 3 Avenida Norte No. 4; 8-323-721. MODERATE.

There are several low-budget *hospedajes* between the Parque Central and the market. A good bet is the **Hospedaje Primavera**, on a little box-canyon side street off 4 Calle Poniente. The ten small rooms in this two-story hotel share two baths and have two beds each plus a small table and white walls without decor. The management is friendly and helpful. ~ 3 Callejón No. 3. BUDGET.

A more comfortable reasonably priced hotel is the nine-room **Hotel Cortés y Larraz** on a usually quiet side street less than two blocks from the Parque Central. The clean white rooms have two beds each with private baths. There are few windows, but some rooms have small fireplaces for those chilly Antigua evenings. There is parking in the hotel courtyard for one or two cars. ~ 6 Avenida Sur No. 3; 8-320-276. BUDGET TO MODERATE.

A small, friendly bed and breakfast in a colonial home two blocks from the Parque Central, **La Casa de la Musica** has a comfortable sitting room with a fireplace and cable TV, as well as a rooftop patio with spectacular views of the surrounding volcanoes. Three of the four guest rooms have private sitting areas with fireplaces, and all have private baths. ~ 7 Calle Poniente No. 3; 8-320-335, fax 8-323-690; e-mail ginger@guate.net. MODERATE

◄ HIDDEN

Then there's Antigua's largest hotel, the **Radisson Villa Antigua**. This modern 156-room hotel on the outskirts of town along the road to Ciudad Vieja is totally devoid of the colonial ambience the other hotels listed here provide in abundance. Instead, it offers an array of resort-style amenities including three pools, tennis courts, saunas, a workout room, a children's playground, bicycle rentals, and a restaurant, bar, disco and shopping complex. The rooms are impressively large, bright and contemporary, with TVs, fireplaces, bathtubs and balconies that give guests spectacular volcano views. Rates are at least as much as you would pay for comparable accommodations in the United States. ~ 9 Calle Final at Carretera Ciudad Vieja; 8-320-011, fax 8-320-237. DELUXE TO ULTRA-DELUXE.

Near the outskirts of town, the **Posada del Angel**'s claim to fame is that U.S. President Bill Clinton stayed there while visiting Antigua in 1998. The five luxurious suites are individually decorated with colonial-style furnishings and Maya folk art. All have fireplaces and cable TV and overlook a lovely patio and swimming pool surrounded by palm trees and pines. Special touches include bathrobes and fresh flowers. ~ 4 Avenida Sur No. 24A; 8-325-305, fax 8-320-260; e-mail elangel@ibm.net. ULTRA-DELUXE.

Also on the edge of town, the **Antigua Spa Resort** has a row of five hotel suites in a nicely landscaped compound surrounded by high ivy-covered walls topped with barbed wire. The spacious, quiet suites are new-looking and colorfully decorated, but the real attraction here is the spa facility, which includes a steam bath, sauna, jacuzzi, indoor swimming pool and exercise room. Services including massages, facials and manicures are available. The spa is also open to non-guests, and the charges are far less than you'd expect to pay at a comparable spa in the United States. There is a complimentary shuttle to take guests into town. ~ Camino a Ciudad Vieja; 8-323-960, fax 8-323-968; e-mail antgspa@infovia. com.gt. DELUXE.

Even more than in other Guatemalan cities, most of Antigua's restaurants shun anything resembling regional cuisine in favor of food with an international flair intended to attract foreign visitors. The only problem with dining out in Antigua is choosing between the many outstanding restaurants. Check your bill before

DINING

leaving a tip; it is standard practice in almost all Antigua restaurants to add a 10 percent *propina* to the total.

An inexpensive place geared for a young international crowd is the long-established **Café Librería**, more commonly known as the Rainbow Reading Room. In back of a used book shop, it has a courtyard with flowers, incessant Fleetwood Mac on the sound system and lots of designer *típica* clothing displayed for sale. Here you'll find bagels, fruit salads and good coffee for breakfast and an eclectic lunch and dinner menu. ~ 7 Avenida Sur No. 8. BUDGET.

Hidden away behind the Casa del Conde bookstore on the west side of the parque central, the **Café Condesa** offers such peace and quiet that it seems far removed from the bustling town center. Flower gardens and waterfall fountains set the ambience for a restful break and a cup of good Guatemalan coffee or a Moza beer. The food is healthy, featuring organic vegetables and low-fat ingredients. The sandwiches are unimpressive, but the Sunday brunch is the best in town. ~ 5 Avenida No. 4; 8-325-274. MODERATE.

The **Fonda de la Calle Real** is where students at Antigua's dozens of language schools congregate. The large, rather plain restaurant has a friendly, though almost completely Spanish-speaking, atmosphere and features live music on weekends. House specialties include fondue and *caldo real* (royal soup), a rich chicken soup with lots of trimmings. There is also a full menu of more substantial chicken, pork and beef entrées. The prices are set with students in mind, though the portions tend to run smaller here than at other restaurants nearby, making this place a dubious bargain for anyone with a big appetite. ~ 5 Avenida Norte No. 5, upstairs; 8-322-696. BUDGET.

Farther up 5 Avenida Norte next to the Nim Po't textile center, **Frida's** serves exceptional Mexican cuisine ranging from *pollo en mole* (chicken in chocolate-and-chile sauce) to vegetarian tacos. The decor features posters of paintings by the restaurant's namesake, Mexican painter Frida Kahlo, and a hodge-podge of almost-antiques including an old-fashioned gas pump, and the atmosphere tends to be boisterously fun. ~ 5 Avenida Norte No. 29; 832-5274. MODERATE.

HIDDEN ▶ It's alarmingly easy to travel the length and breadth of Guatemala without ever discovering that the country has its own distinctive cuisine beyond tortillas and black beans. You can rectify that with a visit to **Café Panchoy**, a big, brightly lit restaurant where white-coated waiters serve such local favorites as *pepián* (a spicy chicken and pumpkin seed stew) and *parrilla mixta* (assorted barbecued meats) to a clientele that consists mainly of well-heeled Guatemalans. ~ 6 Avenida Norte No. 1B; 8-321-4-249. MODERATE.

The **Café Flor**, a split-level Thai and Szechuan restaurant—is one of the few places in town to get spicy food. Several bright, cheerful little dining areas have three or four tables each. Sink your chopsticks into the yellow curry with veggies and your choice of chicken or tofu. ~ 4 Avenida Sur No 1. BUDGET.

A great place for truly hungry travelers, the **Restaurant Katok** is loud, funky and full of that tattered-yet-dignified ambience that is peculiarly Guatemalan. Old photos on the walls show Antigua as it was in the early decades of the 20th century. The food selection consists of various *carnes parrilladas* (grilled meats) including beef, lamb, rabbit, sausage and ham. The best bet is a platter for one or several people containing a substantial portion of each meat along with salad, potatoes, beans and fried bananas. ~ 4 Avenida Norte No. 3-C; 8-320-524. MODERATE.

The traditional gringo hangout in Antigua is **Restaurant Doña Luisa Xicotencatl**, generally called just "Doña Luisa's," a few blocks east of the Parque Central. Travelers gather at tables in the open-air courtyard to exchange new discoveries and words of encouragement, and often to arrange ride-sharing for excursions to other parts of Guatemala. The English-language bulletin board here is the town's largest, and there is a fair-sized lending library of paperbacks in English. CNN broadcasts play constantly on the TV in the room behind the courtyard. There are other, more secluded dining areas upstairs. Breakfast options include a heaping fruit salad of pineapple, mango, banana and assorted melon slices served with yogurt and granola on the side. The coffee, from locally grown beans, is some of the best in town. Lunch and dinner entrées include Reuben sandwiches, Texas-style chile con carne, and stuffed baked potatoes. The best takeout bakery in town is at the front of the restaurant. ~ 4 Calle Oriente No. 12; 8-322-578. BUDGET.

For a big splurge, the place to go is **El Sereno**, a longtime Antigua legend recently relocated to the classically colonial Casa de la Pirámide. Often rated as the finest restaurant in Guatemala, this mansion restaurant has upstairs dining areas with views of the nearby volcanoes and more intimate rooms that set the stage for a romantic candlelight dinner. Typical of the classic French fare is baked ham in a rich *crème de cassis et moûtard* sauce, served as the main event in a multicourse feast with potato soup, a salad du jour, exquisitely prepared steamed vegetables and a choice of fine wines, with a chocolate mousse for dessert. Prices are prohibitive by Guatemalan standards but, thanks to the U.S. dollar's high buying power, really about the same as you would pay for dinner at a typical steakhouse in the United States. This is practically the only restaurant in Guatemala that takes advance reservations. ~ 4 Avenida Norte No. 16; 8-320-501. DELUXE.

SHOPPING   In some ways, Antigua is the best shopping town in Guatemala. Asking prices for *típica* and *traje* clothing are much higher than in Panajachel or Chichicastenango, so if you plan to venture to those highland towns or to more remote villages, save your shopping dollars until you get there. But for a day of last-minute gift and souvenir shopping before you head back to the Guatemala City airport and home, the selection to be found in Antigua is hard to beat. And Antigua is the only place in the country with a lot of art galleries, designer boutiques and specialty shops.

Two words used over and over in this book are *típica* and *traje*, separate types of clothing you'll find for sale in just about every corner of Guatemala. *Típica* clothing, exported throughout the industrialized world, is made by Guatemalan women, Indian and ladino alike, who own hand looms or sewing machines and work in their own homes. They can make as much as US$1.50 a day, which is considered a good wage for women in Guatemala. This low labor cost, together with favorable foreign currency exchange rates, makes Guatemalan clothing an incredible bargain. Quality is variable, though. There is a big difference between these commercial clothing products and *traje*, or traditional village clothing. Each village throughout central and western Guatemala has its own style and pattern of clothing, which is unlike that of any other village. Although at first glance all *traje* of a particular village looks alike, small differences in detail make each garment unique in the eyes of other village women. In a few villages, men as well as women still wear *traje*. Designs woven or embroidered into the clothing often have symbolic significance, though in some villages the meaning of a stylized design has been lost to memory. Careful craft goes into each garment, and a single *huipil* with a cash value of US$30 or $40 can take several months to make. You can wear *típica* in public anywhere in Guatemala, but as for *traje,* Indians take offense at foreigners who wear traditional village clothing even though they are eager to sell it to you—assuming, no doubt, that you plan to display it on your wall as folk art.

In addition to the **Mercado de Artesanías**, mentioned in Sights above, another truly exceptional place to shop for high quality Maya traje is **Centro de Textiles Tradicionales Nim Po't**. This museumlike consignment store displays thousands of ceremonial *huipiles* grouped by region, with maps and displays telling about the areas they come from. Prices are fixed and range from $30 or so to as much as $800 for museum-quality pieces. Spend some time here developing an eye for fine workmanship before shopping with street vendors. ~ 5 Avenida Norte No. 29; phone/fax 8-322-681.

Other places in Antigua where many vendors sell *típica* clothing from all over Guatemala include the old public market site in the ruins of the **Church and Convent of Compañía de Jesús** on 4

Calle Poniente and the center median of 8 Calle Oriente near the **Church of San Francisco**.

Of the many retail stores in town that sell highland Maya folk art, the best is **Casa de los Gigantes**. A shopper can spend hours browsing among the shelves piled high with masks, wood carvings, textiles and other items. ~ 7 Calle Oriente No. 18; 8-320-685. Another great shop, geared to more expensive, museum-quality collectibles, is the **Casa de Artes** across the street from the Hotel Antigua. ~ 4 Avenida Sur No. 11; 8-320-792.

Antigua is also noteworthy for its designer shops. Dozens of residents, most of them foreign expatriates, are in the business of creating original clothing and accessory designs and hiring local women to make them. Although much of the apparel made this way is exported to stores in the United States and Europe, a fair sampling is displayed in boutiques around Guatemala. Stylish shops can be found along 5 Avenida Norte. For one of the most interesting selections of women's clothing and accessories made from handwoven native fabrics, check out **Al Pie del Volcán**. ~ 5 Calle Poniente No. 13; 8-323-684. To buy the same handmade fabrics by the yard, visit **Textiles Plus**, under the same management as Al Pie del Volcán. ~ 6 Calle Poniente at Alameda de Santa Lucia. Check out the cotton casual "wearable folklore" at ¡**Que Bárbara!** ~ 4 Calle Oriente No. 37. One-of-a-kind designer clothing, lambswool blankets and hand-carved bone jewelry are among the offerings at **El Nicho**. ~ 4 Calle Oriente No. 23.

Some of the hardest, finest-quality jade in the world is mined in Guatemala. The art of jade cutting has been passed down through the centuries, and today several companies in Antigua operate jade mines, factories and showrooms that are the most elegant stores in town. Just east of the Parque Central is the ritzy **Casa de Jades**, where, in addition to luxury-priced jewelry, the stock includes more modest gift items such as cassette tapes of Guatemalan Maya music. ~ 4 Calle Oriente No. 3.

A little way up the street at the oldest and largest of the jade factory showrooms is **Jades, S.A.**, where the showpieces are magnificent and exorbitantly expensive replicas of royal burial masks like the one found in King Pacal's tomb under a pyramid temple at the Maya ruins of Palenque in Chiapas, Mexico. ~ 4 Calle Oriente No. 34; 32-07-52. Perhaps the most interesting jade factory to tour is **Jades J.C.**, operated in a family home on the outskirts of town; their showroom is just north of the Parque Central. *Jades* is pronounced "HA-days" in Spanish. ~ 9 Calle Oriente No. 2-A; showroom: 5 Avenida Sur No. 6.

You'll find fine quality handmade silver and gold jewelry incorporating ancient Maya designs at **Platería Típica La Antigüeña** ~ Callejón Los Horcones No. 46; 8-320-411, located north of town near Iglesia San Felipe de Jesús. Another good jewelry source is **Platería Típica Maya**. ~ 7 Calle Oriente No. 9; 8-322-883.

Although Guatemala produces some of the world's finest coffee, until recently it was entirely for export and virtually unavailable within the country. In fact, it was so scarce that most restaurants made their *"café"* from a blend of about 10 percent ground coffee beans and 90 percent roasted wheat. Looks convincing, but . . . yuck! Recently, entrepreneurs have set up *tostadurías* to supply the restaurants in towns where a lot of international travelers go. They buy fresh coffee direct from small farmers on the slopes of the volcanoes above Antigua, roast it fresh daily, grind it to order. In Antigua, the place to go for souvenir bags of coffee is the **Tostaduría Antigua**. ~ 6 Avenida Sur No. 12-A.

HIDDEN ▶

Specialty food shops are good to know about, especially if you are packing a picnic lunch for a volcano climb or preparing for a trip to the eastern part of the country, where restaurants are few and far between. Several places in Antigua deal in cheeses and wines, gourmet items and commonplace American foods, which are sold here as cures for homesickness. When students have been away from the States for a month or so, their eyes can grow misty at the sight of a box of Triscuits. You can get them at **Deliciosa** ~ 4 Avenida Norte No. 10-D, 8-320-713; or **Peregrinos Deli** ~ 5 Calle No. 4, 8-322-832.

NIGHTLIFE

Cultural entertainment in Antigua got a big boost with the recent opening of **El Sitio**, a non-profit cultural project that presents film festivals in English and Spanish, theater performances, indigenous dance groups, photo and painting exhibitions and other events. There's something going on just about every afternoon and evening except Monday and Friday. Monthly schedules are posted around town and published in *The Revue*.

Antigua's usually sedate nightclub scene can become lively when a lot of visitors are in town. The **Café Picasso**, one of Antigua's oldest bars, is an artsy meet-you-there-later sort of place where lilting guitar strains create a soundtrack behind your conversation. ~ 7 Avenida Norte No. 3. There's live jazz, salsa, blues and rock-and-roll at **El Afro**. ~ 6 Calle Poniente No. 9. Latin disco music is featured at **La Casbah**, which has a flashy light show on Saturday night. ~ 5 Avenida Norte No. 30, 8-322-640. Look for more Latin disco rhythms at **La Canoa**. ~ 5 Calle Poniente No. 6. **Mangos** is another Latin disco club. ~ 6 Avenida Norte No. 2. For a mellow piano bar ambience, try **Nicolas**. ~1 Calle Poniente No. 3. Or if drinking beer in a pool hall suits your taste, head for **El Atico de Frida**, upstairs from Frida's restaurant. ~ 5 Avenida Norte No. 29; 8-320-504.

Some of the most rewarding short side trips from Antigua are to villages on the slopes of Volcán de Agua. **Ciudad Vieja**, 6 kilometers south of the city **Outlying Villages**
on Route 14, was the capital of Guatemala before it was destroyed by floods in 1541 and the government moved to what is now Antigua. The town was washed away so completely that archaeologists are unsure where the original plaza, palace and cathedral were located. Today, visitors to this coffee-growing community of about 10,000 people will find plenty of guides eager to tell the tragic story of the old capital for a modest *propina*, but there really isn't much to see.

On a different road from Antigua, the Cakchiquel village of **Santa María de Jesús** is a colorful community of thatch-roofed huts where the women wear lovely purple *huipiles* and some men still wear traditional red shirts lavishly embroidered with flower designs. The view from this village high on the northeast slope of the volcano is spectacular. Santa María is the starting point for hikers to climb Volcán de Agua (see Outdoor Adventures). The village is 12 kilometers south of Antigua on the road that extends from 1 Avenida Sur.

A kilometer or so to the north on a side road that leaves the highway at Ciudad Vieja is the Cakchiquel village of **San Antonio Aguas Calientes**, renowned for some of the finest traditional backstrap weaving in Guatemala. Visitors often have a chance to watch the women weaving.

Just a short distance past Ciudad Vieja is another side road that turns off toward San Miguel Dueñas. About 2.5 kilometers down this road you will find the **Jardín Botánico y Estación Experimental Valhalla**, a government-chartered organic test farm where 400 different subspecies of macadamia trees are being grown to determine which are most suitable for Guatemala's climate. The botanical garden has a beautiful picnic area with volcano views, and the small admission charge includes a tour and samples of the farm's specialty products, which include macadamia chocolates, roasted macadamia nuts and natural nut oil antiwrinkle creams. Admission.

◄ HIDDEN

Although the beautiful *huipiles* for sale in stalls on **San Antonio Aguas Calientes'** plaza can also be found for about the same price in Antigua's public market, there is a certain appeal to buying them in the village where they are made.

SHOPPING

You can rent a mountain bike by the hour, day or week in Antigua at **Bike Center Antigua**. ~ **Outdoor Adventures**
6 Calle Poniente at 6 Avenida Sur No. 21; 8-322-768. Or try **Escley Rent-A-Bike**. ~ 4a Avenida Norte No.

BIKING

4-C; 8-320-762. **Antigua Mountain Bike** has rentals, too. ~ 5 Avenida Sur No. 36. A substantial deposit is required. **Mayan Bike Tours** offers guided tours ranging from four-hour trips around nearby coffee *fincas* to three-to-five-day trips around Lago de Atitlán, including all meals and van transportation. ~ 1 Avenida Sur 15; 8-323-383.

HIKING

HIDDEN ►

You can get a great bird's-eye view of Antigua from the **Cruz del Cerro**, a monumental wooden cross that stands on the hillside east of town. A trail designed for religious processions climbs by switchbacks up to the cross. Until recently, visitors were warned against using this trail because of the high risk of robbery, and it is still unwise to climb it solo. Antigua's Tourist Police—those young, English-fluent cops in white T-shirts who patrol the Parque Central armed with walkie-talkies—are happy to accompany sightseers up to the cross. Contact them at the Tourist Police station, 4 Avenida Norte just off the main plaza; 8-320-533.

For a much more ambitious hike, the most popular volcano climb is on **Volcán Agua** south of town. The 6-kilometer climb from the village of Santa María de Jesús to the summit of the 12,350-foot volcano can easily be done up and back in a single day. The smoking, rumbling **Volcán Fuego** west of town, standing 12,350 feet high, can also be climbed in a day, while nearby **Volcán Acatenango**, at 13,040 feet in height, takes two days for a roundtrip and has a hikers' hut at the summit. The shortest trails up both volcanoes start at the village of Yepocapá on the west slope. Information on guide services and current safety bulletins are available at the INGUAT office in Antigua. The **Club de Andinismo Chicag** in Antigua organizes hiking trips in the region. ~ 6 Avenida Norte No. 34; 8-323-343. The **Casa Andinista** sells trail maps and guidebooks for hikers. ~ 4 Calle Oriente No. 5-A.

In Antigua, horses can be rented for private rides or guided tours to the volcanoes at the stables of R. Roland Pérez. ~ San Pedro El Panorama No. 228; 8-322-809.

Transportation

CAR

Antigua is on **Route 10**, a winding mountain road that branches off **Route 1** (the Panamerican Highway) west of Guatemala City. It's 26 kilometers from Guatemala City's center to the turnoff and another 14 kilometers to Antigua.

Carretera Ciudad Vieja leaves town to the south, from the public market and past the Radisson hotel, and goes to Ciudad Vieja and other outlying villages on the slopes of Volcán de Agua.

CAR RENTALS

Among the car rental agencies in Antigua are **Avis** (5 Avenida Norte No. 22; 8-322-692), **Tabarini** (2 Calle Poniente 19A; 8-323-091), and **Ahorrent** (5 Calle Oriente No. 11; 8-320-787).

Antigua has no airport. If you have just arrived by plane at Guatemala City's airport, there is no reason to rent a car at the airport. Renting a car is just as easy in Antigua, and driving it away is much easier. Simply take the hour-long ride from the airport to Antigua on one of the shuttle vans that meet all international flights.

AIR

Buses run to and from 15 Calle 3-65, Zona 1 in downtown Guatemala City every 15 minutes during daylight hours. If you are traveling to Antigua from Quezaltenango, Huehuetenango or other points west, you'll usually need to change to a local bus at Chimaltenango, a large town on the Panamerican Highway. Buses from Antigua pass through Ciudad Vieja on the way to the more distant village of Alotenango, and still others serve most villages in the department of Sacatepéquez. All buses load and unload in the street south of the public market.

BUS

Taxis can just about always be found at the cab stand by the northeast corner of the Parque Central. You won't need them to get around Antigua unless you're loaded down with luggage, but they present a reasonable alternative if you need to get to the Guatemala City airport at a time when there's no shuttle scheduled.

PUBLIC TRANSIT

Any of the many travel agencies that line the streets of central Antigua can arrange shuttle service to Guatemala City, Panajachel or Chichicastenango. Prices are the same everywhere, and schedules don't vary much. Buy a ticket in advance and the shuttle van will pick you up at your hotel.

Addresses & Phone Numbers

INGUAT (tourist information) ~ Palace of the Captain-Generals; 8-320-763

Tourist police ~ 4 Avenida Norte; 8-320-533 or 8-320-577

Policía Nacional ~ Palace of the Captain-Generals; 8-320-251

Fire department and ambulance ~ Bomberos Voluntarios, public market bus area; 8-320-251

Hospital ~ 6 Calle Oriente No. 20; 8-320-883

Post office ~ 4 Calle Poniente across from the public market; 8-320-485

SIX

Lago de Atitlán

 A hypnotic wind rolls across Lago de Atitlán in midafternoon, chopping the stainless steel surface of the water into sparkling waves behind a sharply defined line that moves toward Pana- jachel with the eerie grace of some ancient, unseen Maya god. The wind front is so usual that the local Indians have a name for it: *Xocomil.* You can sit under a *palapa* at the Sunset Café and watch it come toward you for an hour. In fact, this is one of the more popular pastimes in Panajachel. Down the hill, barefoot women wearing identical black skirts and bright pink *huipiles* balance bundles of clothing the size of elephants on their heads as they wait silently for the ferry that will take them home to their village across the lake. Tall, steep Volcán Tolimán stands outlined in the hazy distance and appears to be the wind's source. Time stops, almost. The wind front reaches you at last, snapping the long, slow, silent moment with a whispered roar and blowing your paper napkin away.

It's easy to see why Lago de Atitlán is Guatemala's premier tourist destination. While Antigua is certainly one of the best places in Guatemala to visit, it is unlike any other place else in the country. It has more Spanish colonial buildings and in- ternational restaurants than all the rest of Guatemala put together. Lago de Atit- lán, however, wraps the best of the backcountry in a package so exotic that just being there can make you feel like you're in a movie of your own making. The part of the lakeshore between Santiago Atitlán and San Pedro La Laguna, along with the three major volcanoes on the south side of the lake, make up Atitlán National Park, while another part of the shoreline nearby is a nature reserve protecting the habitat of the rare, flightless Atitlán grebe. The area offers a mixed bag of just about everything one goes to Guatemala to see.

To begin with, there's the big, beautiful lake, which is for all practical purposes "bottomless." Soundings to a depth of more than 1000 feet have proved this an- cient, rain-filled volcano crater to be the deepest lake in North America—and no- body is certain how much deeper it may be. Scientists puzzle over the fact that sev- eral rivers run into the lake and none flow out, yet the water of Lago de Atitlán is fresh instead of salty like Utah's Great Salt Lake, as it would be if it lost water only through evaporation. Many believe that the lake must drain to the sea by way of a great, undiscovered underground river.

Lago de Atitlán measures 12 miles long by 6 miles wide—just big enough so that as you gaze across the lake from Panajachel's beachfront you can see the huge volcano that looms above the Maya village of Santiago Atitlán, the largest town on the lake, on the far horizon. The lake wraps around the bases of several volcanoes that reach altitudes of up to 11,700 feet (3500 meters) against the clear blue highland sky. The ferry trip across the lake, which takes less than an hour, transports you to a mirrored world where Maya villages endure, little changed over the centuries. A road runs partway around the lake, and ferries run regularly to the larger villages. Other traditional villages are only accessible by canoe or foot trail.

The word *atitlán* ("lake") is Nahuatl, the language of Aztec slaves who came to Guatemala with the first Spanish conquistadors. The fact that Lago de Atitlán should be a beach resort at all is curious, since the entire beachfront is narrow and rocky. The water is chilly for swimming, and pollution may pose health risks since raw sewage drains into the lake, which has no known outlet. Yet the lake does have a lively beach scene, especially on weekends, when Guatemalans flock here from the city. The rest of the week, the waterfront around the town of Panajachel is one of those rare places where you can while away hour after hour just staring in wonder at the water and the mysterious volcanic landscape beyond.

En Route to Panajachel

On the way from Antigua to Panajachel you pass the neighboring sites of the greatest Postclassic Maya cities and the first Spanish capital of Guatemala. The town of Tecpán (pop. 7000), just off the Pan-American Highway (Route 1), 48 kilometers from Panajachel and 71 kilometers from Antigua Guatemala, is a village that served briefly as Guatemala's first Spanish colonial capital, which was then called Santiago de los Caballeros de Guatemala. Conquistador Pedro de Alvarado held court there for three years before a Maya uprising drove him to move the capital to a safer location.

SIGHTS

The only thing to see around Tecpán today is the ruined fortress city of **Iximché**, located five kilometers south on an unpaved side road. Iximché was the short-lived capital of the Cakchiquel Maya, who were the ancestors of the people who live in several Lago de Atitlán area towns and villages such as San Pedro La Laguna and Sololá today. Admission.

At the southeasternmost reach of the Aztec Empire, the Cakchiquel people of Iximché paid tribute to the Mexicans and adopted Aztec customs, notably mass human sacrifice of prisoners of war. Their main enemies were the Quiché at K'umarcaaj, who dominated the highlands at the time of Iximché's founding in 1470. The Spanish army arrived just 54 years later and, following a bloody six-year war against the Cakchiquels, destroyed the city. Like the other major highland Maya ruins at Zaculeu and K'umarcaaj, Iximché even in its heyday was unimpressive compared with fabulous lowland ceremonial centers such as Copán and Tikal. The largest temple pyramids were only 30 feet in height. The ceremonial center at Iximché was extraordinarily spacious and open, with temple mounds and altars graded from the hilly natural landscape around four large plazas. Several temples and one of the two large ball courts at Iximché are better preserved than anything at K'umarcaaj, though, and visitors can see faint remnants of paintings on two of them. Although the structures here were devoid of sculpture, the walls were covered with bright-colored murals inside and out. Iximché, perhaps better than any other highland ruin, imparts a feel for the warlord era that marked the declining Maya civilization in the last centuries before it fell to Spanish invaders.

Located about three kilometers from Panajachel and 600 feet higher in elevation, **Sololá** (pop. 10,000), capital of the department of the same name that encompasses the Lago de Atitlán area, is a steep hillside town spilling over the edge of a mesa above the lake. It is a Cakchiquel town, inhabited by the descendants of the Maya people who built Iximché. Today the town's main claim to fame is tofu. An experimental factory built here in the 1970s by Americans from The Farm, a large Tennessee commune, who idealistically saw tofu as the solution to hunger in Guatemala, a cheap source of protein in the Indian diet. The experiment flopped: local Indians, who reject even more mundane foreign foods such as wheat, were less than impressed by tofu. Locals bought the equipment and went into the business of marketing tofu and tempeh to the growing number of vegetarian-friendly restaurants in Panajachel, Antigua and even Guatemala City.

There is a spectacular view of Lago de Atitlán from the cemetery at the lower end of town.

LODGING   Travelers looking for low budget rates in the Lake Atitlán area can check into their choice of two hotels, both cramped and minimally furnished. The **Posada del Viajero** has rooms with a shared bath. ~ South side of the Parque Central, Sololá. BUDGET.

The **Hotel El Pasaje**, located one block east and one-half block north of the Parque Central, also rents units with shared baths. ~ Sololá. BUDGET.

DINING   Both the **Posada del Viajero** and the **Hotel El Pasaje** have small *comedor*-style restaurants. BUDGET.

SHOPPING   Market days, Friday and Tuesday, fill the streets of town with vendors selling fruits and vegetables, live turkeys and healing herbs. Onions are the top crop around here, so you'll often find more

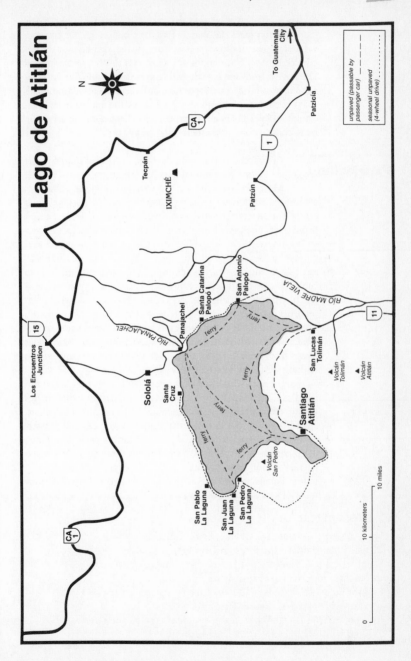

onions in the Sololá market than you can imagine in one place. Although this market is mainly for locals, not gringo gift and souvenir shoppers, it draws people from villages throughout the department of Sololá, making for a colorful display of traditional dress. Men from some of the villages wear traditional *traje*—colorful tunics and short pants or wraparound garments like women's skirts but shorter. Veteran textile collectors and market buffs often claim that the Sololá market, where prices have not been driven up by tourism, is one of the best in Guatemala.

▼▼▼▼▼▼▼▼▼▼
Panajachel

Panajachel (pop. 5000), the most developed tourist resort area along the shore of Lago de Atitlán, has a dual nature.

Most weekends the town, referred to by locals as Pana, is packed to overflowing with recreationers from Guatemala City. It can be quite a scene. Prominent businessmen from Guatemala City bring their mistresses here. Young ladinos, including lots of self-styled gangsters, are drawn here by Pana's reputation as an international jet-set hotbed of drugs, sex and rock-and-roll. (In truth, most of the hippie-druggie action has moved across the lake to cheaper, more cop-free San Pedro la Laguna, and anyone who offers to sell you drugs in Panajachel these days is most likely a rip-off artist or an undercover Guatemalan policeman.) While there's nothing particularly sexy about this scene by United States or European standards, in a country where people keep their skin under wraps from neck to ankle, the prospect of bodies on the beach in bathing suits may be excitement enough.

From Sunday night through Friday night, Panajachel is lazy and laid-back, the kind of away-from-the-world paradise that invites you to get an early start on watching the sunset. At these times, Pana belongs to the international dropouts, retirees and import-export entrepreneurs who provided the town's passé nickname, "Gringotenango," in the days when this was the only place in the Guatemalan highlands where you'd ever expect to see a foreign visitor. Panajachel presents one of the most unusual cross-sections

◆◆

✔ **CHECK THESE OUT**

- Stroll among the butterflies, monkeys and coffee bushes at the idyllic **Nima'yá de Atitlán** nature reserve near Panajachel. *page 149*
- Slumber in a luxurious medieval castle–like setting at the **Posada de Santiago** near Santiago Atitlán. *page 157*
- Enjoy a sandwich, a drink, and one of the most spectacular views on earth at Panajachel's **Sunset Café**. *page 153*
- Ride horseback through the coffee fields and up the side of a volcano with **Aventura en Atitlán**. *page 160*

of humanity in Guatemala. Indians from the dozen Tzutuhil, Quiché and Cakchiquel villages around the lake come to Panajachel to sell things to tourists and shop at the grocery stores and pharmacies. In Panajachel, you will encounter a sizable percentage of all the foreigners in Guatemala at any given time, including bus tour groups and backpackers from every part of the industrialized world and a number of older North American expatriates who have found that retirement checks go a long way in this funky little piece of never-never land.

Panajachel's commercial district is basically X-shaped. There are no street signs because the Guatemalan government several years ago directed that Panajachel, like all other towns in the country, should have numbered *calles* and *avenidas*. Rejecting the whole concept, the local people continue to call the streets by their old, familiar names, but have taken the street signs down. You enter the village on a road called **Calle Principal** (Spanish for "Main Street") or sometimes Calle Real. It goes *away* from the lake and intersects the other main streets in the center of town. If you continue on the same street straight through town, it will eventually take you around the lake to San Lucas Tolimán and continue to Santiago Atitlán. Intersecting Calle Principal at a sharp angle, **Calle Santander**, a wide street entirely lined with perhaps the widest array of *típica* clothing to be found at any permanent market in Guatemala, runs back toward the lake. Jogging half a block east as it crosses Calle Principal, Santander becomes Calle Los Arboles, a continuation of the commercial district that eventually wanders off into the residential back streets of the village.

SIGHTS

Calle Santander takes you directly to the waterfront, where a cobblestone **promenade** runs for five blocks along the edge of a mesa that slopes down to the public beach and ferry docks. The promenade ends at the Río Panajachel. To see the semirural suburbs and cemetery beyond, the river can usually be crossed easily on a log footbridge—though the wide, rocky arroyo through which it flows bears mute witness to the size of flash floods that come occasionally during the wet season.

Panajachel dates back to the year 1567, when Franciscan missionaries built a church and monastery at the site of a makeshift Spanish fort that had been established to wage war against the local Tzutuhil Maya population. The original stone church facade still stands along Calle Principal across from the town hall, though the church building behind it was replaced after an earthquake. Nearby, the public market is just about the only place in town to buy practical household items. Although it operates every day, Sunday is the official market day.

North of Panajachel on the lakeshore road, just past the entrance to Hotel Atitlán, is the **Nima'yá de Atitlán** nature reserve.

◀ HIDDEN

This wonderful facility got its start as a butterfly breeding facility where some three dozen species of Central American butterflies are grown for export to zoos and butterfly parks around the world. The reserve has grown to include a monkey rescue center and a network of nature trails through an idyllic setting of native flowers and trees, waterfalls, hanging bridges, coffee groves and herb gardens. Admission.

LODGING　The finest hotel on the lake is the **Hotel Atitlán**, situated on the edge of a coffee *finca* (plantation) 1.5 kilometers north of town. This beautiful colonial-style hotel, full of fancy tilework and carved hardwood trim, has 60 guest rooms on three floors. The rooms have private baths (though hot water is sporadic), twin beds and balconies overlooking the lake with fantastic views of the volcanoes. The grounds blaze with colorful tropical flowers and overflow with magenta cascades of bougainvillea. You'll find a swimming pool and a guests-only beach. ~ Sololá Road; 3-608-405, fax 3-340-640 in Guatemala City. ULTRA-DELUXE.

The newest resort hotel in town, the **Posada de Don Rodrigo** is centrally located on the *malecón*, or pedestrian promenade, above the beach and ferry docks. There are lake views from the balconies of most guest rooms, which surround a swimming pool and a large grassy expanse of recently landscaped grounds with hammocks for guests' use. Other facilities at the hotel include squash courts, a sauna and a comfortable solarium. The rooms are modern and bright, with colonial-style furniture, fireplaces and cable TV. Run by the owners of the elegant colonial-style inn of the same name in Antigua, the hotel's rates are about $10 a night less than those in Antigua. Price and location make this hotel a bargain. ~ Camino Santander; 7-622-326; reservations: fax 3-316-338; e-mail chotelera@c.net.gt. DELUXE.

The other expensive hotel in Panajachel is the **Hotel Del Lago**. Operated by the Biltmore International hotel chain, this six-story high-rise tourist facility lacks the lush colonial atmosphere of the Hotel Atitlán, but makes up for it with a perfect location on the waterfront just down the hill from town. With 100 guest rooms, all with private baths, the hotel has nearly half of all the tourist beds in Panajachel and often fills up with tour groups. The rooms are fairly lavish, with bathtubs and marble fixtures, as well as balconies overlooking the lake. The hotel's dock is where the boats leave for Santiago Atitlán and other villages around the lake. ~ Calle Rancho Grande; 7-621-555, fax 2-621-562 in Guatemala City, or 800-327-3573 in the U.S. ULTRA-DELUXE.

Very nice accommodations, almost on the beachfront, are at the small **Hotel Visión Azul**, located less than half a kilometer from town where the Hotel Atitlán entrance road forks off the Sololá Road. The 24-room white stucco hotel, nestled on a hillside amid banana trees and bougainvillea, features a riding stable and the best beach on Lake Atitlán. All guest rooms are large and sunny, with private baths and terraces facing the lake across a grassy pasture. ~ Sololá Road; phone/fax 7-621-426. DELUXE.

Another very nice midrange hotel, closer to the center of things, is the **Cacique Inn** on the waterfront between Calle Principal and Calle Santander. Each of the 33 large rooms, decorated with native weavings, has its own private bath and fireplace. The rooms are in a compound of pseudo-rustic buildings with Mediterranean-style tile roofs surrounding a beautifully landscaped courtyard with a small swimming pool. ~ Calle Embarcadero; phone/fax 7-621-205; fax 7-622-053. DELUXE.

A good bet, particularly for families or small groups traveling together, is **Bungalows El Aguacatel**, across the street from the *malecón* and one block south of the Posada de Don Rodrigo. Most of the 12 units here are two-bedroom suites with separate living rooms, some with kitchens. The furnishings have a Salvation Army look, and some units are more spacious and better lit than others, so it's wise to look before you rent, but the location and price are outstanding. ~ Calle Embarcadero; 7-621-482. MODERATE.

An old-fashioned hotel with red tile roofs and a country feel, the **Hotel Regis** is located right in the heart of town off lively Calle Santander. The hotel consists of 14 guest rooms in duplexes and bungalows set around an attractive colonial-style main building, which houses a lobby area and dining room adorned with local arts and crafts. Each guest room has a private bath and veranda that looks out on a green lawn landscaped with palm trees. Some rooms have kitchenettes, and televisions are available at an additional charge. For children, there is a playground with a wading pool, a swing and a slide. ~ Calle Santander; phone/fax 7-621-149. MODERATE.

The **Hotel Las Casitas**, a large motel-style place far from the lake but close to the market, has 24 rooms with large windows, dark wood furnishings and thick wool blankets. ~ Calle Principal; 7-621-224. BUDGET.

Another good low-priced option away from the lake is **La Zanahoría Chic**, with seven guest rooms that are not so chic but are certainly adequate and have reliable hot water. Also on the premises is a small restaurant specializing in fruit pies and budget-priced Guatemalan fare with a TV that shows CNN news all day long. ~ Calle de los Arboles; 7-621-249, fax 7-622-138. BUDGET.

◄ HIDDEN

In the center of the village, along Calle Principal near where it intersects Calle Santander and Calle Los Arboles, is the **Mayan Palace Hotel**, which has 22 scantily furnished rooms. The rooms overlooking the street can be noisy, especially on weekends, but all have private baths, big windows and good views of town and the hills beyond; some have cable TV. ~ Calle Principal at Calle Santander; 7-621-028. BUDGET TO MODERATE.

A long block east of the town center on the road into Panajachel, the **Fonda del Sol** offers a selection of rooms in varied price ranges. The older part of the inn has ten basic budget-priced rooms with minimal furnishings. The shared bathrooms are clean and modern. The new addition has 15 very attractive motel-style units with red-brick floors, contemporary furnishings and bright-colored accents. ~ Calle Principal; 7-621-162. MODERATE.

One block past the Los Arboles intersection on Calle Principal, the **Hotel Galindo** makes a postcard-perfect first impression with its lush courtyard gardens and white-stucco-and-red-tile architecture. The guest room situation is strangely divided between 15 fair-sized, plain rooms with beds, private baths and not much else, and three very nice suites with fireplaces and separate bedrooms. ~ Calle Principal; 7-621-168, fax 7-621-178. BUDGET TO DELUXE.

Two blocks past the Los Arboles intersection on Calle Principal, near the church, the owners of **Hotel Maya Kanek** have also spruced up the appearance of their no-frills concrete hotel built around a courtyard used as off-street parking. The 20 smallish rooms (some with private bath) have narrow beds and not much light, but if it's basic you want, here's a good place to find it. ~ Calle Principal; 7-621-104. BUDGET.

Many local people rent out rooms in their homes at very modest prices—probably the best bet for low-budget travelers. These places change constantly and usually don't have phones. The best plan is to arrive early in the day and look for signs that say "Rooms" in English.

HIDDEN ►

One unique little hostelry that isn't in Panajachel but can only be reached by boat from Pana is **Noah's Ark**, an animal-loving kind of place that has bungalows with one double bed and one single bed as well as smaller rooms with two singles, and is about as remote as you can get even at Lago de Atitlán. The managers are gourmet cooks, and eating here is half the fun. ~ Santa Cruz La Laguna; reservations and transportation, 7-621-196 in Panajachel.

DINING

Panajachel is full of restaurants. Almost none of them has a telephone; reservations are unheard of. In Panajachel, there's no such thing as street addresses, but you'll have no trouble finding the places listed here.

The longtime favorite "elegant" restaurant in town (which is not to suggest that you can't come here in a T-shirt) is **Casablanca** near the town center. The two-story dining area has big picture windows overlooking the main street, hanging plants and paintings by top local artists on the walls. The fare consists primarily of steaks and seafood, and you'll find the lobster a real bargain. Salads and sandwiches are also available. Casablanca is under German management and for some not-too-obvious reason seems to be a favorite of German tourists. Dinner only. ~ Calle Principal. MODERATE.

La Laguna offers indoor and outdoor dining. The indoor seating area is elaborately decorated with native arts and handicrafts, and one wall is muraled with the best map in town of Lago de Atitlán, while the outdoor patio faces a nicely landscaped front yard. The menu offers a good selection of native and foreign dishes, from black bean soup to pepper steak. This is a good place to try *pepián de pollo*, the national dish of Guatemala. ~ Calle Principal at Calle Los Arboles. BUDGET.

A laid-back Panajachel institution, the longstanding gringo hippie hangout is **Al Chisme**, one block off Calle Principal. The restaurant manages to be funky and spotless at the same time. It earned its reputation as *the* place to go if you're a gringo in Guatemala by being the first restaurant in the entire country to sell good coffee. It's still good. There are tables on a streetside patio, as well as indoors. The menu consists of an eclectic assortment of international dishes—crêpes, Belgian waffles, borscht, lasagna, shrimp scampi, stuffed breast of chicken and lots more. Service can be on the slow side, but there are piles of vintage American and German magazines to keep you occupied while you wait, and this is probably the best place in town to ask around for hiking and sightseeing suggestions and up-to-date info on your next destination. ~ Calle Los Arboles. BUDGET TO MODERATE.

For low-priced shrimp, ceviche and other seafood delights, try the no-frills **Comedor y Cafeteria Costa Sur**. ~ Calle Principal. BUDGET.

If you prefer a more elegant atmosphere with your seafood, the place to go is **La Terraza**, an upstairs restaurant with a bird's-eye view of the street. Located above a mini-mall next to the Maya Palace hotel, it features seafood platters with shrimp, fish, scallops and squid. Chateaubriand is another specialty. ~ Calle Santander at Calle Principal. MODERATE TO DELUXE.

Nearby, the **Bar/Restaurante Socrates** serves good steaks and imported Italian pasta in an atmosphere so clean and polished you may not believe you're in Guatemala. ~ Calle Principal. MODERATE.

The **Sunset Café** serves drinks, snacks and sandwiches under an open-air *palapa* overlooking the lake. The sandwiches are just okay, but the view is one of the finest in Guatemala. ~ Calle Santander at the *malecón*. BUDGET.

If red meat is your passion, head for **Los Gauchos**, a Uruguayan restaurant where white-coated waiters serve South American-style beef steaks in a lush flowering courtyard. The menu also in-

cludes a few fish and shrimp options. ~ Calle Santander. MODER-
ATE TO DELUXE.

On the other hand, if your preference is for vegetarian fare,
head up the street to a tree-shaded mini-mall with a tree-shaded
patio shared by two outdoor restaurants, **Sevananda** and the **Bom-
bay Pub & Café**, both serving Asian-style cuisine, most of it built
around tofu. ~ Avenida de los Arboles. BUDGET.

Most of the casually fancy, tourist-oriented restaurants in town
are affiliated with the bigger hotels. One of the best is the dining
room at the **Hotel Atitlán**. Floor-to-ceiling windows provide diners with a panoramic view of the lake and the volcanoes. The
menu, which changes seasonally, features an international assortment of beef, chicken, pork and shrimp dishes, as well as fresh-
caught bass broiled to a turn. ~ Located 1.5 kilometers out of town
on the road to Sololá; 9-621-429. MODERATE.

SHOPPING   You would think that Panajachel's status as the premier tourist
destination in Guatemala would translate into higher prices for gift
and souvenir items, but in fact the opposite is true. Panajachel is
home base for virtually all dealers who export Guatemalan clothing to the United States, Canada and Europe. Vendors come to
Panajachel not only from villages around the lake but also from
villages in distant parts of the highlands, and the intense competition keeps prices down at the street vendors' stalls and small,
nameless shops selling *típica* up and down Calle Santander. Asking prices are incredible bargains by U.S. standards. They are also
very flexible. Negotiation is appropriate and expected.

Other art-and-craft specialties found in Panajachel include
wood carving and leatherwork by native artisans, along with
hand-painted T-shirts, landscape paintings and silver jewelry made
by North American and European expatriates who make their
homes around Lago de Atitlán. Also seen in small shops around
Panajachel (though far less than in Antigua) is high-fashion clothing handmade by local Indian seamstresses from designs created
by American emigrés who live in the area.

NIGHTLIFE   The sizable American expatriate community in Panajachel has
given rise to an odd phenomenon—the video bar. These are small
theaters where gringos sit in the dark in front of a large television
screen and watch recent English-language movies on videotape.
Three different videos are shown each afternoon and evening, re-
peating in a different order every week until the owner gets more
from the United States. Video bars come and go; the video bars
at the moment are at **La Zanahoría Chic** (Avenida de los Arboles)
and **Centro Commercial Rincon Sai** (Calle Santander near Calle
Principal).

The best spot in town for dancing is **Chapiteau,** where a mixed crowd of locals and foreign visitors mingles to live, loud Latin music most evenings. ~ Calle Los Arboles. Just down the street, **Nuan's Dance Bar,** the only discotheque in Panajachel, has a deejay armed with a solid international selection of rock, world beat and salsa records. ~ Calle Los Arboles.

On some evenings, you'll find live piano music at the **Circus Bar,** a rustic saloon with circus posters on the walls. ~ Calle Santander. **The Last Resort** is where a lot of expatriates go to waste away the late evening in this remote corner of Margaritaville. ~ Calle Santander.

PLAYA PANAJACHEL The chilly water off Panajachel's rocky public beach, where the Panajachel River flows into Lago de Atitlán, is noxious, evil smelling and disturbingly unsanitary. Locals do their laundry, wash their hair and their trucks, and clean fish there. Untreated sewage drips into the water upriver. There is a lot of social sunbathing on the beach, making it a fun place to spend the morning—as long as you don't go in the water. ~ South end of the *malecón.*

▲ The camping policy varies: sometimes whole colonies of tents line the beach on both sides of the river, while at other times the police roust campers and may search them for drugs.

PLAYA DEL NORTE ⟿ A cleaner beach, at the **Hotel Visión Azul** off the Sololá Road north of town, is open to nonguests for a nominal fee.

▲ Camping is permitted here.

Passenger ferries that dock at Panajachel provide service several times daily to the traditional highland Maya villages situated on other parts of Lake Atitlán's shoreline. They seem to have been established on the lake almost by coincidence, for most village people here do not catch fish from the lake or depend on canoes for transportation, preferring to carry their burdens along the rough dirt tracks that link the villages; nor do they know how to swim. Santiago Atitlán is also accessible by road, though the rough ride from Panajachel takes much longer than the boat trip. It's 36 kilometers (22 miles) of recently resurfaced but steep and winding paved road from Pana to the mainly ladino town of San Lucas Tolimán, a commercial center for local coffee growers, on the south side of the lake. From there, the road makes its way around the base of Volcán Tolimán, a distance of 15 kilometers that takes about an hour to drive, to Santiago Atitlán. The road is paved to within a couple of kilometers of Santiago Atitlán. From there, it continues as an unpaved road, gradually deteriorating until it reaches San Pedro la Laguna, where it ends. The villages on the north side of the lake can only be reached by boat or by foot trails.

SIGHTS   The largest village on the lake, three times the size of Panajachel, is Santiago Atitlán, the home of the Tzutuhil Maya people since pre-Hispanic times, with its spectacular setting at the foot of **Volcán Tolimán** (10,400 feet) and across the bay from **Volcán San Pedro** (11,800 feet).

Upon arrival in Santiago Atitlán, stepping off onto the rickety wooden ferry dock puts you in a world that feels medieval. Many men and virtually all women wear *traje*, the official clothing of the village. Women balance bundles of laundry atop their elaborate headdresses as they descend the ancient stone stairway to the rocky cove where wash is done. Boats glide along trails through the cornfields and cow pastures to the rocky stretch of shoreline used for laundry and bathing. People pole strange angular canoes along the shallows near the shore to make their way to other villages along the lake. It is a different world, but one that has grown quite accustomed to visitors and apparently regards us as . . . well . . . better than the army, anyway.

After walking up the hill from the ferry docks into town, bear left to reach the town plaza, which is filled with street vendors most days. The big white **church** has stood facing the plaza since 1568, when it was built as the headquarters for Franciscan missionary efforts in the region. As elsewhere in the highlands, this church reveals a strange fusion of Catholic and pre-Hispanic Maya religious beliefs. Besides the saints dressed in village *traje*, signs of ancient influences include carvings of the corn god Yum-Kax on the pulpit and throne. On a more contemporary note, a plaque behind the altar commemorates Father Stanley Francis Rother, an American-born village priest who was assassinated by a government death squad in 1981 during Guatemala's civil war. The government had antiguerrilla troops stationed in Santiago Atitlán until 1990, when the army massacred local townspeople. The elders of Santiago Atitlán decided to banish the military from the town. Amazingly enough, the government honored the ban and removed all troops from Lago de Atitlán villages except for the army base with the guardhouse in front shaped like a pair of army boots and a helmet on the main road to Lago de Atitlán.

LODGING   After the day's last excursion boat leaves, the people of Santiago Atitlán settle back into the ancient language and stately rhythms of everyday life in one of the world's most isolated and beautiful spots. To experience this peaceful village without the selling frenzy, plan to spend a night here. Santiago Atitlán has bargains in low-budget hotels, as well as an environment that is at once more peaceful and more memorable than Panajachel's, on the far side of the lake in the Maya village of Santiago Atitlán. The **Backpackers' Hostel**, located on the lakefront, has 12 rooms with very basic furnishings. One, at a slightly higher rate, has a private bath, while the others share the same bathroom. Guests have kitchen privileges, and camping is permitted. To get there from the ferry dock, turn left and follow the waterfront to the house with the red roof. ~ BUDGET.

Pensión Rosita, next to the church, costs about the same and has more primitive plumbing. The guest rooms offer a bed and nothing else. Baths are shared. Adventuresome travelers should look at a stay in this or any other Indian village as a cultural experience, bearing in mind that even the crudest accommodations are a cut above the conditions in which the local villagers spend their whole lives. ~ BUDGET.

◀ HIDDEN

The **Posada de Santiago**, located one kilometer past the center of town along the main road, has eight nicely furnished stone cabañas and duplexes set in nicely landscaped grounds. Built by local stonemasons in a traditional style, the rooms are beautifully appointed with handmade furniture, and many have fireplaces. Accommodations vary in size, with singles, doubles, triples and suites available. The grounds include a gazebo overlooking the water, beautiful flower gardens and a grove of avocado trees and coffee bushes whose beans are roasted on the premises and used to make the coffee served in the restaurant. The inn's small size enhances the feeling of being far away from the known world. ~ Phone/fax 7-217-167; e-mail posdesantiago@guate.net. MODERATE TO DELUXE.

DINING

There are several small *comedores* and slightly larger restaurants in Santiago Atitlán, from fast-food stands like the **Restaurante Texas Burger** (budget) and the **Restaurante Regiomontano** (budget) overlooking the ferry dock to the relatively nice **Restaurante Tzutuhil** (moderate) in the center of town. Most restaurants operate only during tourist hours—from the first ferry arrival of the morning to the last departure in the afternoon. All restaurants in Santiago Atitlán, without exception, are more expensive for what you get than those in Panajachel. Reasonable alternatives are to bring along a picnic dinner from a deli before you leave Pana or to eat fruits and vegetables from the public market.

The restaurant at the **Posada de Santiago**, by far the best on this side of the lake, serves a varying gourmet menu of beef, fish and vegetarian dishes in the front part of the large comfortable lobby/library/bar overlooking the lake. ~ 7-217-167. MODERATE.

SHOPPING

Santiago Atitlán is the commercial center for all the Indian villages around the lake, and every day is market day. Fridays and Tuesdays are the busiest. When boatloads of tourists are in town—roughly from 10 a.m. to 1p.m.—the hawking of *típica* and curios reaches a fever pitch all the way from the boat landing to the market on the north side of the town plaza. The selection and prices are not much different than you would find in Panajachel.

▼▼▼▼▼▼▼▼▼▼▼▼▼▼▼▼
San Pedro La Laguna

HIDDEN ►

To experience the rhythms of modern village life, with its somewhat less traditional but much less touristy atmosphere, catch a ferry from Panajachel to **San Pedro La Laguna**, a Tzutuhil-speaking community around the other side of the San Pedro volcano from Santiago Atitlán. *Evangélico* church influence is very much in evidence here, eroding traditional folkways; also taking its toll is the growing presence of drugs, which resident hippies offer to sell to almost any American or European who steps off the ferry. With fewer tourists than Santiago Atitlán and really cheap accommodations, this village has become the new darling of the backpacker set. At the curve in the road just before you enter the village is the trailhead for climbing Volcán San Pedro, the easiest of the big Lago de Atitlán volcanoes to climb. The hike takes about three hours each way.

The rough road through Santiago Atitlán continues for 18 more kilometers (11 miles) to San Pedro La Laguna. The road does not follow the lakeshore, where the volcano's steep slope plunges straight into the water, but skirts the other side of Volcán Tolimán, taking you into the wildest backcountry that can be reached by road around Lago de Atitlán. The road around the lake, which goes through a number of smaller, picturesque Maya villages in addition to Santiago Atitlán and San Pedro La Laguna, is *difficult*. I would not recommend taking a rental passenger car, though it's an exciting trip by mountain bike (rent one in Panajachel at **Bicicletas Gaby** on Calle Santander) or by motorcycle or four-wheel-drive jeep (both available in Panajachel from **Pana Sol Moto Rent**, Avenida Los Arboles; 9-621-253). It is a long, long hike around the lake, but every part of the lake is accessible on foot from one of the towns with ferry service.

LODGING

The lowest-priced lodging on the lake is found in several *hospedajes* scattered through San Pedro La Laguna. All are low-budget, with rooms ranging from US$2 to $4. All are small and minimally furnished. Children meet every arriving boat and try to get guests for the various *hospedajes*.

Try the **Hospedaje Chuazinahi** or the **Hospedaje Ti-Kaaj**, both located near the village center and have shared baths. ~ BUDGET.

DINING

Simple and very inexpensive meals can be had for less than US$1 at any of two dozen small *comedores* around town. Try **La Ultima Cena**, a longtime favorite where most of the gringos in town can be found from time to time. ~ BUDGET.

The Saint
of Bad Habits

Santiago Atitlán is the home of Maximón, the reprobate saint, who has been revered here since the mid-19th century. He is represented by a three-and-a-half-foot-tall statue wearing a cowboy hat and many colorful scarves that hang down almost to his feet.

A direct descendent of Ma'am, the ancient Maya Lord of the Earth who reigned over the five-day period between the end of one year and the beginning of the next, he became merged with St. Simon (the disciple Simon Peter) in a phenomenon known as "transfer of magic" whereby the old gods were identified with Catholic saints to form a uniquely Mayan syncretic religion. He is also identified with Judas Iscariot, with the Antichrist of Revelation, and with Spanish conquistador Pedro de Alvarado. The cult of Maximón spread rapidly from Santiago Atitlán to many other towns around the highlands, where he is known by different names including San Simón, San Judas, Rijlaj Mam and Ca Tatá.

Maximón's fundamental trait is the enjoyment of vices. His *cofradía,* or caretaker, regularly plies him with offerings of cigars and liquor, and he is reputed to seduce the single women of the village after dark. Believers pray to him for money or practical items like garden tractors and mountain bikes.

The procession of Maximón during Semana Santa reveals just how different Maya beliefs are from conventional Catholicism. After other saint figures have been placed around the plaza and the Christ figure has been lowered from his cross and carried from the church on a funeral bier, Maximón's *cofradía* carries him to confront the dead Jesus amid fireworks and music. During the brief contact between Christ and Antichrist, it is said, Maximón "gives his seed" to Jesus, thus allowing the new year to be born. Afterwards Maximon is hung from a tree, symbolizing the death of Judas Iscariot. To traditional Maya people, there is no dichotomy of good versus evil; both are inseparable parts of the way the world works.

Maximón is never allowed inside the church. Instead, he resides in his own small building uphill behind the church. In the 1950s, Maximón's mask was stolen and later sold to the Musée de L'Homme in Paris. It took nearly two decades for the people of Santiago Atitlán to negotiate its return, and thereafter for many years he was kept in storage away from public view except during Semana Santa. In recent years, though, as many villagers have been converted by evangelical sects, the *cofradía* has run short of money to satisfy Maximón's tastes for tobacco and booze. As a result, when you visit Santiago Atitlán you are sure to be approached by young tour guides eager to introduce you to Maximón (and give you the chance to make a cash donation).

SHOPPING Sunday is San Pedro La Laguna's market day. The village is known for its rugs, which local women weave on backstrap looms, and its T-shirts, silk-screened in a village factory for sale in Panajachel. You can visit both the weavers' workshops and the T-shirt factory.

▼▼▼▼▼▼▼▼▼▼▼▼▼▼▼
Outdoor Adventures

FISHING Several Panajachel hotels, including the **Hotel Atitlán** and the **Hotel Visión Azul**, offer rental motorboats so you can explore Lago de Atitlán on your own. Rowboats, canoes and kayaks can be rented on the beach at **Lake Recreation Services**. However, there is no fishing tackle for rent. Fishermen will find that the native fish of Lago de Atitlán have all been displaced by black bass, which were introduced by the government as a sport fish during the 1980s.

WIND-SURFING & KAYAKING Lago de Atitlán is the place for both kayaking and windsurfing. There is almost always a breeze. Morning is the time to go; in the afternoon, the unpredictable *xocomil* wind can make both sports quite dangerous. Sailboards and kayaks are rented on the beach at **Lake Recreation Services**.

RIDING STABLES Horses are rarely seen in the Lago de Atitlán area because there are no veterinarian services available to treat the tropical diseases horses are vulnerable to. An American couple who have a homestead on the road beyond Santiago Atitlán operate **Aventura en Atitlán**, offering both hourly horse rentals and three- to six-hour guided rides through coffee fields along the lake and up the side of a volcano. ~ Santiago Atitlán; 2-015-527, or inquire at Posada de Santiago.

BIKING By renting a bicycle in Panajachel at **Hotel del Lago** or **Los Geranios Turicentro**, both on the waterfront, you can spend the day exploring the back roads that connect the villages along the shores of Lago de Atitlán.

HIKING The three volcanoes around Lago de Atitlán that make up Atitlán National Park are probably the most-often hiked peaks in Guatemala. The easiest climb is **Volcán San Pedro**, 9900 feet high, the only Lago de Atitlán volcano that can be climbed up and back the same day. The 9-kilometer trail starts at the village of San Pedro La Laguna. The six- to eight-hour trek to the summit of **Volcán Tolimán**, 10,280 feet high, is considered the most difficult climb, and **Volcán Atitlán**, the highest of the three volcanoes at 11,600 feet, has a hut on top where climbers can spend the night. The trails to both volcanoes start on the south shore of the lake at the village of San Lucas Tolimán, where hikers' maps of the national park are sold at the American Pie restaurant.

The distance from Antigua to Panajachel is 117 kilometers (70 miles). If you're driving, go north from Antigua to join Route 1 at Chimaltenango, then west to Los Encuentros Junction, where the good, recently paved and widened road to Lago de Atitlán turns off from Route 1. (Coming from the west, it's also 117 kilometers from Huehuetenango, or 90 kilometers from Quetzaltenango.) The road from the Pan-American Highway to the lake—also designated Route 1—passes through Sololá, and then descends abruptly, with several switchbacks and dramatic overlooks, into Panajachel on the shoreline.

Transportation

CAR

BUS

Frequent buses and vans stop in Sololá on their way to or from Panajachel.

The trip to Lago de Atitlán by public bus is time-consuming. From Antigua, you must change buses at Chimaltenango, then again at Los Encuentros Junction. From Guatemala City, Quetzaltenango or Huehuetenango, you also change buses at Los Encuentros Junction. You can simplify the trip considerably by taking one of the affordable two-and-a-half-hour shuttle van trips that leave from Antigua for Panajachel several times daily, making it possible to take the beautiful hour-long walk down the road to the lake and catch a cheap ride back.

BOAT

The usual way to get to Santiago Atitlán is to take one of the passenger ferries that run between Panajachel and Santiago Atitlán five times daily, from early morning to midafternoon. The inexpensive scenic boat trip takes a little more than an hour each way and is beautiful, particularly on the approach to Santiago Atitlán. Current ferry schedules are posted at the INGUAT office on Calle Santander and on signs at the docks of the various ferry companies. Smaller water taxis that hire out to individual parties and cost more come and go all day. You pay for the round-trip when you board the ferry at Panajachel and pay nothing on the return trip.

Five ferries daily run from Panajachel to San Pedro La Laguna and back. Consult the schedule posted at the INGUAT office on Calle Santander or the signs posted at the boat docks for current departure times.

Addresses & Phone Numbers

INGUAT (tourist information) ~ Calle Santander at Calle Principal, Panajachel; 7-621-392

Police ~ Calle Principal, Panajachel; 7-621-120

Medical clinic ~ Calle Principal, Panajachel

Post office ~ Off Calle Principal, left at the Catholic church, Panajachel

SEVEN

El Altiplano

 People mark Holy Week in the most remote Maya towns of Guatemala's western mountains with as much religious fervor as in Antigua. It feels different because the region is rural and purely Maya. A dirt footpath leads between modest homesteads, each with a small cornfield behind the house and a yard full of chickens and maybe a pig. Here and there, steep trails lead away from the main footpath to the summits of ancient temple pyramids. Young boys guard some of the trails, keeping outsiders away from the shamanic ceremonies that are still conducted on top of the pyramids. In times past, it was the old men of the village who kept their ancestral religious traditions alive while teaching their sons. Now, as a result of government massacres in the 1980s, many members of the ancient brotherhoods are barely out of their teens.

It's Good Friday. Earlier in the day, villagers dressed as Roman soldiers whipped a local man through the streets before mock-crucifying him on another old pyramid. A person who climbs to the top of a grass-covered temple pyramid that is not in use can see the whole town below, its whitewashed walls and red tile roofs gleaming against the green of the forested mountains beyond. A procession makes its slow way from the church across the plaza and through the streets with somber chants. As if on cue, an evangelical missionary church bursts into hymns in Maya accompanied by an electric guitar. And against the clamor as more churches chime in with different hymns come the shouted prayers of Maya holy men, carried to the old gods on black, fragrant wisps of smoke from burning copal.

Travelers who explore the Guatemalan Altiplano, or highlands, find themselves immersed in a world of surpassing strangeness and more than a little secrecy. The region is home to the majority of all Maya Indians, the largest American Indian group anywhere. The Maya population of Guatemala outnumbers the entire American Indian population of the United States. The plight of indigenous people in Guatemala is far worse than in Mexico, the United States or Canada, though a distinct improvement over places like neighboring El Salvador, where the entire Indian population has been exterminated. The people of the highlands speak 22 different languages, each one unintelligible outside its own particular valley, and follow a way of life that has changed relatively little in all the centuries since the first Spanish conquistadors arrived in Guatemala.

There are several highland towns with travel accommodations comfortable enough to make them natural bases for exploring villages in the surrounding mountains. More people visit Chichicastenango than any other purely Maya town in Guatemala, drawn by its world-famous public market. Travelers who continue northward, deeper into the mountains, reach fascinating Indian villages such as Santa Cruz del Quiché and Nebaj. Tourist accommodations are limited because these towns have only recently welcomed outsiders again after nearly two decades caught in the crossfire of a civil war that killed many times more Indian bystanders than government soldiers and guerrillas combined. Now the region is safe, and a trip there offers maximum adventure at minimal expense.

To the west, Huehuetenango is a more run-down and "real" town than Chichicastenango, a low-cost starting point for ventures to the Maya ruins of Zaculeu and to towns like Todos Santos situated in the distant reaches of Guatemala's highest mountain range. Farther south, Quetzaltenango has its own unique historical charms, city conveniences, plus hot springs and some of the most colorful Maya villages. Many language students claim it's like Antigua—without the tourist crowds.

Every place described in this chapter can be reached easily, if not always comfortably, by second-class local buses. Market days are the times to visit all Maya villages, and if you plan to spend the night, arrive early the day before. Expect cool (in fact, sometimes chilly) weather throughout the region, especially in Todos Santos with its high altitude and Nebaj with its damp climate.

▼▼▼▼▼▼▼▼▼▼▼▼ Chichicastenango

Once you're at Lago de Atitlán, it's just a short trip to Chichicastenango (pop. 9000), the third major travel destination in the Guatemalan highlands and perhaps the most famous of all present-day Maya towns. Chichicastenango is just 32 kilometers to the north of Panajachel, crossing the Pan-American Highway at Los Encuentros; the distance from Antigua to Chichicastenango is 119 kilometers. Go there on a market day—Thursday or Sunday—to see the biggest and most colorful public market in Guatemala. Just be warned that on market days, a small fee is charged to enter the town by car, and you may have to pay from Q5 to Q10 to park. The night before a market day, hundreds of vendors fill the town plaza with stands built of pine poles. In the morning, thousands of people—locals, buyers and sellers from other villages, and plenty of gringo tourists—turn the town into a kaleidoscope of bright-hued clothing and a babel of many languages.

SIGHTS

The **Church of Santo Tomás** on Chichicastenango's plaza dates back to 1540. Day and night, people burn copal incense in a *quemada*, or altar-like burner, on the platform atop the steps that lead to the church's front entrance. Women walk slowly around the platforms swinging incense balls that pour forth more of the pungent copal smoke, until a cloud hangs over the plaza. It is customary for Indians to ask the sun or moon for permission before entering the front doors of the church. Non-Maya visitors should enter by the side door through the *atrio*, or walled churchyard.

As in many other highland village churches, this one is used constantly for prayers and ceremonies that involve offerings of incense and candles, liquor and flowers made on square altars in the center aisle—but no priests. What is unusual about this church is the presence of *chuchkajaues*, native prayer men who know the exact words and phrases that will most effectively invoke a saint's help. Instead of speaking directly to the saints as in most other Maya churches, the people hire one of the *chuchkajaues* who wait at the front door of the church to speak for them. The saints and other religious statues lining the walls embody strange symbolisms. In one small shrine, for instance, there is a pair of cherubim—each with one arm and the opposite wing broken off. The idea that they are half human and half divine suggests that they represent the legendary twins who, according to the *Popol Vuh,* were the first ancestors of the Quiché Maya. It was in a former chapel adjoining the church and now used as offices that a priest discovered the sacred book of the Quiché in 1680.

On market days, the church stairway both affords the best overview of the teeming market and, crowded as it is with Indians and tourists, becomes a spectacle in itself. If the three-sided, semirounded shape of the steps reminds you of an ancient Maya pyramid, you can be sure that it's no coincidence. Chichicastenango was here long before Spanish missionaries brought Catholicism to town.

The **Museo Regional**, on the south side of the plaza, features artifacts from around the department of Quiché, including pottery, stone points and other relics from the areas around Iximché and K'umarcaaj, some of which date back to the Preclassic Period (1500 B.C.–A.D. 250). The museum's primary exhibit is the Ildefonso Rossbach jade collection, consisting of carvings given by villagers to the accountant-turned-priest, who resided in Chichicastenango for 50 years until his death in 1944.

Ceremonial offerings are still held at Rossbach's large tomb, which dominates the **town cemetery**. Some tombs are the size of small houses, complete with Roman columns and garish paint jobs. Throughout the highlands, a big tomb is considered the ultimate status symbol of the locally wealthy and powerful. At the other extreme, on the outskirts where the cemetery spills into the surrounding arroyos, are the burial grounds of traditional Maya people who reject church burial customs. Those who follow the old ways are buried wrapped in blankets, casketless, in dirt mounds

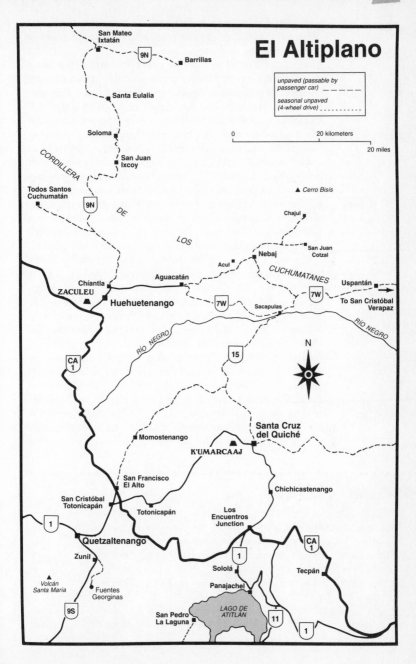

El Altiplano

| unpaved (passable by passenger car) | – – – – – – |
| seasonal unpaved (4-wheel drive) | .... |

0   20 kilometers

                    20 miles

San Mateo Ixtatán

9N   Barrillas

Santa Eulalia

Soloma

San Juan Ixcoy

CORDILLERA

Todos Santos Cuchumatán

9N

DE

LOS

▲ Cerro Bisis

Chajul

Nebaj   San Juan Cotzal

Acul

CUCHUMATANES

Chíantla
ZACULEU
▲   Huehuetenango   7W   Uspantán   7W   To San Cristóbal Verapaz

Aguacatán

Sacapulas

RÍO NEGRO

RÍO NEGRO

CA 1

15

N

Santa Cruz del Quiché

Momostenango

K'UMARCAAJ

San Francisco El Alto

Chichicastenango

San Cristóbal Totonicapán

Totonicapán

Los Encuentros Junction

1

Quetzaltenango

CA 1

Zunil

▲ Volcán Santa María

Fuentes Georginas

Sololá

Tecpán

9S

Panajachel

San Pedro La Laguna

LAGO DE ATITLÁN

11

1

with a small stone cross at the foot and a type of treelike cactus planted at the head. After many years, when the cactus has grown to full height and died, the body that nurtures it is deemed to be gone; the cross is removed and the same plot of ground is used for a new burial. ~ Located on a hill at the southwest corner of town.

Much of the spiritual life of Chichicastenango takes place outside jurisdiction of the church and without the slightest veneer of Christianity. Prohibited on pain of death for centuries, traditional Maya religious ceremonies have only lately—and cautiously— emerged from secrecy. Although Maya people generally refuse to discuss the meanings of specific practices even with serious ethnologists who try to study them, in many cases they permit outsiders to visit sacred sites and even be present at routine rituals. Just west **HIDDEN ▶** of town at the hilltop shrine of **Pascual Abaj**, for instance, an ancient stone head turned black by centuries of copal smoke stands over a series of altars and stone fire circles. The head is smoothly carved on one half and terribly battered on the other; missionaries tried to smash it in colonial times, and it existed in hiding for at least a century. The purpose of the copal smoke is to carry prayers to the gods. Child tour guides will offer to show you the way up to the shrine, promising that a ceremony is about to take place there. In fact, rituals seem to go on there almost constantly. Besides the usual offerings—candles, flowers, Pepsi Cola—the *chuchkajaues* sometimes sacrifice live chickens here, beheading them in elaborate rituals and pouring the blood over the stone head. After people leave, local dogs come and eat the chicken. They're lucky beasts; most Maya dogs are fed fermented corncobs. Because so many tourists come to Chichicastenango, the people who use the Pascual Abaj shrine have come to allow outsiders at ceremonies. Even photography is usually allowed. But the rituals are not simply fluted up for the tourists. The same kind of thing

✔ **CHECK THESE OUT**

• Explore the incense-filled depths of the cave beneath **K'umarcaaj**, where fresh flowers and offerings honor ancient Maya kings. *page 170*

• Spend a luxurious night at Chichicastenango's **Hotel Santo Tomás**, where you can enjoy a hot tub—in a town where most homes have no running water. *page 168*

• Ask around Nebaj for **Juana Marcos**, who cooks Maya meals for travelers in her home. *page 177*

• Trek the steep trail to the summit of **Volcán Santa María** near Quetzaltenango for the ultimate view of the Guatemalan highlands. *page 188* goes on at similar crude shrines on hilltops and remains of ancient pyramid temples near every village in the Maya highlands.

Even without a guide, getting to Pascual Abaj is easy. Follow 9 Calle south out of town, where it becomes an unpaved road that curves around and runs in front of two houses occupied by the town's ceremonial-mask makers, who also operate museums and retail shops there. To climb Cerro Pascual Abaj on your own, turn up the path to either Morería Santo Tomás or Artesanías de Diego Ignacio, both marked by big roadside signs. The paths lead right through the mask makers' yards and past their stores. Nobody will ask you for an admission charge, though the younger children of the families may ask whether you'll give them a pen for their school. (This request is often heard by gringo travelers all over Guatemala.) Once past the *morerías* (mask makers' houses), the trail curves up the high pine-covered hill to the shrine at the summit, offering good views of the town along the way.

Improbably enough, Chichicastenango has two of the finest hotels in all of Guatemala. The original luxury hotel here was **Mayan Inn**. It was built more than 60 years ago by package tour pioneer Alfred S. Clark, whose decision to include Chichicastenango on his tour groups' route helped the town's market boom to its present size and gave generations of international travelers a once-in-a-lifetime glimpse of Maya life. This 30-room colonial-style hotel three blocks west of the town plaza has antique furnishings, lush gardens and lovely views. The guest rooms, set around beautifully landscaped courtyards, have massive hand-carved furniture, fireplaces and handwoven textiles everywhere you look. If you're traveling first-class, the American plan (meals included) is worth considering since the town has little to offer in the way of fine dining. ~ 8 Calle at 3 Avenida; 7-561-176, fax 7-561-212. DELUXE.

LODGING

In the same price range, also within easy walking distance of the market, the **Hotel Santo Tomás** is a competitor for the title of Guatemala's Finest Hotel. It has 43 modern, spacious rooms. Dark colonial reproduction furnishings accented by colorful Maya textiles set off the white walls. Fireplaces warm chilly Chichi nights. All guest rooms open onto central courtyards with flowers, parrots and a fountain. The abundant, mostly Maya hotel staff dresses so picture-perfectly in village *traje* that the whole hotel, with its reinterpretation of Spanish colonial architecture, can feel not quite real. It often hosts bus tours, and it is one of the very few places in Guatemala that has a heated swimming pool and a jacuzzi hot tub. ~ 6 Calle at 7 Avenida; 7-561-061, fax 7-561-306. DELUXE.

Because it is a market town, Chichicastenango has quite a few affordable accommodations. One low-cost option is the **Maya**

Lodge. The ten rooms are simple, with just a bed, a table and a chair. A few rooms have private baths and fireplaces at higher, budget-to-moderate rates. Staying here puts you right in the middle of the action on market day: when you leave the hotel, you immediately find yourself elbow to elbow in the frenzied crowd. Needless to say, it's noisy. Meals in the hotel's tiny restaurant are also in the budget price range. ~ On the northwest corner of the central plaza; 7-561-167. BUDGET.

The longtime backpackers' favorite in Chichicastenango is the **Hospedaje Salvador**, two long blocks south of the town center. This crazy labyrinth of a hotel offers 35 claustrophobically small rooms with minimal furnishings and private baths, and cheaper ones with shared baths—a good deal if you're willing to overlook the funny odor (possibly the result of a rustic patchwork plumbing system) that seems to permeate the place. ~ 10 Calle at 5 Avenida; 7-561-329. BUDGET TO MODERATE.

A better budget bet despite slightly higher rates is the **Posada Belen**, on the south edge of town about five blocks from the central plaza. Rooms in this three-story hostelry are plain but spacious and open onto large shared balconies that face away from town, toward the hilltop site of Pascual Abaj and the mountains beyond. There are seven rooms with private baths and nine with shared baths. ~ 12 Calle at 6 Avenida; 7-561-244. BUDGET.

Seemingly out of place in this part of the country, the big ultramodern **Villa Grande Hotel** sprawls across a hillside just out of town on the highway from Los Encuentros. Designed to cater to bus tour groups, this German-built hotel also has full conference center facilities—something of an oddity given the setting. It seems to be empty a good part of the time. Accommodations are in 40 spacious rooms, each with two double beds, and 35 two-room suites. All are sparely furnished with ultra-chic contemporary styling, and all have fireplaces, private baths with tubs, and sliding glass doors opening onto terraces with views of the town below. ~ Phone/fax 7-561-053. DELUXE.

DINING   Each of the expensive hotels in town—the **Hotel Santo Tomás**, the **Mayan Inn** and the **Villa Grande Hotel**—has its own dining room serving a different Continental fixed menu each night. Prices are expensive, the quality of the food far surpasses that found elsewhere in town, and there's no reason to eat at the Santo Tomás if you're staying at the Mayan Inn or vice-versa.

For plain good restaurant food with a view, eat at the **Restaurante La Fonda del Tzijolaj**, on the second floor of the produce market building on the north side of the plaza. You can't see much from here on market day except a sea of plastic tarps that shade the booths, but if you eat dinner on the restaurant's large balcony the evening before market day, you can watch as vendors set up their stalls. Or the next evening as they tear them down. This is the only restaurant right on the plaza, and it's a good choice. The menu includes several shrimp entrées and vegetarian stir-fry, along with chicken, pasta and local versions of *chile rellenos* (stuffed chili poblano peppers) and tamales. ~ North Parque Central; 7-561-013. BUDGET.

Most of the other indoor, sit-down restaurants in town are located in a cluster three blocks north of the plaza on 5 Avenida, near a muraled archway called Arco Gucumatz, just far enough away from the epicenter of the market to be at the edge of the crowds. It's simple to wander over to this corner of town, down a street lined with sidewalk honey sellers, and compare the menus posted out front. There is not much difference between the **Restaurante Kato Cok** (5 Avenida at Arco Gucumatz), **Restaurante Tapena** (5 Avenida) and the **Restaurante Tziguam Tinamit** (5 Avenida at 6 Calle). All have a certain plastic-tablecloth charm that shows they're trying to be better than the corner *comedores*. The Tinamit has more "international" specialties such as pizza and *pollo frito* (fried chicken), while Kato Cok has an impressive selection of meat dishes and sandwiches, and serves American-style breakfasts. ~ BUDGET.

Around the corner, the somewhat tonier **Restaurante El Torito** specializes in thin, tasty grilled beefsteaks. ~ 6 Calle between 4 and 5 Avenidas, upstairs; 7-561-006. BUDGET.

On market days, you can eat Maya food (mainly corn dishes) very inexpensively at the numerous open-air *comedores* that set up around the northwest corner of the plaza.

The famous public market at Chichicastenango is held on Thursday and Sunday. Though the market is the local people's main source for household necessities, the shaded stalls on the plaza are increasingly given over to clothing, textiles and other arts and crafts. Specialties of the town, in addition to the beautiful hand-embroidered *huipiles* made by the village women, include masks, hand-carved wooden saints and decorative boxes.

SHOPPING

Because of the market's enormous popularity, vendors from all over the country come here to sell, and asking prices for many items run higher than in Panajachel or Antigua. It is not the goods for sale but the sheer spectacle of so many people in bright-hued *traje* from all over Guatemala that makes market days in Chichi so special. Don't miss the fruit and vegetable market inside the big building on the north side of the plaza opposite the church, where you can stand on the second floor and watch the dazzle of color below. The market also spills into the surrounding side streets, where women show off arrays of *huipiles* spread across the hoods of trucks, and others sit cross-legged on the sidewalk selling medicinal herbs and whiskey bottles full of fresh honey.

In the Chichicastenango market, if you walk away from a deal (as a bargaining strategy or just to think it over), when you return you may find that the price has been *raised*. It's nothing personal. Vendors often raise their prices as the day goes on, perhaps as a tactic to stimulate buyers' eagerness to buy now—or perhaps not. Many highland Maya customs defy attempts at simple explanation.

▼▼▼▼▼▼▼▼▼▼▼▼▼▼▼▼
Santa Cruz del Quiché and K'umarcaaj

Santa Cruz del Quiché (pop. 15,000), 33 kilometers north of Chichicastenango via paved Route 15, is the capital of the department of Quiché. The bleak, dusty town with its concrete-paved Parque Central holds few charms for the visitor. Other than its authentic, unexciting market and colonial church and colorful religious celebrations ten times a year, there is not much reason to linger in Santa Cruz.

SIGHTS

The main reason to go to Santa Cruz del Quiché is to pay homage to **K'umarcaaj** (admission), the site of the most important city in Guatemala when the Spanish conquistadŏrs arrived. Some maps, including the Guatemalan government's INGUAT tourist map, show the site as Utatlán, the Aztec name given by early Spanish conquerors. The ruins are a short taxi ride or a long walk from the town center. If you're driving, follow the one-way Calle 10 west out of town. It merges with Calle 9, which is one-way back into town. Follow the unpaved road for three hilly, rocky kilometers until you start to suspect you're on the wrong road. Then watch for a steep driveway up the hill on your right. There is no sign, but there's an official-looking open gate at the top of the driveway. Pass through it and you're in the visitors center parking lot.

The locals know K'umarcaaj only by its original Maya name. It was the short-lived capital of the Quiché Maya, a warrior society influenced by Mexico's Toltec civilization. The Quiché people rose up and conquered the Guatemalan highlands in the 1300s. Because the city was at the height of its splendor at the time of the Spanish conquest, and because the record of the Quiché empire was recorded at length in the Popol Vuh, more is known about the history of K'umarcaaj than any other Maya site.

The city's last ruler, Tecún Umán, heard that the Spanish were coming in the form of conquistador Pedro de Alvarado and his army. He assembled one of the largest Indian armies ever known—30,000 warriors—and rode out to meet Alvarado in western Guatemala. Incredibly, Tecún Umán's forces could not stand up to Alvarado's detachment of 200 Aztec slaves and 250 Spanish soldiers with their horses, steel weapons and armor. After hurling thousands of men into the jaws of the Spaniards, Tecún Umán challenged Alvarado to resolve the conflict by one-on-one combat—to the death. Tecún Umán lost, and Guatemala fell to

Spanish colonialism. Alvarado ordered the great city of K'umar-caaj destroyed.

Though never inhabited again, K'umarcaaj still had some stair-ways and smooth-cut stone facing, as well as paintings on stucco walls when John Lloyd Stephens visited during the 1839 expedition through the Maya world that's recounted in his book *Incidents of Travel in Central America, Chiapas and Yucatán*.

K'umarcaaj is one of the few Maya ruins where free camping is allowed.

Today, virtually all of the stonework has been taken away and used as building material elsewhere, leaving only faint echoes of past greatness. A model at the small visitors center shows what Utatlán looked like during its heyday. All through the large site, steep, grass-covered mounds scarred by dozens of archaeological trenches show where great temple pyramids and ball courts once stood. Shamans in shabby western wear can often be seen performing ceremonies in the old central plaza, laying out patterns in white sand on ground dyed black by centuries of ceremonial fires, chanting and making of-ferings of incense smoke and liquor. If this isn't enough to con-vince you that K'umarcaaj is still revered as a holy site, notice how people leave offerings of forest boughs and flowers at the foot of the oldest cedar trees that have grown over the old city.

◄ HIDDEN

Visitors often miss the most interesting part of K'umarcaaj, the **cave** (*la cueva*) beneath the city. Follow the west rim of the mesa, directly across the ruins from the visitors center, until you find a trail marked with a small hand-lettered sign nailed to a tree: "*a la cueva.*" Follow the trail down the slope for a hundred yards or so to the cave entrance, marked by accumulations of the bark wrappers for copal incense. You may see incense smoke wafting from the cave entrance. Entering the cave with a flash-light and following the straight, incense-filled passageway, you may notice that its floor was leveled and its walls smoothed and widened by ancient craftsmen. Eventually the tunnel becomes a labyrinth of passageways to small shrines, often marked by lit candles and fresh flower offerings, which are said to mark the tombs of rulers of ancient K'umarcaaj. The largest shrine is by a narrow hole flanked by the remains of sacrificial doves. Indian tradition holds that this possibly bottomless pit is where the first ancestors of the Quiché people emerged into the present world. It lies directly beneath the main plaza of the K'umarcaaj ruins, where the shamans perform their rituals.

About ten kilometers out of Santa Cruz del Quiché in the other direction, toward the uninteresting old town of Joyabaj, the church at the small town of **Chiché** is virtually identical to the church in Chichicastenango, and ethnologists sometimes study the rituals conducted there because they are exactly the same as those practiced in Chichicastenango—but without the tourist presence.

LODGING　If your only interest in the area is to visit K'umarcaaj, the best plan is to come on a day trip from Lago de Atitlán or Chichicastenango. The town of Santa Cruz del Quiché was a center of Guatemala's guerrilla conflict until quite recently and still lacks accommodations for travelers.

The best hotel in Santa Cruz del Quiché is the 24-room **Posada Calle Real** (**Travel House**), where you'll find clean, underfurnished doubles with shared baths and hot-water showers, opening onto a concrete courtyard. ~ 2 Avenida No. 7-36; 7-551-438. BUDGET.

The 40-room **Hotel San Pascual** has good, basic rooms, including a few with private baths, heated water and even TVs, secured behind steel doors and barred windows. ~ 7 Avenida No. 0-25; 7-551-107. BUDGET.

For super-cheap lodgings, check out the **Hospedaje Tropical** and **Hospedaje Hermano Pedro**, both next to the outdoor bus terminal. Rooms (all with shared baths) cost less than two dollars, but you'll want to stay here only if your travel budget is approaching the desperate level. ~ 9 Calle at 0 Avenida; no phone. BUDGET.

DINING　The cuisine scene in Santa Cruz del Quiché is almost nonexistent. Facing the Parque Central, the **Comedor y Cafeteria Karin** serves a menu that ranges from fried eggs to chicken. ~ 3 Calle No. 1-24. BUDGET. The identical fare is served at **Comedor Las Rosas**. ~ 1 Avenida No. 1-28. BUDGET. In fact, if you order roast chicken with rice and a Coca-Cola in either of these places, I suspect it's the same chicken that will die. Both have seating in crude hand-built wooden booths. They are the fanciest restaurants in town.

A reasonable alternative if you forgot to bring enough food with you is to buy bread at one of the small bakeries on the west side of the plaza and fresh fruit and vegetables at the town marketplace on the opposite side.

SHOPPING　While a few produce sellers are there every day, official market days are Thursday and Sunday, the same as in Chichicastenango, which tends to keep the tourists away. The Santa Cruz market is as practical as can be, a place where local farmers come to sell tropical fruits, vegetables and big slabs of dried fish and buy hand tools, blue jeans, plastic water jugs, bolts of cloth and bright colored thread for embroidering *huipiles*. There are distinctive lace-topped traditional blouses alongside Metallica T-shirts. You'll find that it's not easy to spend money in this part of the country. The only local crafts for sale are heavy, broad-brimmed hats woven from palm fiber. Market day in the nearby village of Chiché is Wednesday.

The Ixil Triangle is the nickname given to a lush, bowl-shaped valley surrounded by the peaks of the Cordillera de los Cuchumatanes. The valley's three

▼▼▼▼▼▼▼▼▼▼▼▼
The Ixil Triangle

villages—Nebaj, Chajul and San Juan Cotzal—form the points of the triangle. The inhabitants of this valley are the only people who speak Ixil, one of the more obscure among the 22 Maya languages spoken in Guatemala today. The language barrier has preserved the Ixil culture as one of the most traditional in the highlands.

The Ixil Triangle was an ultimate destination to an earlier generation of international trekkers. The remoteness of the place, its physical beauty and unspoiled village lifestyles combined to make it a sort of Shangri-la. Beginning in the late 1970s, however, foreigners were barred from the region as the Ixil Triangle became the scene of fierce fighting between army troops and guerrillas that went on intermittently for more than 15 years. Thousands of Ixil men were executed to punish the villages for allegedly giving aid and comfort to the guerrillas. Only since 1993 has the area really been reopened to outsiders. The tourist infrastructure is minimal, and therein lies its charm.

The Ixil Triangle is on the wet north-facing side of the Cuchumatanes mountains, where humid air that rolls off the Caribbean Sea and across the Petén rainforest meets the cool mountains and dumps large amounts of rain—an average of 80 inches a year. Even in the dry season, most days bring afternoon thunderstorms. The weather is cool and drizzly most of the time and can be uncomfortably cold after rainstorms. This is the land where women wear red skirts—a deep red hue from a special German dye that has been in use here for more than a century. Whenever the sun comes out, which in Nebaj is not an everyday event, the lush greenery of farmland and forest seems to blossom with squares of red fabric laid out to dry.

If you're driving, figure on averaging no more than 12 miles per hour on this trip. Follow Route 15 north from Santa Cruz del Quiché for 42 kilometers to the plain little riverside town of Sacapulas. Although there are plans to pave this road sometime soon, it is now deteriorating from lack of maintenance. From Sacapulas, follow the main road, Route 7, eastward for about 6 kilometers and watch for a road that turns off to the left and climbs up the slopes of the mountains. This unnumbered road goes over the crest of the mountains and descends in Nebaj, a distance of 20 kilometers.

Nebaj (pop. 20,000) is the main town of the Ixil Triangle and the only place where you'll find accommodations for travelers. The town center has lost some of its character with a recent postwar

SIGHTS

reconstruction project that has replaced the former cobblestone streets with concrete pavement and lined many sidewalks with concrete walls. As soon as you walk more than three blocks from the town center, though, you will find yourself on narrow pastoral lanes between small homes of adobe with roofs of sheet metal or red tile and stick fences that do little to restrain turkeys, pigs and goats that seem to come and go as they please. There are no real sightseeing highlights in Nebaj, only the opportunity to experience the slow, timeless rhythms of traditional Maya life.

As a townsite, Nebaj is estimated to date back about 1000 years, and some 30 Postclassic pyramid temples rise from the cornfields along the northwest edge of town. The stone facings were stripped away centuries ago to build the impressive cathedral on the main plaza, and the pyramids are not very noticeable. Spot them first from the hill of the cemetery just outside town, then follow the narrow lanes to find footpaths that lead to the tops of the pyramids, which are still used regularly for shamanic rituals.

Outside Nebaj, small pastures and cornfields fill the valley, broken here and there by intrusions of tall, dense forest that spill down the mountainsides. The small **United Nations Peace Park** has swimming pools and a children's playground on a hillside just north of town. A two-kilometer trail from the park follows a creek up a narrow green valley and past a stone dam that creates another pool locals use for swimming, to a growing government-planned community called Las Violetas where stairways climb high up the steep mountainsides between homesteads.

Although **Acul**, another government project village, may not be much to look at, the two-hour hike from Nebaj to Acul over a mountain ridge and through stands of high cloud forest is the most beautiful trail in the Ixil area. Near Acul, the **Finca San Antonio** is owned by an Italian family that has been making cheese there for three generations. It is widely reputed to be the finest cheese in Guatemala. Visitors are welcome at the *finca* and cheese factory. Along the much longer route to Acul by road, which goes around the mountain instead of over it, is a fabulous double waterfall flanked by tall forest and banana trees; unfortunately, animal grazing upstream makes it unsafe for bathing.

The second point of the Ixil Triangle is the village of **Chajul** (pop. 17,000), situated 15 kilometers (9 miles) east of Nebaj on a good unpaved road. This attractive village centers on a triangular, multilevel cement plaza with flowering trees, which leads up the hill to the gleaming white church, Chajul's only real point of interest. A life-size black Christ figure in the middle of the large gold-painted *retablo* draws pilgrims from all parts of the highlands on the second Friday of Lent. Two other life-size figures the local people refer to as angels stand at the sides of the *retablo*, guarding the Christ figure with blowpipes, the traditional weapon formerly used for hunting and war in the Ixil area. The angels now wear traditional village dress, as they have ever since a men's *traje* maker donated the angels and their original wardrobe to the church in the 1920s—except during the recent conflict, when they were clothed in military uniforms for several years. (Of which army was never quite clear.) To the right of the altar, a big painting crudely and graphically depicts peasant men being shot as women look on in anguish. The caption translates as "Blessed are the persecuted, for theirs is the kingdom of heaven." The painting recalls a massacre of village men by government troops in the 1980s. Its public display exemplifies the more open expression of postconflict Guatemala.

From Chajul, a foot trail leads north and climbs about 10 kilometers to the summit of 9000-foot **Cerro Bisís**, then descends   ◀ *HIDDEN* into a cool, dark forest wilderness dotted with tiny Maya settlements that cannot be reached by road. The Cerro Bisís wilderness has been proposed for preservation as a nature reserve, though so far no international agency has put up the funding necessary to make it a reality.

In contrast to Chajul, **San Juan Cotzal** (pop. 12,000)—the third point of the Ixil Triangle—seems blanketed in despair. At the village center stands the facade of an old gold-colored mission church that has been bombed out and never restored. During Holy Week, the enigmatic figure of San Judas (the same one known elsewhere as Maximón or San Simón) holds court in front of the church doors to receive offerings of liquor and cigar smoke and, many Guatemalans believe, to dispense prosperity. The rest of the year, the shell of the old church stands abandoned. More than the other towns of the Ixil Triangle, Cotzal seems to be inhabited only by women and children, and a deeper level of poverty is evident. Homes around the village are patchworks of old boards and salvaged sheet metal. Local *traje* is sold at market but not common on the streets of town, where most women wear ragged Indian-style clothing made from nondescript cloth. Cotzal is 13 kilometers (8 miles) from Nebaj by a good unpaved mountain road. There is also a rough 12-kilometer four-wheel-drive road connecting Cotzal with Chajul.

Sacapulas, a hillside town along a stretch of river that is variously called the Río Negro or the Río Chixoy (two names used for the same river in different areas), is a key crossroads in this part of the highlands.

From Sacapulas, the Santa Cruz del Quiché and Nebaj roads meet Route 7, the rough, unpaved "highway" that runs from Huehuetenango in the west to Cobán in the east. Turning west on this road will take you to the large, traditional Maya village of Aguacatán, discussed further in the Huehuetenango section later in this chapter.

Heading east from Sacapulas takes you through the Quiché Maya town of **Uspantán,** whose most noteworthy feature is the row of topiary tree sculptures in the median of the pretentious paved main boulevard, which turns back into a rocky, narrow mountain road at the other edge of town. Nobel Peace Prize recipient Rigoberta Menchú was born and raised in a now-vanished village near Uspantán. Farther along Route 7, **San Cristóbal Verapaz,** the main town of an ancient Maya people who call themselves the Pokomchí, who are known for dark superstitions and hostility toward foreigners. This route makes for a good, slow, adventurous shortcut from the highland areas covered in this chapter to the Cobán area (Chapter Nine), bypassing Guatemala City.

LODGING The only hotels in the Ixil Triangle are in Nebaj. The "best" hotel in town is the **Hotel Ixil,** which has seven large but spartan rooms with two to four beds each, all sharing one bathroom and shower. The rooms surround a pretty enclosed courtyard with flower gardens, parking for two or three vehicles, and clotheslines with Spanish moss hanging from them. ~ 5 Avenida at 10 Calle; no phone. BUDGET.

The best-known lodging in Nebaj is the low-budget **Posada de las Tres Hermanas,** which enjoyed a brief reputation as an international backpackers' hangout in the mid-1970s, before military violence put Nebaj off-limits to tourists. Travelers revisiting the area today will discover that the place hasn't changed much, though one of the three octogenarian sisters who run it has passed on. The six-room inn is organized around a landscaped courtyard full of flowers. Although the rooms themselves are dark and a little cramped, and all share a single bath, the courtyard is often lively with student travelers as well as women displaying *huipiles* for sale. The fact that meals are served on the premises makes this a more social place than the Hotel Ixil. ~ 5 Avenida at 4 Calle; no phone. BUDGET.

Sacapulas has just one hotel/restaurant, the **Posada Río Negro,** a low-budget place with two simple, steel-doored second-floor guest rooms that could easily pass for jail cells. Hot springs along the river near the hotel are used by the local residents for bathing—men in the morning, women and children in the afternoon, generally not by anyone after dark. ~ No phone. BUDGET.

DINING The **Posada de las Tres Hermanas** serves American-style egg breakfasts and sometimes other meals. While you eat, women will display *huipiles* in hope of selling you one. ~ 5 Avenida at 4 Calle. BUDGET.

Otherwise, dining in Nebaj is pretty much limited to the small *comedores* around the *parque central*. The best of them is the **Cafetería y Comedor Irene**, an indoor-outdoor eatery paneled in unfinished lumber, located one block west of the plaza. The little restaurant claims to specialize in raw seafood *ceviche*, but considering the distance from the ocean and the unreliability of refrigeration, I'd give it a miss in favor of beef, chicken or vegetarian Guatemalan dishes. ~ Calle 5. BUDGET.

Because of the restaurant shortage, some women around town approach visitors and offer to serve lunch or dinner in their homes. Prices are in the budget range, and the meals (which may include a local homemade corn wine that tastes something like Japanese *sake*) are more interesting than at the *comedores*. One of these women, widow **Juana Marcos**, offers a package deal that combines a typical Maya meal with a "sauna" in the traditional sweat bath behind her house. ~ BUDGET.

◄ HIDDEN

SHOPPING

The three Ixil villages stagger their market days so that there is something going on at one or another of them every day except Wednesday. Markets are held in Nebaj on Thursday and Sunday, in Chajul on Friday and Monday, and in Cotzal on Saturday and Tuesday. The distinctive *huipiles* of the region, elaborately embroidered in many colors on white cloth in Nebaj and on red cloth in Chajul, are considered by many to be some of the most collectible in Guatemala. It takes a woman about two months to make one. Most Ixil people are too poor to take their work to Chichicastenango's lucrative arts and crafts market for sale, so visitors to Nebaj can expect to encounter street vendors selling their own handiwork at very good prices all over town.

▼▼▼▼▼▼▼▼▼▼▼▼▼▼▼▼▼

Quetzaltenango (Xela)

The Guatemalan tourism agency INGUAT has recently been working hard to promote Quetzaltenango (pop. 100,000) as a tourist destination. The only problem is that the city lacks much in the way of sightseeing. Recently, Quetzaltenango has become a favorite place for serious Spanish students—like Antigua without the tourists. Quetzaltenango is on the southern branch of Route 1, the Pan-American Highway. (Both the highway from Tapachula, Mexico, through Quetzaltenango and the one that crosses the border at La Mesilla and goes through Huehuetenango are designated as Route 1 and referred to as the *Carretera Panamericana*. The two routes join 11 kilometers north of Quetzaltenango.) The city is 206 kilometers west of Guatemala City, 118 kilometers east of Tapachula, Mexico, and 90 kilometers south of Huehuetenango; all three routes are paved two-lane highways with potholes.

Although Quetzaltenango is the second-biggest city in Guatemala, its population is only one-twentieth that of Guatemala City.

Its official name was Quetzaltenango for nearly five centuries, though most people who live here (and any travelers who want to sound cool) still call it Xela (pronounced "SHAY-la"), from Xelaju, the Quiché name for the ancient Maya capital that once occupied the site. The old name has stuck thanks to the most important historical event that ever took place here: the defeat by Spanish conquistador Pedro de Alvarado of the great Quiché Maya hero Tecún Umán in 1524, which opened the route from Mexico to the Guatemalan interior and spelled the beginning of the end for the Maya people as an independent nation. Following Central America's independence from Spain, Quetzaltenango became the capital of the independent republic of Los Altos, which included most of western Guatemala. Formed in 1847, the new nation lasted for only two years before it was absorbed by Guatemala. In 1991, for obscure reasons, the Guatemalan government changed the city's official name from Quezaltenango to Quetzaltenango.

SIGHTS

The city's central plaza, called the **Parque Centroamérica**, is surrounded by gray neoclassical buildings with Greek columns made of concrete. Other columns stand alone as monoliths around the plaza. Though the architects sought to imbue the city center with a colonial feeling, all the buildings—many of them banks—are actually of recent origin, as the city was destroyed by an earthquake in 1902.

On the south end of the plaza, the **Casa de Cultura del Occidente** contains the **Museo de Historia Natural**, a packrat hodgepodge of curiosities ranging from examples of pre-Hispanic pottery, village *traje* and documents from various revolutions to bad taxidermy and such bizarre curiosities as a human brain in formaldehyde. Downstairs in the **Casa de Cultura** is an excellent exhibit of highland Maya dance masks and musical instruments. There is also a gallery where paintings by regional artists are sometimes shown. On the second floor is an office of INGUAT. Admission. ~ Calle 7.

Quetzaltenango's second-best point of interest, located on the northwest side of town about one kilometer from the central plaza, is the **Templo de Minerva**. This concrete replica of an ancient Greek temple dedicated to the goddess of learning, built in the early years of the 20th century by Manuel Estrada Cabrera (Guatemala's "education president"), is one of the largest among several such temples that he built all over the country, few of which are still standing. It is said that Estrada Cabrera built more Roman temples than schools. ~ Calle Rodolfo Robles.

Near the temple is the **Parque Zoológico**, a modest and not particularly humane little zoo and children's playground.

A stay at the **Pensión Bonifaz** will spirit you back to an earlier era of elegance. This 62-room hotel facing the central plaza is divided between two buildings—the original turn-of-the-century hotel and a modern annex. Rooms in the old section have been refurbished, and some have balconies overlooking the plaza. All the rooms are large and many have tubs; all have private baths. There are no in-room televisions or telephones, but the central TV lounge is a popular gathering place. ~ Calle 4 No. 10-50; 7-612-279. MODERATE.

For drivers, the **Hotel Del Campo** (with more than 100 rooms, it's the largest lodging establishment in Quetzaltenango) is located a long way from the city center but close to where routes 9S and 2 intersect. Rooms all have private baths and cable TVs. They are modern and carpeted, with furnishings comparable to those in good motor inns in the United States. There's a pool on site. ~ Camino a Cantel at Las Rosas Junction; 7-612-064. BUDGET.

A good bet for lower-priced rooms is the **Hotel Modelo**, located five blocks from the central plaza, around the block from the pizzerias Pastelería Bombonier and Pizza Ricca. The guest rooms here are small but colorfully decorated and they have private baths. If you've never huddled around a big fireplace in the tropics before, the best place I can think of trying it is in the cozy lobby of this family-operated hotel, a favorite with Guatemalan businessmen and families. ~ Avenida 14-A No. 2-31; 7-612-529, fax 7-631-376. BUDGET.

Quetzaltenango's best restaurant is at the **Pensión Bonifaz**, facing the Parque Centroamérica. This old-fashioned grand hotel has three dining rooms, all with the same menu. The cuisine is Continental, with selections that range from spaghetti to filet mignon. The colonial-style decor features heavy wooden furniture and lots of wrought iron, and the staff dresses in traditional highland Maya *traje*. In the afternoon, the last of Quetzaltenango's German coffee-plantation high society congregates around the fireplace. Budget prices notwithstanding, it's one of the most elegant places in this part of Guatemala. ~ Calle 4 No. 10-50; 7-612-279. BUDGET.

A more modest place—where you can sample an assortment of regional foods at a low budget price—is the **Cafetería El Kopetin**. The specialty at this modern family-style restaurant is the *parrillada* (barbecue), a platter of five different meats with all the trimmings. Other entrées run the gamut from cheeseburgers to seafood. ~ Avenida 14 No. 3-31; 7-612-401. BUDGET.

Pizza places are special in Guatemala. They're where local families eat out on special occasions and foreign travelers hang out to lose those culture shock blues. Quetzaltenango's two popular pizzerias, which also serve burgers and fries and such, are neighbors two blocks west and two blocks north of the Parque Centroamérica. **Pizza Ricca** has wooden booths and pizza bakers dressed in white. ~ Avenida 14 No. 2-52; 7-618-162. BUDGET. Nearby **Pastelería Bombonier** has equally good food at even lower prices, but is quite small, with seating for only three parties at one time. ~ Avenida 14 No. 2-20; 7-616-225. BUDGET.

SHOPPING   The old **Mercadito** (Little Market) off Quetzaltenango's central plaza still operates on a small scale. It is mostly tourist-oriented, with a fair selection of commercial-quality clothing and jewelry. The larger public market is **La Democracia**, ten blocks northwest of the city center. This is the place where the locals go for food and furniture, kitchenware and bolts of blue denim, imported all the way from the United States. ~ Avenida 16 and Calle Rodolfo Robles in Zona 3.

One of the best *artesanía* shops in Quetzaltenango is **Mujeres al Año 2000**, a women-owned crafts cooperative selling unique and beautiful *huipiles* and a wide range of other products. ~ 2 Calle No. 12-13, Zona 1. Also check out **Utzil**, a shop that sells handmade dolls dressed in more than 100 distinct *típica* patterns. ~ 7 Avenida No. 15-17, Zona 5; 7-616-214.

You can buy bags of coffee grown by the owners and roasted in your presence at **Bazar del Café**, C.C. Mont Blanc, Nivel 3; 7-654-870.

In many cases, the best souvenir and gift shopping bets are market days at outlying villages, described below.

▼▼▼▼▼▼▼▼▼▼▼▼▼▼▼▼▼▼▼▼
Quetzaltenango Area Villages

Quetzaltenango's top attractions are the numerous traditional Maya villages secluded in the mountains around the city. Here are markets as large as Chichicastenango's and ancient customs as powerful as Santiago Atitlán's—without the effects of large-scale tourism that have altered the character of those villages closer to Guatemala City and Antigua. All of these villages are within easy day-trip distance of Quetzaltenango either by car or by the second-class buses that run back and forth constantly from the city's La Democracia market.

SIGHTS   **San Cristóbal Totonicapán**, 12 kilometers north of Quetzaltenango on Route 1, is best known for its mask makers. Ceremonial dance masks from this plain little town are used all over southern Guatemala. The market is on Saturday. From there, an un-

HIDDEN ►   paved road leads to **San Francisco El Alto**, where the Friday market is among the largest in Guatemala.

Fifteen kilometers farther on the same road will bring you to **Momostenango**, a village famous for its thick, warm wool blankets, ponchos and jackets. There are several hot springs in the hills around town, including **Pala Grande** (about four kilometers up the road) and **Pala Chiquita** (six kilometers from town). The altar mounds on **Chuitmesabal**, a hill about two kilometers out of town, are part of a strange highland Maya tradition that is still practiced around Momostenango. On "Eight Monkey," the New Year's Day of the 260-day Maya religious calendar that has been in use since ancient times, the people of the village leave pieces of pottery that has broken during the year as offerings to the old gods. Outsiders are not allowed at the ceremonies, but you can see the mounds that have built up over centuries of ceremonies. For non-drivers, buses run regularly from the Templo de Minerva in Quetzaltenango to both San Francisco el Alto and Momostenango.

Ten kilometers south of Quetzaltenango on Route 9S, **Zunil** may be the most colorful village in the Guatemalan highlands. The village women dress in *huipiles* and long shawls in a full range of pink, red and purple hues. The village church has an ornate old white facade and, inside, an altar made of pure silver. For a firsthand look at one of the strangest aspects of highland Maya folk religion, walk up to the small house behind the church, which serves as a shrine to Maximón. Known here also as San Simón or Alvarado, this effigy—a seated mannequin dressed in a stylized Spanish suit, a cowboy hat, sunglasses and many scarves—does not live in the church because he is considered an "evil saint" by the Catholic clergy, perhaps a manifestation of Judas Iscariot. The local people see him as an incarnation of the ancient Maya god Mam and believe he has the power to heal the sick and answer prayers for money. Visitors are expected to make small offerings of cash. At the shrine in Zunil, it is customary to make offerings to Maximón by blowing cigar smoke in his face and pouring liquor down his throat. Buses to Zunil run regularly from Quetzaltenango.

From the highway near Zunil, a rugged nine-kilometer unpaved road leads over a ridge and down a deep ravine to **Fuentes**   ◄ *HIDDEN*
Georginas, a beautiful hot-springs spa owned by the Guatemalan government. It has a pool and a moderately-priced restaurant, along with a few budget-priced cabins, in a setting that couldn't be more idyllic. Sulfurous steam drifts through a landscape of cedars and giant ferns scattered with fountains and statues of unclad women. The spa is set on the edge of a precipice overlooking a cool pine forest valley. In October 1998 a massive mudslide engulfed Fuentes Georginas, destroying the restaurant and filling the hot-springs pools with muck. It took the better part of a year to restore the facilities, and some of the elegant neoclassical statuary that graced the grounds has never been found, but today Fuentes Georginas looks better than ever. Admission.

SHOPPING   The Saturday market at **San Cristóbal Totonicapán** is known for its fine dance masks, as well as for wooden toys and pottery.

Every Friday, **San Francisco El Alto** hosts the largest village market in Guatemala. Unlike such well-known weekly markets as the one at Chichicastenango, this is mainly a genuine Indian market with few concessions to tourism. You'll find lots of pigs for sale, as well as fruits and vegetables from all over the country, handwoven and imported fabrics and strange herbs. Blankets and all kinds of woolen goods are an excellent buy here. The market starts early, with some vendors doing business by candlelight before dawn, and by noon it's all over.

If you can make it to **Momostenango** for the Sunday market, you'll find the best buys imaginable on wool blankets, a challenge to carry back home but worth it for their warmth. There's a second market day on Wednesday. If you go to this village on any day other than market day, you'll find that most of the places in Momostenango that represent themselves as blanket factories are actually retail stores with hefty markups. For the best selection and prices, visit the cooperative in the center of town or the *fábrica de chamarras* (the real blanket factory) on the outskirts of town.

▼▼▼▼▼▼▼▼▼▼▼▼
Huehuetenango

Most travelers who enter Guatemala by road from Chiapas, Mexico, make their first night's stopover at Huehuetenango, the first large town. Visitors who arrive in Guatemala by air rarely go near the place—and don't know what they're missing. Although Indian and ladino alike are poor in this remote mountain state—it was a guerrilla stronghold in the 1970s and early 1980s—on my recent visit there was not the slightest hint of political unrest or even random lawlessness—just some of the most cheerful and friendly people in Guatemala. Huehuetenango has several language schools, and its popularity as a place to study Spanish is growing because, unlike Antigua Guatemala where language instruction has become a major industry, little English is spoken anywhere in Huehuetenango.

Huehuetenango (pop. 50,000), commonly called "Huehue" (pronounced "WAY-way"), is the capital of the department (like a state) of the same name. The 88-kilometer trip from the border to town on paved Route 1, climbing from 2500 to 6300 feet in elevation, unveils dry, dusty, played-out hillside farms in the claustrophobic valley of Río Selegua. Foot trails disappearing up into ravines barely hint at the grand mountain ranges just a few kilometers away.

Your first impression on arrival in the town of Huehuetenango may well be of a place in hopeless disorder and disrepair, of brightly painted buildings peeled until they are half-gray and battered old cars and trucks, many pocked with bullet holes, chugging through the streets as if each trip might be their last.

Small people, exotically dressed in colorful clothing, walk bare-foot down the middle of narrow streets roughly cobbled with round rocks, carrying improbable burdens such as four-by-eight-foot sheets of tin roofing and net bags full of live baby chicks, or sit in open doorways and curbs of crumbling sidewalks gazing fixedly with black, unreadable eyes at any foreign traveler who may wander past.

All second-class buses (and all buses from the border *are* second-class) let you off on Avenida 1 near the **public market**. The market itself is inside a dim old building, but the local color spills out into all the surrounding streets, for this is the center of town as far as the Indians are concerned. You'll find produce, clothing, low-priced cookware and hardware, and even livestock for sale here, along with prayer candles, used bottles and green (unroasted) coffee beans. ~ Between Avenidas 1 and 2 and Calles 3 and 4.

For the ladino population, as well as for travelers, the center of town is the concrete **parque central**, located four blocks west of the market. A ponderous old colonial-style cathedral with a facade full of decorative columns looms over the plaza, but the main point of interest is in the middle of the park, a giant relief map of the Department of Huehuetenango painted with vegetation zones and roads, with flags marking the locations of major villages. As you can see from the map, the 12,800-foot high point in the Cordillera de los Cuchumatanes, the highest mountain range in Central America, looms in the center of the department just above the village of Todos Santos Cuchumatán, 54 kilometers from Huehuetenango. ~ Between Avenidas 4 and 5 and Calles 2 and 3.

Seventy percent of the population of the town of Huehuetenango and the surrounding villages is Maya Indian. Almost all are descendants of the Mam Maya, whose rugged domain at the time the Spanish first arrived had almost exactly the same boundaries as the Department of Huehuetenango today.

About four kilometers out of Huehuetenango is the closest thing to a tourist attraction in the area—the more-or-less restored ruins of **Zaculeu** (admission), which was the Mam Maya capital of the region until Spanish conquistadors arrived in the year 1525. It is generally considered to be one of the worst restoration jobs in the history of archaeology. The United Fruit Company, which virtually owned Guatemala for much of the 20th century, rebuilt Zaculeu as a set for publicity photos in 1946 and 1947, hastily slathering the old walls and temple mounds with concrete. Even the ball court was completely paved, creating an entirely different impression than other ball courts found throughout the region. Today, the concrete is as cracked and cockeyed as the sidewalks of Huehuetenango, and a streaky gray patina of not-so-great age has settled over the ruins. The stark, streaked planes of Zaculeu pose a wonderful challenge for photographers. Put a human subject in bright-colored clothing anywhere within these ruins and you can't help but take an unusual and dramatic picture.

Many Maya buffs dismiss Zaculeu as a downright boring place to spend an afternoon. But I've found it well worth visiting (once, anyway), for its historical interest, as well as for the dramatic visual effect of its square, unadorned contours set against a backdrop of Guatemala's highest mountains. As a series of paintings and interpretive displays in Spanish in the museum at the site recounts, Zaculeu was the last bastion of the highland Maya people against Spanish soldiers led by Gonzalo de Alvarado, younger brother of the conqueror of Guatemala. Its location on a bluff flanked by deep ravines made it unassailable, and finally the Spanish resorted to a six-month siege to starve the Mam people into submission and finish their conquest of the Maya empire in 1525.

It is a long, gradual uphill walk, which takes slightly more than an hour, from the plaza in Huehuetenango to the Zaculeu ruins, but we would not recommend it to anyone who has doubts about asking and understanding directions in Spanish, because the route has several forks and intersections. Taxi fares are quite reasonable around Huehue, and a shuttle bus runs back and forth on the road past the ruins periodically. The same route is much easier to follow on the way back to town. The people who live along the road, several of whom you will undoubtedly meet if you walk, are remarkably open and friendly toward strangers.

Slate plaques covered with shiny pyrite were made in Zaculeu and traded throughout the Maya world. Although no one knows for sure, they may have had the same significance as the mirrors that hang around saints' necks in Maya churches today.

LODGING   The best place to stay in Huehuetenango is the **Hotel Zaculeu**, a comfortable low-rise hotel just a block from the central plaza. Don't expect American-style amenities such as televisions, in-room phones or air conditioning. Instead, this hotel has quiet, cozy rooms with bright-colored bedspreads, private bathrooms with reliable hot water and a lovely, peaceful interior courtyard with a big fountain and lots of flowers. ~ 5 Avenida No. 1-14; 7-641-086. BUDGET.

If the Hotel Zaculeu is full, the best alternative is the **Hotel Central** across the street. Rooms here are big but dark, baths are down the hall and the courtyard is bare and paved with concrete, but this low-budget, bare-bones lodging is a cut above the other hotels in town. Most guests here are young American and European budget travelers. ~ 5 Avenida No. 1-33; no phone. BUDGET.

If you are driving a rental car or your own vehicle, staying downtown can pose a serious parking problem. The best alternative is the **Centro Turístico Pino Montano**, a roadside motel on Route 1, two kilometers northwest of the turnoff to Huehuetenango. The 20 rooms are in bungalows in a pleasant enough landscaped setting. There is a small, none-too-clean unheated swimming pool. Rates are about the same as at the nicer Hotel Zaculeu. This is actually one of the better motels to be found along the highways of Guatemala, a nation where so few people have automobiles that the whole concept of motels doesn't make much sense. ~ Carretera Panamericana Km. 259; 7-531-394. BUDGET.

Huehuetenango has nothing even close to a fancy restaurant. It's no problem at all to eat cheaply in Huehuetenango; eating well is more challenging. The best meal bargain in town is at the plain, simple restaurant in the **Hotel Central**, where fixed menus offer *comida corrida* fare, typically including fruit, a beverage, roast chicken, spaghetti, potatoes, a vegetable, plenty of handmade tortillas and dessert, all for less than you'd pay for a quarter pounder with cheese back in the United States. ~ 5 Avenida No. 1-33. BUDGET.

DINING

The nicer **Hotel Zaculeu** across the street also has a restaurant, but it seems to be empty most of the time. The decor is intriguing—a big mural of Maya huts in the highlands on one wall dominates the room—but the food is just okay and the prices, while still in the budget range, are outrageously high by Huehuetenango standards. ~ 5 Avenida No. 1-14; 7-641-086. BUDGET.

A place where a lot of foreign visitors in the know hang out is **Pizza Hogareña**, an unpretentious establishment that looks like a hole-in-the-wall from the street, but has a huge back room. Besides pizzas, the menu includes sandwiches, *churrascos* (meat-filled fried pastries) and a wide variety of spaghetti dishes. ~ 6 Avenida No. 4-45. BUDGET.

The same management operates a similar eatery, **Restaurante Rincón** three blocks farther south. ~ 6 Avenida No. 7-21. BUDGET.

Visitors who have just arrived from Mexico should rest assured that they will find much better restaurants in other parts of Guatemala where more tourists stay.

In and around Huehuetenango, you can find some of the best buys in Guatemala for native *traje*, though it takes a little looking.

SHOPPING

Commercial Guatemalan clothing is available in several shops around Huehuetenango. There is an unusually nice selection of blouses, *huipiles* and bags of all sizes at **Artesanías Ixquil**, next door to the Hotel Zaculeu and half a block from the central plaza. ~ 5 Avenida No. 1-30. For the most part, however, you'll find a much better selection at equally good prices in tourist centers like Lago de Atitlán and Antigua Guatemala.

In the **Huehuetenango public market**, you can find *huipiles* and other *traje* from every village in the department if you ask around. Indian women trade both newly made and used *huipiles* to market vendors and shops, for sewing supplies or household items. A good plan is to look at the clothing people wear to market and, when you see a style you like, find out what village it comes from. Then ask around to find out who has it for sale.

▼▼▼▼▼▼▼▼▼▼▼▼▼▼
Cuchumatán Villages

There are about 30 major Maya villages in the department of Huehuetenango, some of them almost as large as the capital town. The easiest Indian villages to visit are Chiantla and Aguacatán, both on a wide, recently paved road that runs north and then east of Huehuetenango. Chiantla is just about four kilometers out of town, and Aguacatán is 18 kilometers farther on. You can easily make a round-trip by bus to both villages in a single day.

SIGHTS

Chiantla is most famous throughout the Maya highlands as a religious center. It is widely believed that the image of the Virgin Mary kept here possesses miraculous healing powers, and the faithful from all over the region make a pilgrimage here on February 2 each year. The main industry in the village of Chiantla is cattle grazing, and leather goods are a specialty.

Aguacatán is a unique village whose people speak a language unlike any other in the Maya world. The people, who are unusually small even by Maya standards, wear some of the most distinctive *traje* in the Maya highlands, especially the women's blouses of white satin festooned with glittery ribbonwork and simple symbolic embroidered figures. The village is so rural in character that there hardly seems to be a town center. The main cash crop is avocados. A visit is most interesting on market days, which in Aguacatán are twice weekly—on Sunday and Thursday. The unexcavated ruin of **Chalchitán** lies buried near the banks of the Río San Juan, about two kilometers north of the village.

HIDDEN ►

By far the most memorable of the Maya villages in Huehuetenango is a lot harder to reach. **Todos Santos Cuchumatán**, a true Central American Shangri-la in the heart of Guatemala's proposed Los Cuchumatanes National Park, is set at an 8200-foot elevation in a valley within shouting distance of a craggy peak that towers above the village. There was no road access to Todos Santos until the 1970s, and even today visitors are likely to feel they have stepped back into medieval times. It's a 54-kilometer trip from Huehuetenango, but the journey can take almost half a day since the road is as bad as any that visitors are likely to find themselves on anywhere in Guatemala. You would not want to drive your own vehicle or dare to drive a rental car on this road.

Lingering memories of the Postclassic Maya world are still strong here. Recent anthropological studies claim that Todos Santos is one of the few places where the 260-times-365-day "short-count" calendar of the ancient Olmec, Maya and Toltec civilizations is still in use. To confirm this fact for yourself, you would probably have to engage in lengthy discussions in the Mam language. Another remnant of ancient times is more tangible: a series of burial mounds from the Preclassic ceremonial site of Tecumanchún can be seen by looking south up the ridgeline from the center of town.

The men of Todos Santos, who stand taller and seem prouder than the residents of other highland villages, dress in a style unique to this valley, with red-and-white striped trousers, homespun shirts with crimson collars, and warm black-wool cloaks and leggings. They are often seen in Huehuetenango, while men from other villages, dressed in remarkably different *traje* and carrying bundles of trade goods on their backs, trek in and out of Todos Santos on a daily basis.

Other villages of special interest in the highlands around Huehuetenango include **San Juan Ixcoy**, 64 kilometers from the capital over the crest of the mountain range, where they specialize in growing temperate-zone fruits such as apples and cherries, which are rare and expensive delicacies in the tropics; **Santa Eulalia**, 84 kilometers by slow paved road, where shrines and ceremonial caves are maintained just outside the village; and **San Mateo Ixtatán**, 112 kilometers away, the farthest place in the Cuchumatán Mountains that can be reached by road, where mineral salt from a local spring is believed to have magical powers.

LODGING

In the village of Todos Santos Cuchumatán, where visitors by bus have no choice but to spend the night, the only accommodations are in two primitive guest houses—the **Hospedaje La Paz** and the **Pensión Lucía**, both near where the buses stop. You get a mattress and a roof over your head but no indoor plumbing. You will want to bring camping gear—preferably a sleeping bag. Chill air pours down from the mountaintops at night, dropping temperatures in Todos Santos perilously close to the freezing mark almost every night of the year. The cost to stay is minimal. ~ BUDGET.

DINING

Two no-name *comedores* at the Todos Santos marketplace are open daily. Otherwise, this area's tourism infrastructure is non-existent, so finding food can be a problem.

SHOPPING   Market days are Saturday in Todos Santos Cuchumatán and Sunday in Chiantla, Aguacatán, Santa Eulalia, San Mateo Ixtatán and Barillas. Both Aguacatán and San Mateo Ixtatán hold a second market day on Thursday.

▼▼▼▼▼▼▼▼▼▼▼▼▼
Outdoor Adventures

BIKING

The rugged, unpaved backcountry roads of the Altiplano are ideal for mountain bike touring. Increasing numbers of highland peasants are riding mountain bikes, outnumbering cars and trucks by a wide margin.

HIKING   South of Quetzaltenango, the **Volcán Santa María** reaches an elevation of 12,375 feet and commands a view of all of Guatemala's highest mountains, including the Cuchumatán Mountains above Huehuetenango and the volcanoes around Lago de Atitlán and Antigua, as well as the lowlands that spill south to the Pacific coast. A lower crater known as **Santiaguito**, standing at 8166-feet elevation on the big volcano's south slope, has been steadily active since 1902 and continues to spew forth ash and noxious fumes fairly regularly. A very steep seven-kilometer trail climbs to the Santa María summit from the village of Llano del Pinal on the north slope, which can be reached by local bus. The distance may not sound like much, but it is a difficult all-day round-trip to the top of the volcano and back. Also in the Quetzaltenango area, San Martín Chile Verde is the starting point for a four-kilometer (one-way) hike up **Volcán Chicabal** to the lake of the same name, which fills the volcano's crater.

▼▼▼▼▼▼▼▼▼▼▼▼
Transportation

CAR

Chichicastenango is on **Route 15**, a distance of 17 kilometers north of Los Encuentros Junction on **Route 1**. It is just 32 mountainous kilometers from Panajachel and 119 kilometers from Antigua. Parking has become a big problem here on market days, and streetcorner entrepreneurs charge a fee of several dollars to find you a parking space in the back streets of town.

Continuing beyond Chichi on Route 15 another 33 kilometers will bring you to Santa Cruz del Quiché, where a side road leads to the ruins of K'umarcaaj. Beyond Santa Cruz, the pavement ends, but Route 15 continues—very slowly—to Nebaj and the Ixil Triangle.

Quetzaltenango is on the southern branch of Route 1, the PanAmerican Highway, a distance of 206 kilometers from Guatemala City and 118 kilometers from the Mexican border. **Route 9S** continues south from Quetzaltenango to Zunil and eventually to the coast.

Huehuetenango is 90 kilometers north of Quetzaltenango, 266 kilometers west of Guatemala City and 84 kilometers east of the Mexican border at La Mesilla. All three routes are paved two-lane roads.

Buses run frequently to Chichicastenango from Panajachel and Los Encuentros. There are also buses to and from many other villages in the area. To get to Chichicastenango from Antigua by public bus means changing at Chimaltenango and again at Los Encuentros. It's much simpler, and not very costly, to take one of the shuttle vans that run from Antigua (as well as Panajachel) to Chichicastenango most days.

Buses run regularly between Santa Cruz del Quiché and Chichicastenango.

For bus travelers, there is first-class service several times daily from Guatemala City, with departures from 7 Avenida No. 19-44, 2 Avenida No. 18-47 and 2 Avenida No. 20-49, all in Zona 1. First-class buses also run between Panajachel and Quetzaltenango, and second-class buses come from Huehuetenango and from the Mexican border at Talismán bridge.

Buses that go to San Cristóbal Totonicapán, San Francisco El Alto and Momostenango leave the Quetzaltenango bus terminal about once an hour. Zunil, located 10 kilometers south of Quetzaltenango on Route 9S, is easy to reach by bus, with departures from downtown Quetzaltenango about twice an hour. There is no regularly scheduled bus service to Fuentes Georginas, but it's possible to walk or hitchhike from Zunil.

First-class buses run from Huehuetenango to Guatemala City and Quetzaltenango. Second-class buses link the town with the Mexican border.

Two beat-up second-class buses a day—one before dawn and the other shortly after noon, with additional buses for the Saturday market—leave from Huehuetenango's market area, reaching Todos Santos in the late afternoon. They do not start the return trip until the next morning, so outsiders who visit Todos Santos must be prepared to spend the night.

▼▼▼▼▼▼▼▼▼▼▼▼▼▼▼▼▼▼▼▼▼
Addresses & Phone Numbers

INGUAT tourist information (Quetzaltenango) ~ 12 Avenida No. 11-35, Zona 1; 7-614-931
Police (Quetzaltenango) ~ 14 Avenida, Zona 1; 7-654-994
Police (Huehuetenango) ~ 5 Avenida between 6 and 7 Calles; 7-641-366

Cruz Roja/Red Cross (Quetzaltenango) ~ 8 Avenida 6-62, Zona 1; dial 125

Fire department and ambulance (Chichicastenango) ~ 7 Avenida at 6 Calle; 7-561-214

Medical clinic (Chichicastenango) ~ 5 Calle No. 6-32; 7-561-309

Hospital and ambulance (Quetzaltenango) ~ 9 Calle No. 10-41, Zona 1; 7-614-414

Hospital (Huehuetenango) ~ Las Lagunas, Zona 10; 7-641-414

Post office (Chichicastenango) ~ 7 Avenida No. 8-47

Post office (Quetzaltenango) ~ 4 Calle No. 15-07, Zona 1; 7-612-671

Post office (Huehuetenango) ~ 2 Calle between 3 and 4 Avenidas

EIGHT

La Costa del Sur

Black volcanic sand absorbs heat from sunlight so that by midday the beach is hot enough to fry an egg on. If you tried to cross it wearing sandals, the sizzling heat would raise blisters right through the soles. If you put on hiking boots and thick socks, you can hotfoot it over to the water's edge and take them off when you reach the sand that's wet and cool from the Pacific surf. Then you can have the straight, empty beach to yourself for as many miles as you wish to walk.

When Guatemalans speak of *La Costa del Sur*, the South Coast, they mean not only the beaches and wetlands where the ocean meets the land but also the wide shelf of tropical hotlands that lies between the mountains and the sea. For the most part, the land is given over to ranches and plantations. African zebu cattle graze in pastures bordered by cotton fields. Seas of sugar cane rustle at the slightest breeze. After a morning of driving and searching, casual sightseers are likely to be disappointed by the archaeological sites that were discovered while clearing some of these plantations, but those with a serious interest may find in these stones some puzzling clues about the origins of Maya civilization.

The Pacific coast does not figure prominently in most travel itineraries. Much of it is inaccessible, and tourist facilities are limited. Perhaps the most likely reason to find yourself in the region is that the *Carretera Costa Pacífica*, Route 2, is the fastest and easiest way to return from the western highlands to Guatemala City. Although it's called the Pacific Coast Highway, it actually runs along the northern edge of the coastal plain, 30 miles inland. It can take you from Quetzaltenango to Guatemala City in four hours without crossing a single mountain range. If you prefer to take your time, three coastal areas are reached easily by car or bus; all three have some kind of lodging. Champerico is "the beach" for people who live in Quetzaltenango. The Puerto San José area has the closest ocean beaches to Guatemala City, and although the run-down old port has nothing to recommend it, beach lodging of variable quality has sprung up in several former fishing villages nearby. Monterrico is the most remote and secluded of Guatemala's beaches and offers the best chance to view wildlife.

Don't even think of going to any of these beaches on a weekend, when hordes of city people descend on all of these areas, bringing lots of noise, some crime and unbelievable quantities of paper wrapping, beer bottles and other debris. On weekdays, however, the "resort" beaches are absolutely deserted except for lodging and food-stand operators, who clean up the beach little by little for next Saturday. Walk a little way down the beach and you may feel alone with your footprints on the edge of the world.

▼▼▼▼▼▼▼▼▼▼
Retalhuleu and Champerico

The warm climate, far enough inland to be free of the insects that plague the coastal wetlands, makes Retalhuleu (pop. 50,000) a popular summer weekend getaway for businessmen and plantation owners from the chilly, gray highlands around Quetzaltenango. There are better hotels and restaurants than you would expect, but not much to see. The fact that Guatemalans on holiday opt to stay in this unexceptional town of squat, square highwayside buildings is an indication of how bad the lodging is at Champerico on the coast.

SIGHTS   Retalhuleu lies off the main highway on the road to Champerico, and the best reason to go there is to find food or lodging in this untouristy area.

Reached by a 26-kilometer trip from Retalhuleu that begins as a highway drive and ends on a narrow, rocky road through the foothills, **Abaj Takalik** is best reached by booking a tour in either Retalhuleu or Quetzaltenango. Archaeologists working at the site have found about 170 pieces of ancient sculpture, including Maya-style carvings that date back to the Preclassic era alongside giant Olmec-style stone heads that may date back as far as 4000 years—long before the rise of the Olmec civilization in Mexico. Structures that once stood at the site are thought to have been built around 235 B.C. Considerable controversy surrounds this and other South Coast archaeological sites. Some archaeologists believe that the area provides a "missing link" between the Olmec and Maya cultures, explaining how early Maya groups came to adopt the Olmec calendar, religious practices and a crude form of writing that would evolve into Maya glyphs. In fact, some patterns carved in stone here may be the earliest known examples of writing in the Western Hemisphere. Some scientists dismiss the supposed Olmec-Maya connection, pointing out that the two groups might have lived in the area at different times, as much as a thousand years apart, while others cite the great age of some Olmec-like carvings to support the idea that an earlier people—possibly of Polynesian origin—may have been the ancestors of both the Olmec and the Maya. ~ To reach Abaj Takalik, follow Route 2 for eight kilometers west of the intersection with Route 9S and turn north on the road that goes nine kilometers to the

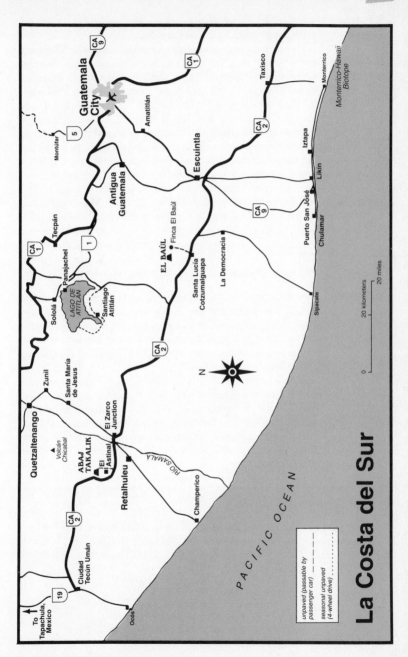

La Costa del Sur

village of El Asintal and then gradually deteriorates into a dirt
track before reaching the archaeological zone.

A half-hour drive or bus ride south from Retalhuleu brings you
to the Pacific coast and the shantytown has-been coffee port of
Champerico (pop. 8000), a grubby little town that nonetheless
draws its share of beachgoers from Quetzaltenango on weekends.
The old seaport here has deteriorated from disuse and decay,
though there are plans to restore it—some day—under a joint
agreement with Mexico. The beach is wide, and though it tends
to be dirty near town (pigs graze on the beach, dining on tourist
leftovers), a walk of less than a mile in either direction will bring
you to pristine expanses of sand.

HIDDEN ►

The truly intrepid outdoorsperson will find boatmen willing
to take anglers or sightseers up the coast to **El Manchón Nature
Reserve**, a vast, isolated, rarely seen wetland inhabited by myriad
birds, caymans and mosquitoes. If all you want to do is see the
ocean, though, you might wait and go to a resort community like
Likín, on the coast south of Guatemala City, or Monterrico farther
to the east, where you can sunbathe in more pleasant surroundings.

LODGING

Retalhuleu has one of the nicest hotels on the South Coast, the **Posada de Don José**, which has 25 spacious guest rooms with private
baths, air conditioning, phones and cable TV. There's also a pool.
It's located across from the train station, two blocks northwest
of the *parque central*. ~ 5 Calle No. 3-67, Zona 1, Retalhuleu;
7-710-080. MODERATE.

Midway between the Parque Central and the train station, the
Hotel Astor is a grand old turn-of-the-century mansion divided
into 13 large, comfortable units; some have private baths. The
rooms are not air conditioned, a drawback in this climate, though
they do have ceiling fans. The rooms open onto a courtyard with
flower gardens. ~ 5 Calle No. 4-60, Zona 1, Retalhuleu; 7-710-
475. MODERATE.

✔ CHECK THESE OUT

- Take a side trip to **La Democracia** to see stone heads left by one of
the most ancient and mysterious civilizations in the Americas. *page 195*
- Sleep in a modern thatch-roofed hut on the beach at **Cabañas Pez
de Oro** in Monterrico. *page 199*
- Feast on a fried fish big enough to feed a family at the **Divino
Maestro** in Monterrico, where they personally catch the fish they
serve. *page 199*
- Book a guided boat trip into the **El Manchón Nature Reserve** for
great birding and cayman-watching. *page 200*

In Champerico, the nicest of the three dubious *hospedajes* along the waterfront is the ten-room **Hotel Martita**, where the rooms are plain but reasonably comfortable, a big improvement over the other options. Baths are shared, and there are no fans to provide relief from the heat, which is sweltering on most days. ~ Champerico. BUDGET.

The best food in Retalhuleu is in the dining rooms at the **Posada de Don José** (5 Calle No. 3-67, Zona 1; 7-710-180) and the **Hotel Astor** (5 Calle No. 4-60, Zona 1; 7-710-475). Both serve fixed-menu lunches and dinners that change daily. Entrées are usually beefsteak or fish. Otherwise, dining is limited to a few small *comedores* around the plaza that serve tortillas, beans and mystery meat at low prices. ~ BUDGET TO MODERATE.

DINING

In Champerico, too, the only restaurants are hotel dining rooms, but here the hotels are of lower quality. You'll find basic roast chicken dinners at the **Hotel Martita** and the **Hotel Miramar**. There are also a number of food vendor stands along the beach. ~ BUDGET.

Like Abaj Takalik, the area around Santa Lucía Cotzumalguapa and La Democracia is rich with artifacts of an ancient culture that remains one of the greatest mysteries in Central American archaeology. Some experts now believe the oldest civilization in Mesoamerica might trace its roots to this region. The mystery culture has been dubbed the Cotzumalguapa-Pipil culture. Many of the stone heads found in this area date back as much as 4000 years and are among the oldest large sculptures in the Western Hemisphere. Besides the heads, there are zoomorphs and stelae hundreds of years older than any known Maya monuments and containing what some experts believe are early non-Maya hieroglyphs.

▼▼▼▼▼▼▼▼▼▼▼▼▼▼▼▼
La Democracia, Likín and Iztapa

The small village of **La Democracia** has a museum exhibiting stone artifacts found at nearby Finca Monte Alto. The most remarkable of the Monte Alto finds are a group of giant stone head sculptures set around a towering ceiba tree in La Democracia's central plaza. The heads, along with those discovered at Abaj Takalik and other sites in the area, closely resemble the Olmec heads of southern Veracruz, Mexico (many of the Mexican Olmec heads are larger, however). ~ To reach La Democracia, go 25 kilometers west from Escuintla on Route 2 and then 10 kilometers south on the road toward Sipascate.

SIGHTS

◄ *HIDDEN*

More Olmec-like sculpture carved from volcanic rock has been found all around the town of **Santa Lucía Cotzumalguapa** (pop. 16,000), located 33 kilometers west of Escuintla on Route 2. Archaeologists find this area interesting not only because of the mysterious Olmec link but also because of the broad array of artistic styles. Some incorporate designs and motifs that also appear in Mexican Toltec or Yucatecan Maya sculpture; others, including some that contain non-Maya glyph inscriptions, are unique to the countryside around this town. Several archaeological digs have been undertaken around Santa Lucía, revealing pottery and tools, but the artifacts have provided scant clues about the people who built a civilization here centuries before the emergence of the Classic Maya culture.

Santa Lucía's central park contains replicas of several strange stone monuments found in the area. Many of the originals stand in the fields of nearby *fincas*. The plantations have grown mostly coffee until recently, and the mysterious stone carvings are still being unearthed as new lower fields are cleared to expand sugar cane production. One of the main archaeological sites, **Bilbao**, is on a small dirt road at the north end of town near the start of 4 Avenida (a southbound street). Several foot trails lead off this road to clearings in the cane fields where the ancient sculptures stand.

Continue west on the Bilbao road, turn right on a wider road and right again on the road to Ingenio Los Tarros, and you'll come to **Finca El Baúl**, where many of the monuments found on the plantation have been moved to a small open-air museum not far from the main house. **Monument 13** at El Baúl, one of the most puzzling, is a giant head with a full beard. Scientists have long puzzled over bearded figures depicted in ancient artwork not only here but also at Copán and Quiriguá and in the Olmec region of Veracruz, Mexico, since most Indians today cannot grow such beards. Ask at Finca El Baúl for directions to other sculpture groups and temple mounds concealed by the El Baúl cane fields, especially the haunting visage of Monument 3.

Another collection of these strange stone carvings can be found at **Las Ilusiones**, a sugar cane plantation two kilometers east of Santa Lucía, where the owners maintain a small private museum and can provide a guide to take you to the spots where artifacts have been unearthed. Admission.

Puerto San José (pop. 10,000) was Guatemala's largest shipping port in the 19th century, but no longer sees many ships. Now the town's main attraction is the long, white beach, which is on the other side of the intracoastal canal. Boats are waiting to take you there.

If you have a car, you can reach more secluded beaches nearby. **Balneario Chulamar**, five kilometers to the west, is wider and quieter than Puerto San José. A similar distance to the east is **Balneario Likín**, a planned community of posh vacation homes owned by Guatemala's moneyed elite. Another seven kilometers to the east, the laid-back village of **Iztapa** (pop. 2000) was Guatemala's first seaport, established by Pedro de Alvarado in the mid-

16th century and used for 300 years before Puerto San José was built. Although tourism is also the main industry here, the place is much less developed than Puerto San José and enjoys a mellower atmosphere, though the mosquitoes are fierce at times.

Santa Lucía Cotzumalguapa is a decent spot to spend a night while exploring nearby archaeological sites. The better lodgings are at two motels located across the highway from each other outside of town. The **Caminohotel Santiaguito** has 21 simple painted-concrete rooms and a swimming pool surrounded by palm trees. They feature ceiling fans and shared baths. ~ Route 2, Kilometer 90.4, Santa Lucía Cotzumalguapa; 8-825-435, fax 8-825-438. MODERATE.

LODGING

If Caminohotel Santiaguito is full, the **Hotel El Camino** has 15 rooms with private baths. ~ Route 2, Kilometer 90.5, Santa Lucía Cotzumalguapa; 8-825-316. BUDGET.

Guatemala's beach resorts cater to two kinds of visitors—daytrippers and vacation-home owners. Lodging is minimal. Both Chulamar and Iztapa have clusters of very basic cabañas for rates that are shockingly high compared to lodging costs in any other part of Guatemala. Thatch-roofed huts without private baths may run in the deluxe range. Iztapa also has two funky little hotels. The **Hotel Brasilia** is a simple, johns-down-the-hall place, while the nearby **María del Mar** has small, dark concrete-block rooms (with private baths) arranged motel-style around a swimming pool. ~ BUDGET.

If you're spending the night in Santa Lucía Cotsumalguapa, the only restaurant other than the dining rooms of the two motels on the highway is the **Rincón Huehueteco**, across the street from the southeast corner of the *parque central*. The menu there is sturdy and unexceptional, with such mainstays as roast chicken and spaghetti topped with garlic butter. ~ BUDGET.

DINING

Guatemala's Pacific beach resorts have no real sit-down restaurants. All of the beaches from Chulamar to Iztapa have food stands that sell fruit, fish tacos and whole fried fish at very inexpensive prices. Wise travelers stock up on picnic supplies before embarking on a trip south from Guatemala City or Antigua.

The small village of Monterrico (pop. 700) got its start more than a century ago as a place where fugitives from the law could go and never be found. Most of the *palapa*-style beach bungalows that make up the village were originally built by squatters, and title to most real estate here is murky. Today, the tiny community serves as a hideaway for fugitives from modern life. It is located on a barrier island with a straight sandy brown beach on the ocean side and a verdant mangrove-lined

▼▼▼▼▼▼▼▼
Monterrico

lagoon that's part of the Chiquimulilla Canal on the inland side. Monterrico can only be reached by a 20-minute boat trip down the canal. Turn off Route 2 at the village of Taxisco, 48 kilometers east of Escuintla. From Taxisco, it is 19 kilometers to the dock for ferries waiting to take you—and, if you wish, your vehicle—down the canal to Monterrico for a nominal charge. Both passenger launches and small car ferries that carry one or two vehicles each make the trip constantly on weekends and snooze in the sun at the mainland port on weekdays hoping for a customer or two. The trip takes you through an area teaming with bird life, including snowy egrets, great blue and great white herons and pelicans. If you are driving, the idea of cruising the canal on the ferry and birdwatching from the comfort of your own car is so novel as to be practically irresistible. When you arrive in Monterrico, however, you discover that deep sand traps in the village's few roads render vehicles without four-wheel-drive all but useless on the island. Unless you are staying at the Monterrico Paradise Hotel, far from the village, you'll find that a car is more of a hindrance than a convenience here. There's plenty of parking space in fields near the ferry dock. The landowner will charge you a few quetzales, and your car will be safe.

SIGHTS   The entire area is part of the **Monterrico-Hawaii Biotope**, which was originally established as a reserve for sea turtles. Two species—the endangered olive ridley turtle and the near-extinct leatherback turtle—lay eggs in the beach sand here. The turtle eggs had always been a favorite food of the local population, so a turtle research center was set up by the University of San Marcos and the World Wildlife Fund to educate the locals about the turtles and ask them to keep only half the turtle eggs they found and bring the rest to the center for incubation, which would increase the baby turtles' survival rate. Unfortunately, a scandal in the administration of the research center gave anti-environmental forces in the government an excuse to cut the center's funding and transform it from a save-the-turtles center to an experimental shrimp farm. Today, the government tourist agency INGUAT is working to publicize Monterrico as a beach resort. They have a long way to go. Monterrico is way off the beaten track, so tourist facilities and even public utilities are minimal. A single electric line serves the entire island. There are no phones and no TV reception.

LODGING   Don't expect to find phones or street addresses in Monterrico: there aren't any. Some of the hotels here have contact phones in Guatemala City where you can make reservations; others are simply first-come, first-served. If you visit during the week, you won't encounter any room availability problems.

The original Monterrico lodging is the **Hotel El Baule**. Owned and operated by a woman who came to Guatemala as a U.S. Peace Corps volunteer, married a Guatemalan and stayed, the hotel has eight basic two-bed huts with mosquito nets and hammocks on the porches; all have private baths. More huts are under construction. The hotel also serves as a sort of information center about the sea turtles. ("Baule" is the Spanish name for the leatherback sea turtle, which is sighted about ten times a year during the December–January nesting season. Leatherbacks grow to seven feet in length and weigh up to 1500 pounds.) Room rates are the lowest you'll find in this low-budget version of paradise. ~ On the beach. BUDGET.

There are three other small, *palapa*-hut hotels along the beach near the Hotel El Baule. The cheerfully painted **Cabañas Pez de Oro** has spacious rooms with private baths and handcrafted rustic furniture. There's also a pool. ~ On the beach; reservations: 3-323-768 in Guatemala City. BUDGET.

Johnny's Place has six large cabañas with three or four beds each, private baths and small individual wading pools in front. ~ On the beach; reservations: 3-364-193 in Guatemala City. BUDGET.

The European-run **Kaiman Inn** has spacious huts with private baths in a nicely landscaped compound picture-perfect for lazy hammock siestas. Rates are higher on weekends. ~ On the beach. BUDGET TO MODERATE.

The most luxurious accommodations in Monterrico are at the **Monterrico Paradise Hotel**. This beautiful little resort hotel was the dream of an American doctor, who went bankrupt from the delays and cost overruns involved in making it a reality. Today, it belongs to nonresident owners in Guatemala City, and the on-site management is sometimes less than hospitable. The hotel has 34 guest units in very nice *palapa*-roofed duplex cabañas surrounding a large swimming pool. The location, about one-and-a-half kilometers west of the village, is isolated, so guests are pretty much stuck eating in the hotel dining room—not bad food, but ridiculously overpriced in comparison with the other places to eat in town. ~ Aldea El Pumpo; reservations: 2-384-690. MODERATE.

DINING

All of the Monterrico hotels listed above except Johnny's Place have restaurants that specialize in seafood and pasta. The restaurants at the **Hotel El Baule** and the **Pez de Oro** are both excellent, featuring shrimp and fish entrées. ~ BUDGET.

The only other restaurant in the village is the **Divino Maestro**, where the family both fishes and cooks, giving them first pick of the day's catch. A fried fish bigger than the plate it's served on is in the budget range. ~ BUDGET.

NIGHTLIFE   Watch the sunset and stay all evening at the only bar on the island, the superfunky beachfront **Pig Pen**, where the amenities include Pink Floyd on the sound system and more hammocks than tables.

▼▼▼▼▼▼▼▼▼▼▼▼▼▼▼

Outdoor Adventures

Monterrico and San José offer excellent sport fishing. Marlin, sailfish and sawfish are plentiful, since these waters have not been overfished like more popular areas in the Caribbean and Mexico, Also common are dorado (mahi-mahi) and sharks. Sport fishing expeditions can be arranged through **Guatemala Offshore Fishing**. ~ 5 Avenida No. 11-63, Zona 9, Guatemala City; 2-317-222. Hotel managers in Monterrico and San José can also make informal arrangements with local fishing guides for you.

FISHING

BIRD-WATCHING   **El Manchon Nature Reserve** near Champerico has a great abundance of water bird life and is a major breeding area for several species including the rare jaribu stork, the largest flying bird in the Western Hemisphere. The area is also inhabited by jaguars and tropical caymans. Guides for boat trips into the reserve can be arranged through hotels in Champerico. If you visit the reserve, you'll quickly discover why it is one of the most pristine wildlife habitats in Guatemala: biting insects and steamy humidity keep humans away.

An easier place for birdwatching is the **Chiquimulilla Canal**, which separates the beaches of Monterrico from the mainland. The canal drains large areas of wetlands for farming, and wading birds abound along its banks.

▼▼▼▼▼▼▼▼▼▼▼▼

Transportation

The main crossroads for reaching all the destinations in this chapter is Escuintla (pop. 50,000), a town with agricultural processing plants and oil refineries but not much to attract visitors. Here, **Route 9** from Guatemala City to the coast intersects **Route 2**, the Carretera Costa Pacífica, which skirts the base of the highlands all the way from the Mexican border to El Salvador. (Another road, **Route 14**, runs directly from Antigua to Escuintla, but the steep, unpaved descent from the highlands is not for the fainthearted.)

CAR

Retalhuleu lies 127 kilometers west of Escuintla; follow Route 2 west to the intersection with **Route 9S** and go a short distance south into town. Continue another 38 kilometers south on Route 9S to Champerico.

The archaeological sites of La Democracia, Bilbao and El Baul are in the vicinity of Santa Lucía Cotzumalguapa, 33 kilometers west of Excuintla on Route 2. (See the Sights section for specific directions on how to reach the archaeological zones. Puerto San José, Iztapa and Likín are at the end of Route 9, 49 kilometers south of Escuintla.

To reach Monterrico, follow Route 2 east from Escuintla for 48 kilometers to Taxisco, then take **Route 5** south for 18 kilometers to the coast, where wooden pangas decked out as ferries carry people and cars down the Chiquimulilla Canal to Monterrico. Of course, a car is pretty useless in Monterrico, but the experience of sailing down a jungle river in a car is one you won't soon forget.

BUS

Second-class buses run regularly from the Quetzaltenango bus terminal, on 16 Avenida in Zone 3, to Retalhuleu and Champerico. First-class buses leave from the station at 19 Calle and 9 Avenida, Zona 1, in Guatemala City.

First-class buses from Guatemala City to Retalhuleu, Quetzaltenango and the Mexican border stop in Escuintla. Local, second-class buses go from there to Santa Lucía Cotzumalguapa and Puerto San José.

▼▼▼▼▼▼▼▼▼▼▼▼▼▼▼▼▼▼▼▼▼▼▼
Addresses & Phone Numbers

Police ~ Retaluleu; 7-710-120
Post office ~ 6 Avenida at 6 Calle, Retaluleu; no phone
Pharmacy ~ 5 Avenida at 6 Calle, Retaluleu; 7-710-453

NINE

Las Verapaces

In the silence of the cloud forest, the air is cool and wet with the drizzling rain the local Kekchí Maya call *chipi-chipi*. Ferns taller than a human arc from the bases of pine trees of immense height. Spanish moss, woven with flowering bougainvillea vines hangs from the branches; orchids spill from the crooks of the trees' limbs. It is a strange Jurassic-like forest, completely unlike the dry pine forests of the Altiplano or the hot rainforest of the Petén. It grows in the place where Caribbean humidity that comes up the Río Dulce and across Lago de Izabal hits the cool air of the high mountains and turns to rain at the rate of 80 inches per year. Visitors come here mainly for one reason: to watch for a kind of trogon known as the quetzal, the sacred bird of the ancient Maya and the national symbol of Guatemala. You walk softly through the cloud forest, scarcely breathing, alert for a glimpse of the legendary bird. Most travelers—and most Guatemalans—have never seen one.

Only a few areas of cloud forest remain. The same climate that created this forest subsequently proved perfect for growing coffee. The cloud forest that is left has been the focus of environmentalist efforts to preserve it since around 1980. Timber interests have fought every move to save the cloud forest and are blamed for the assassination of at least one Guatemalan professor who championed this cause. Yet now, after two decades, ecologists have succeeded in winning protection for three large expanses of forest in Baja Verapaz as quetzal habitat.

Los Verapaces is the collective name for two large departments in central Guatemala—Baja Verapaz and neighboring Alta Verapaz. The word "Verapaz" means "True Peace," and the name commemorates a change in the policy of the Spanish toward the Indians in 1542. When the bloody Spanish conquests that had decimated other Maya tribes throughout the Guatemala highlands had failed to penetrate the rugged homeland of the Rabinal and Kekchí Maya, Dominican friar Bartolomé de las Casas persuaded Pedro de Alvarado, captain-general of Guatemala, to let him prove he could pacify the Rabinal Indians in five years through gentle Christian persuasion. His approach worked (largely because the people who were unwilling to accept foreign domination and a new religion were moved out of the district to a relocation camp that eventually became the village of San Lucas Sacatepéquez near Antigua). The successful conversion of the Indians who stayed set the example for a new strategy of nonviolence in the Spanish conquest. Although even today the treatment of Indians in Guatemala does not measure up to international human rights standards, it is the policy first tried with the wild people of Las Verapaces by this man appointed as Spain's official Protector of the Indians that explains why Guatemala's Indians were not exterminated centuries ago like the native people of other Central American countries.

By far the fastest (though not the most enjoyable) way to reach Las Verapaces is to follow congested Route 9, the *Carretera Atlántica*, east from Guatemala City to El Rancho Junction, roughly a two-hour drive depending on traffic and road conditions. Turning at this junction puts you on a well-paved highway northward through Baja Verapaz. As the road crests a pass to the north slope of the mountains, it crosses into Alta Verapaz. Beyond the department capital and largest town, Cobán, the pavement ends and the road continues into a world of coffee plantations, caves and tiny Kekchí villages.

Sierra de las Minas

The Sierra de las Minas, the highest mountain range in eastern Guatemala, divides the hot, tropical valleys of the Montagua and Polochic Rivers like an impassable wall. No road has ever been built over the top. The mountains form the natural barrier marking the boundary between no fewer than five departments—Baja Verapaz, Alta Verapaz, Izabal, El Progreso and Zacapa. The range is so steep that it rises from 15 feet above sea level at its base to 10,050 feet above sea level at Cerro Raxón, only 17 kilometers away.

SIGHTS

◀ *HIDDEN*

The **Sierra de las Minas Biosphere Reserve** was created in 1990 through the efforts of Defensores de la Naturaleza, Guatemala's leading conservation group. Because the upper altitudes of the mountain range were so hard to reach before the days of four-wheel-drive, the reserve contains a greater diversity of animal and plant life than any other area of the country including the Petén rainforest. More than two-thirds of all bird, mammal, reptile and amphibian species in Guatemala are found on the Sierra de las Minas. The mountains also contain an estimated 60 percent of all the remaining cloud forest in Guatemala, including at least 17 species of evergreen trees that are found nowhere else on earth.

The 143,000-acre biosphere reserve remained almost completely inaccessible until the completion of an as-yet-unnamed hiking trail in late 1994. The wilderness trail, developed with assistance from the Swiss and Swedish governments, the World Wildlife Fund and Conservation International, goes for about 30 long, slow kilometers between San Agustín Acasaguastlán, just off Route 9 east of El Rancho Junction, and the tiny village of Chelascó on the northern boundary of the reserve. **San Agustín Acasaguastlán**, the southern end of the trail, is 86 kilometers (52 miles) east of Guatemala City. **Chilascó** is about ten kilometers by four-wheel-drive track from Route 14. At the northern terminus, the four-wheel-drive road to Chilascó is 60 kilometers (36 miles) north of Route 9 on Routes 17 and 14, before you reach the Mario Dary Quetzal Reserve. The first few trekkers who have taken this new trail have returned with excited reports of wildlife sightings including "quetzals as big as hens!"

LODGING　Plan to camp at least one night in the reserve, as the uphill part of the hike takes most of a day. For those hoping to get an early start, the closest lodgings are the two hotels at the Mario Dary Quetzal Reserve (see below) and the low-budget **Hotel Tezulutlán** (which has private baths) in Salamá. Both are within a half-hour's drive of the turnoff to Chilascó.

DINING　If you're hiking in from the San Agustín Acasaguastlán end of the trail, you'll find a number of *comedores* at the junction of Routes 9 and 17 near the turnoff to the village. None of these, however, can compare with the outstanding Mayan and Guatemalan food served at the restaurant in the **Posada Montaña del Quetzal** located fairly close to the trail's northern terminus. ~ Route 14. (See also "Rabinal Lodging.")

▼▼▼▼▼▼▼▼▼▼
Rabinal　Many travelers go out of their way to visit the large Maya village of Rabinal only for its all-week fiesta surrounding January 23. The event holds a special thrill for students of Maya history because of the *Rabinal Achi*, an extended play/dance/ceremony billed by scholars as the only surviving dramatic work of the ancient Maya. Unfortunately, you can't judge for yourself whether it lives up to its reputation, because it hasn't been performed here since 1856. The fiesta features different costumed dance ceremonies each day, which may or may not have once been part of the *Rabinal Achi* as local people claim.

SIGHTS　Rabinal was founded in 1537 by Fray Bartolomé de las Casas, Spain's officially appointed Protector of the Indians. He persuaded the Indians of the region to submit to Spanish rule without a fight, with the result that here more than in other parts of the eastern highlands, ancient traditions have survived the centuries intact. Today, Rabinal is the center of an orange-growing region; harvest season is November and December. Rabinal has a beautiful colonial church and a colorful Sunday market with weaving, clay figurines and painted calabashes. ~ From the Mixco Viejo turnoff, follow Route 5 north. The pavement ends but the road continues, making its slow way over the mountains to Salamá, capital of the

Las Verapaces

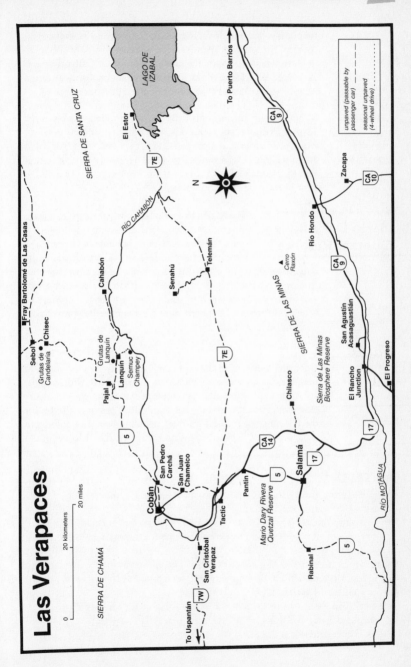

SIERRA DE CHAMÁ

To Uspantán

7W

San Cristóbal Verapaz

Tactic

Cobán

San Pedro Carchá

San Juan Chamelco

Pantín

5

Mario Dary Rivera Quetzal Reserve

Rabinal

5

Salamá

17

17

CA 14

Chilasco

Sierra de Las Minas Biosphere Reserve

SIERRA DE LAS MINAS

Cerro Raxón

San Agustín Acasaguastlán

El Rancho Junction

El Progreso

17

RÍO MOTAGUA

CA 9

Río Hondo

CA 9

Zacapa

CA 10

To Puerto Barrios

N

7E

7E

RÍO CAHABÓN

El Estor

LAGO DE IZABAL

SIERRA DE SANTA CRUZ

Cahabón

Senahú

Telemán

Pajal

Lanquín

Grutas de Lanquín

Semuc Champey

5

Sebol

Grutas de Candelaria

Chisec

Fray Bartolomé de Las Casas

0   20 miles

20 kilometers

unpaved (passable by passenger car) ——

seasonal unpaved (4-wheel drive) ········

department of Baja Verapaz, a distance of 61 kilometers that takes four or five hours to drive. Rabinal is 42 kilometers from the Mixco Viejo turnoff and 19 miles from Salamá.

Just outside town are the unrestored ruins of **Cahyup**, an unexcavated Postclassic Maya fortress-city that probably looked a lot like Mixco Viejo before time crumbled and buried it.

LODGING   Minimally furnished rooms with shared bath are available at the 12-room **Posada San Pablo**. Like the other two hotels in town, which are noisier and more run-down, the rates at the San Pablo are in the low-budget range. The hotel has a very modest restaurant that usually offers a choice of chicken or eggs. ~ Two blocks west of the *parque central*. BUDGET.

▼▼▼▼▼▼▼▼▼▼▼▼▼
Mario Dary Rivera Quetzal Reserve

The Mario Dary Rivera Quetzal Reserve, a magnificent 2900-acre stand of ancient cloud forest, is one of the few remaining habitats of Guatemala's national bird. The reserve was the dream of its namesake, Dr. Mario Dary Rivera, founder of the environmental studies department at the University of San Marcos, who was assassinated—by hit men for the timber interests, according to widely held belief—just months after the government approved protection of this reserve.

SIGHTS   The best time to see the elusive quetzals at **Mario Dary Rivera Quetzal Reserve** is at dawn. Later in the day they are hard to find, but the reserve is worth a visit anyway. Lush with orchids, air ferns and bromeliads that thrive in the damp, cool microclimate under a dense canopy, the cloud forest provides habitat for the full range of tropical wildlife, including peccaries, miniature deer, monkeys, owls, toucans and macaws. The Río Colorado

◆◆

✔ CHECK THESE OUT

- Plunge into the waterfalls and jungle pools of **Semuc Champey** for a taste of the Garden of Eden. *page 213*
- Check into the low-priced **Hostal de Acuña**, which offers a wealth of environmental information as well as lodging for international volunteers in the area. *page 211*
- Indulge in exceptional Mayan and Guatemalan cuisine at the **Posada Montaña del Quetzal** near the entrance of the Mario Dary Quetzal Reserve. *page 207*
- Embark on the wilderness trek through the **Sierra de las Minas Biosphere Reserve**—perhaps the ultimate Guatemalan adventure for serious hikers. *page 215*

tumbles down a mountain slope through the reserve. Two nature trails have been developed. The shorter one takes you two kilometers through impressive forest to a waterfall on the river; allow two hours round-trip. A longer, steeper one follows the river for almost four steep kilometers to its source high in the mountains; allow four hours round-trip. Bring a jacket. Admission. ~ From Salamá, take paved Route 17 east for 13 kilometers to the intersection with Route 14, and then go north for 34 kilometers to the village of Pantín and the entrance to the quetzal reserve.

The **Posada Montaña del Quetzal** is the better of the two inns at the quetzal reserve. A swimming pool, hiking trails, a beautiful cloud forest setting and a monkey mascot combine to provide a rare experience. You can choose among eight small, affordable rooms in the main lodge, with white-textured stucco walls and beamed wood ceilings, or ten higher-priced, large, suite-like two-bedroom bungalows with fireplaces. ~ Route 14, Kilometer 156; in Guatemala City, 2-351-805, fax 2-351-802. BUDGET TO DELUXE.

LODGING

A lower-cost lodging alternative is the **Hospedaje El Ranchito del Quetzal**. More quetzal sightings are reported here than anywhere else in the quetzal reserve and vicinity. The four individual rooms in the new addition rival the small rooms at the Posada Montaña in quality and price, but this *hospedaje* caters mainly to low-budget backpackers who share the rustic accommodations in two large dormitories—one for men, the other for women. ~ Route 14, Kilometer 163; in Guatemala City, 2-313-479. BUDGET.

Overnight camping is permitted in just two campsites in the reserve. No fee.

The **Posada Montaña del Quetzal** has a good restaurant serving traditional Guatemalan dishes. It is one of the few restaurants in the country where you can sample the traditional Maya turkey stew called *cack-ick*—but only on Sunday. ~ BUDGET TO MODERATE.

DINING

The **Comedor Ranchito del Quetzal** at the *hospedaje* offers a variable chicken and spaghetti menu designed for a low-budget clientele. ~ BUDGET.

▼▼▼▼▼▼▼▼▼▼▼▼▼
El Estor and Sierra de Santa Cruz

Unpaved Route 7 turns east from the Cobán highway (Route 5) near the town of Tactic. The 138-kilometer drive to El Estor takes five to six hours. There are no regularly scheduled buses to El Estor. Pickup truck *camionetas* run up and down this road fairly frequently, but it's a long, *long* ride standing up in the back of a truck. El Estor is also the pullout point for raft trips down the Río Polochic, and it is sometimes possible to catch a ride with a rafting company's pickup van.

SIGHTS   There is now a third quetzal reserve in addition to the Mario Dary and Sierra de las Minas reserves. The **Sierra de Santa Cruz Nature Reserve** rises 3500 feet in elevation from the north shore of Lago de Izabal (see Chapter Ten). The reserve, which is believed to contain the largest population of quetzals in Guatemala, is being developed as a joint project between the Guatemalan government and several organizations worldwide including Lions Club International.

Part of the reserve is accessible by 30 kilometers of four-wheel-drive road, better for hiking than driving, that serves several tiny villages in the hills from **El Estor**, an isolated little town that owed its existence to a nickel mine that closed down in 1982 and is still struggling to establish an identity as a tourist destination. Although the nature reserve has no established hiking trails, local guides can lead you through the forest. You can arrange for one at Hugo's in El Estor. Other El Estor attractions include good fishing and, for truly dedicated wildlife watchers, crocodiles. The problem is that it's a long trip on unpaved roads to get there. Of course, the trip takes travelers through one of the most beautiful valleys in Guatemala, flanked by sheer cliffs dripping with jungle vines and ferns along the Río Polochic, before descending into banana plantation country.

Tactic (pop. 4000), the crossroads town where you turn off Route 5 onto the road to El Estor, is the site of **El Pozo Vivo** ("the Living Well"), a small, crystal-clear pool that "comes to life" when a person approaches it, according to local legend. A current supposedly stirs patterns in the sand at the bottom of the pool. I have to admit that when I've visited, the well has shown no signs of life whatsoever, leaving me to feel slightly foolish for making the pilgrimage across the squishy cow pasture and paying the nominal Q2 admission. The Pokomchí people who live in the area consider the well as something of a sacred spot, and some of them can be seen meditating by the pond's edge for hours. Admission. ~ Tactic.

A side trip along the way, turning north at the town of Telemán, takes you to the remote village of **Senahú**, where you'll find one of Guatemala's most beautiful caves, with a large pool inside, on the edge of town.

LODGING   The lodging scene in El Estor is gradually improving. The **Hotel Vista al Lago**, a longtime international backpackers' hangout, has 24 clean, basic rooms with shared bath. ~ 6 Avenida 1-13; 9-497-205, El Estor. MODERATE.

The **Turicentro El Paraiso** offers seven spacious, attractive cabañas with private baths and has a restaurant on the premises. ~ El Estor; no phone. MODERATE.

There are also several very low budget *hospedajes* that I can't bring myself to recommend.

The *palapa*-style restaurant at the **Turicentro El Paraiso** has the best food in town, though it's way overpriced. ~ On the lake, El Estor. MODERATE.

DINING

Hugo's specializes in fresh fish. The English-speaking Guatemalan owner is your best source of information on fishing, boating, hiking and birding in the Lake Izabal area. ~ 5 Avenida at 3 Calle, El Estor. BUDGET.

Cobán (pop. 55,000) is on Route 17, a good paved highway 125 kilometers north of the turnoff from Route 9 at El Rancho Junction. Built along a ridgeline that makes the town seem as triangular as its Parque Central, the town is a world of its own, unlike any other in Guatemala. The population is two-thirds Kekchí Maya, although that fact is not immediately noticeable since cheap ladino clothing has all but replaced village *traje* in this region. In the non-Indian population, many people are of German ancestry.

▼▼▼▼▼▼▼▼▼
Cobán

The land around Cobán was "colonized" in the late 19th century by German coffee planters who shipped their crop down the Río Polochic to Lago de Izabal, Río Dulce and Livingston—and directly to Germany. Economically independent of Guatemala City, Cobán has developed a tradition of keeping its social, political and financial life detached from the rest of the country.

When the United States entered World War II, U.S. diplomats pressured the Guatemalan government to expel all German citizens, which included most of the coffee growers in Alta Verapaz. Guatemala promptly complied, glad for the chance to confiscate the foreigners' coffee plantations. The only Germans allowed to stay were those who had become Guatemalan citizens or qualified to apply for citizenship and could prove anti-Nazi sentiments. It is these German-Guatemalans who give Cobán its distinctive character today.

Cobán's economy has traditionally centered on both coffee and cardamom, a spice mixed with coffee in Middle Eastern countries, but in recent years cardamom prices have declined sharply. The Guatemalan government charters various experimental agriculture stations in the rich farmlands around Cobán, testing new potential cash crops to fill the vacuum left by the falling cardamom market.

The **Parque Central** is a hodgepodge of contemporary fountains, freeform archways and statues of various personages including famous South American poet Gabriela Mistral, who once served

SIGHTS

as a diplomatic consul here, all juxtaposed against the imposing white Moorish facade of the colonial **cathedral** that marks the center of the city. The real points of interest in Cobán, however, are away from the city center.

Three blocks southeast of the *parque* on Calle 1 and then three blocks southwest on Avenida 7 brings you to **El Calvario**, another beautiful colonial-era church on a hillside, reached by climbing 131 steps. Statues of jaguar cubs guard the entrance, reflecting a local Maya legend.

Just down the road to the southeast of the church is the entrance gate to **Las Victorias National Park**, a former coffee *finca* confiscated by the government during World War II that has been allowed to revert to its natural vegetation. More than 14 kilometers of hiking trails loop through the 50-year-old second-growth cloud forest and provide good opportunities for viewing birds and small animals.

HIDDEN ►

Follow the Old Guatemala City Highway (Diagonal 4) for about three kilometers to reach **Vivero Verapaz**, the largest orchid rescue station in Central America. Started in 1989 by a German-Guatemalan family, the station has almost 80,000 orchids of more than 800 species on display. People from Vivero Verapaz go wherever the forests of northern Guatemala are being cleared and salvage orchids from the trees that are cut down. They estimate that they have saved 2 to 3 percent of the orchid species in Guatemala this way; the rest are lost. In addition to a nominal admission charge, the center helps fund its activities by growing and selling orchids—to Guatemalans, but not to foreign travelers. Guatemalan law prohibits taking any orchid out of the country. The orchids reach their fullest bloom from November through January and do not bloom at all in April or May. Admission. ~ Old Guatemala City Highway (Diagonal 4).

The road southeast from the public market area leads to **San Juan Chamelco**, a Kekchí village about ten kilometers out of the city, which has the oldest church in Alta Verapaz and distinctive weavings. About seven kilometers out, the road passes the beautifully landscaped **Balneario Xucaneb** (admission) and **Balneario Chío** (admission), both bathing resorts along the Río Chío with swimming lakes, picnic areas and, on weekends, big crowds.

Also on the Chamelco road, **Té Chilipee** offers an interesting tour of one of the few tea plantations in North America. Originally started by a German exporter in the late 1800s, it was confiscated during World War II and given to Guatemalan farmers during the land reform of the early 1950s to operate as a cooperative. It continues as a cooperative today with a staff of Chinese technical advisors.

The **Museo Regional de la Verapaz**, located eight kilometers (five miles) north of Cobán, is open only on weekends, though if anyone is around the office they will open it for you during the week. It contains archaeology and ethnography exhibits including ancient Maya ceramics and clay figures, Kekchí wood sculptures and regional *artesanía*. There are also rooms containing natural history dioramas and contemporary art, as well as a *"misionología"* room containing documents on missionary efforts in the region over the centuries and a large fresco depicting Fray Bartolomé de las Casas' arrival in Verapaz in 1545. Admission. ~ Route 5, San Pedro Carchá.

LODGING

The **Hostal de Acuña**, operated by one of the region's leading environmentalists, has very clean, modern rooms, each with a table and one or two sets of bunk beds (22 beds in all) with warm Momostenango wool blankets; baths are shared. The grounds have nice lawns, flowering trees and giant rosebushes. The hostel is *the* place to stay for international environmental workers in the region and often sponsors presentations on ecological topics. Beds in shared dorm rooms are the low-budget way to go; or, for privacy, the cost of having a whole room to yourself is still in the budget range. ~ 4 Calle No. 3-11 at Avenida 3, Zona 2; 9-521-547, fax 9-521-268. BUDGET.

The classiest hostelry in Cobán is the old-fashioned **Hotel La Posada**, in the center of downtown at the opposite end of the narrow Parque Central from the cathedral. The 14 guest rooms have antique furnishings and a historic feel. All open onto the colonnade that surrounds the flower gardens of a parklike courtyard much more beautiful than the Parque Central across the street. The noise of the traffic outside comes through, but on a sunny afternoon it's easy to at least imagine birds filling this courtyard with song. ~ 1 Calle No 4-12, Zona 2; 9-521-495. MODERATE.

The **Hotel El Recreo** is on the outskirts of the downtown area, a six-block walk from the Parque Central. The 16-room hotel has a European ambience in its carpeted rooms; all have private baths. After the sparsely furnished hotel rooms that are the norm in many parts of Guatemala, the rooms here seem almost overcrowded with antique-reproduction furniture. The public areas of the hotel center around a dining room, where fixed-menu meals are served at fixed times. ~ 10 Avenida 5-01, Zona 3; 9-521-160, fax 9-521-333. BUDGET.

Don Jeronimo's is a funky, offbeat inn in a country setting half an hour by car or bus from Cobán. Don Jeronimo, a gringo expatriate also known as Jerry, built the inn by hand on a former dairy farm that he has converted into Guatemala's only government-approved experimental blueberry farm. The accommodations—three or four bedrooms with mattresses on the floor—are only slightly more comfortable than camping, but the setting, keep in the woods with an even more secluded stretch of river-

◄ HIDDEN

bank, is magical, and the rates include three scrumptious vegetarian meals a day; bath facilities, of course, are shared. To get there, drive or bus to the village of Chamelco, then change buses (or take the turnoff) to Chamil, ten minutes away. Bus drivers and most people in the area know where Don Jeronimo's is, or you can pick up a map and directions at the Hostal de Acuña in Cobán. ~ Aldea Chajaneb, Chamil. MODERATE.

DINING   Each of the hotels listed in the preceding section has its own food service, and all are good. The excellent open-air **Café Jardin** at the Hostal de Acuña serves a choice of imaginative vegetarian or nonvegetarian entrées from a menu that changes daily. ~ 4 Calle No. 3-11 at Avenida 3, Zona 2; 9-521-547. BUDGET.

One of the few really good restaurants in town that is not part of a hotel is the **Restaurant El Refugio**, a spacious upstairs dining room down the hill from the Parque Central. There is a long menu featuring steaks, seafood and Mexican food. Late in the evening, especially on weekend nights, this place gets busy and lively, sometimes even rowdy. The rest of the time, it's so big and empty it seems to echo. ~ 2 Calle at 2 Avenida. BUDGET TO MODERATE.

The **Café El Tirol**, across the street from the Parque Central, is the place to go for really outstanding coffee in the heart of Guatemala's top coffee-growing area. Food is mostly limited to bakery goods, though there are some sandwich offerings for lunch. ~ 1 Calle No. 3-13. BUDGET.

SHOPPING   The public market, located behind the cathedral, operates daily. It is not very tourist-oriented—a better place to shop for live chickens and cookware than for gifts or souvenirs. There are some interesting mesh *huipiles* that come from nearby villages, and sometimes patterned textiles from Chamelco as well as palm hats and placemats woven by the rural Kekchí people.

A "green store" at the **Hostal de Acuña** sells *artesanía* and nontraditional products from Indian cooperatives developed in the Petén to explores alternatives to slash-and-burn agriculture, from roasted macadamia nuts to scented rainforest potpourris. ~ 4 Calle No. 3-11.

There is little clothing or *artesanía* of interest in most of the local retail stores. Medical herbs, however, are particularly available in the Cobán area. Among the arcane little shops that sell them are the **Centro Naturista El Arbol de la Vida** (1 Calle No. 2-35, Zona 4) and the **Centro Naturista Alfa y Omega** (2 Avenida 4-03, Zona 3).

▼▼▼▼▼▼▼▼▼▼▼▼▼▼▼
Northeast of Cobán

The region northeast of Cobán is wild even by Guatemalan standards, a maze of cloud forest, canyons, ridges, waterfalls, caves, and rivers that suddenly disappear into the ground only to resurface under other names some distance away. Known only to Peace Corps workers and a handful of mostly European backpackers until a few years ago, the attractions of this region have recently captured the attention of adventure travel outfitters, who discover new destinations in the area as quickly as new four-wheel-drive road construction make them accessible.

SIGHTS

The pavement ends at Cobán, but a rough road continues northward, descending among coffee plantations into hot country at lower altitudes. Follow unpaved Route 5 northeast from Cobán for 46 kilometers to the small village of Pajal, then go east for ten kilometers to Lanquín. The route is passable in a passenger car.

Near **Lanquín** (pop. 700), a small Kekchí village built around a colonial mission church, a sign marks the way to **Grutas de Lanquín National Park**. While northern Guatemala is honeycombed with caves, this is one of the few that novice spelunkers can explore on their own. Admission is free if you bring your own flashlight, but the attendant charges a fee if you want him to fire up the small generator that powers the lights inside the cave. The first part of the two-mile-long cave has been made tourist-friendly with lighting, smoothed floors, ladders and chains to hold onto. Beyond that, you're on your own. Though the cave contains no bottomless pits or other seriously dangerous places and is almost impossible to get lost in, its walls and floor are always wet and extremely slippery. As you make your way through the several hot, dank, dripping chambers, you'll see thousands of bats sleeping on the ceiling and discover Maya ceremonial altars centuries old. Some of the altars are still used by the local Kekchí people today for bird sacrifices and copal offerings.

◄ HIDDEN

South of Lanquín along very bad back roads is **Semuc Champey**, a well-hidden little piece of paradise. Hoping to develop the spot as a tourist attraction, the government has begun to improve the roads from Lanquín to Semuc Champey, but the ten-kilometer route is still only suitable for four-wheel-drive vehicles. Tourists in rental cars often wind up stuck along this road after misguided attempts to drive to Semuc Champey on their own. The maze of small roads in the area also makes it easy to get lost. A tourist shuttle runs there from the Hotel El Recreo Lanquín most mornings, returning in the early afternoon. Tours can also be arranged through the Hostal de Acuña in Cobán. Walking from Lanquín to Semuc Champey is hot and unpleasant but not impossible, and by the time you reach your destination you'll be eager to plunge into one of the cool blue pools. A series of brilliant turquoise-hued pools in natural bowls in a natural limestone bridge above the narrow Río Cahabón Gorge, linked by small waterfalls, make for an idyllic swimming spot. The main part of the river disappears into a roaring sinkhole upstream from Semuc Champey and re-emerges farther downstream. Admission. ~ Located ten kilometers south of Lanquín.

If you continued by car or bus two hours farther north from Pajal on Route 5, through coffee-growing country on the Sierra de Chamá, you would reach the village of Chisec and the nearby **Grutas de Candelaria**, the largest-known cave in Guatemala. The cave is only open to tour groups, however, because the Río Candelaria runs through it, and consequently it can be explored only on special rafts equipped with lights. The tour is well worth taking for the unique opportunity to go river rafting underground through a series of huge caverns up to 240 feet high and 360 feet across. An abundance of murals and artifacts shows that the Maya have used the cave for ceremonies since ancient times. Trips can be arranged through **U and I Tours** (Hotel de Acuña, 9-521-547) in Cobán or **Maya Expeditions** (3-634-965, fax 3-374-666) in Guatemala City.

LODGING   The only tourist facility in the Lanquín–Semuc Champey area is the **Hotel El Recreo Lanquín**. Under the same management as the Hotel El Recreo in Cobán, this 25-room inn is simple, rustic and at the same time comfortable, with natural wood throughout, decorated with local Kekchí carvings here and there. The hotel is located along the road before you reach the village of Lanquín. ~ 9-522-160, fax 9-522-333. MODERATE.

Camping is permitted at Semuc Champey. No fee.

DINING   The food at the **Hotel El Recreo Lanquín dining room** is good, though relatively high-priced. ~ 9-512-160. MODERATE.

For basic native food at very low prices, try the comedor **La Divina Providencia** in the village. ~ BUDGET.

▼▼▼▼▼▼▼▼▼▼▼▼▼▼▼   A whitewater raft trip down the Río Cahabón
Outdoor Adventures   in Alta Verapaz takes four days to cover 30 miles of river sheltered by jungle canyons and
RIVER   punctuated by Class III and Class IV rapids. A gentler but no
RAFTING   less adventuresome float trip, the Río de la Pasión winds slowly through the wild jungle of the southern Petén, offering opportunities to visit rarely seen Maya sites and view rainforest wildlife. Trips down these and other rivers are the specialty of **Maya Expeditions**. ~ 15 Calle No. 1-91, Zona 10, Guatemala City; 3-634-965, fax 3-374-666. Another three- or four-day raft expedition takes you down the subterranean portion of the river that flows through the huge caverns of Grutas de Candelaria in Alta Verapaz. These trips are organized by **U and I Tours** ~ Hotel de Acuña, Cobán 9-521-547).

For a gentle walk through the cloud forest, visit the **Mario Dary Rivera Quetzal Reserve**, where there are presently two nature trail loops. One is three kilometers long and the other is half that. Both are steep in places. Of the reserve's 2849 acres, only 62 acres are accessible to hikers. Additional trails were under construction the last time I visited, and more of this unique reserve will gradually be opened to the public. A more extensive trail system, through less pristine forest, is found in **Las Victorias National Park**, a former coffee *finca* gone back to nature on the mountain slopes above Cobán. A 32-kilometer (one-way) trail starts off Route 14 south of the quetzal reserve and leads into the high, lush forest wilderness of **Sierra de las Minas Biosphere Reserve**.

HIKING

◀ HIDDEN

All destinations in Baja and Alta Verapaz are reached by turning off **Route 9** at El Rancho Junction, 81 mountainous kilometers east of Guatemala City. To get to Rabinal, follow **Route 17** for 61 kilometers to Salama and continue west on **Route 5** for another 19 kilometers.

▼▼▼▼▼▼▼▼▼▼▼
Transportation

CAR

To reach the Mario Dary Quetzal Reserve, bear left where the highway divides 48 kilometers north of El Rancho Junction and continue north on **Route 14** for about 20 kilometers. If you're going to El Estor, follow Routes 14 and 5 north for another 29 kilometers beyond the quetzal reserve to the junction with **Route 7E** and follow this unpaved road east for 138 long, slow kilometers.

Coban is on the main highway, which changes its designation from Route 17 to 14 and then to 5, 125 kilometers north of El Rancho Junction. Route 5 continues as an unpaved road beyond Coban, providing access to Grutas de Lanquín, Semuc Champey and the other attractions of northern Alta Verapaz.

Cars and four-wheel-drive vehicles can be rented at **Futura Rent-a-Car**. Rates are reasonable, but the cash or credit card deposit requirement is high—more than US $400. ~ 1 Calle 3-13, Zona 1, Cobán; 9-521-650.

CAR RENTALS

Passenger buses come and go constantly from El Rancho Junction, a few kilometers away from San Agustín Acasaguastlán. Buses between Cobán and Guatemala City pass this way frequently and will stop if you ask them to. The easiest plan for public transportation travelers is to start from the Chilascó end of the trail, where it's easier to get let off than picked up, and end in San Agustín Acasaguastlán, where catching a bus is easier.

BUS

Buses to Rabinal via Salamá board every two hours at the Guatemala City train station (19 Calle and 9 Avenida, Zona 1).

Both first- and second-class buses run through Salamá en route to Cobán. Second-class buses stop at Pantín and can take you to either Salamá or Cobán, where you can get a seat on a more comfortable bus.

First-class buses run to Cobán from Guatemala City, departing from the Escobar y Monja Blanca station at 8 Avenida No. 15-16, Zona 1, in the capital. There is also second-class bus service between Huehuetenango and Cobán along Route 7, an unpaved mountain "highway"; the 150-kilometer journey takes 10 to 12 hours.

Second-class buses run to Lanquín from Cobán four times a day.

▼▼▼▼▼▼▼▼▼▼▼▼▼▼▼▼▼▼▼▼▼▼

Addresses & Phone Numbers

Police ~ 1 Calle No. 3-13, Zona 2, Cobán; 9-521-225
Fire department and ambulance ~ 3 Avenida at 3 Calle, Zona 4, Cobán; 9-523-094
Cruz Roja (Red Cross) ~ 2 Calle 2-13, Zona 3, Cobán; dial 125
Post office ~ 2 Avenida at 3 Calle, Cobán; 9-521-140

TEN

Copán and El Oriente

There are few places as strange as Copán. It makes you want to whisper. Sixteen generations of kings stand larger than life around the parklike Great Plaza, each one so alive that you can look the stone in the eye and feel it looking back. From 12 centuries ago they live on, their elaborate quetzal feather headdresses waving in a breeze that blows through the ages, their words enduring across the vast reaches of time, waiting for our own technology to grow sophisticated enough to make sense of them. Here and there around the outskirts of the ruins, stately ceiba trees stand 150 feet high. The forest giants had not even sprouted when the last of Copán's mighty kings witnessed his city's collapse. Bright red guacamaya macaws glide among the tall treetops, and white-faced monkeys rustle through the branches.

Copán is foremost among several very different destinations reached by way of the Atlantic Highway east of the turnoff at Vado Hondo village. In this region you will also find Copán's smaller rival, Quiriguá, with its 20-foot-tall statues and strangely carved zoomorphs weighing many tons. Farther east lie Lake Izabal and Río Dulce, a region of steep cliffs and dense jungle where white birds stand motionless in the trees while crocodiles and manatees glide silently through the water. Where the river meets the Caribbean Sea is the most unusual of all Guatemala towns, accessible only by boat, the laid-back *garifuna* or Black Carib fishing community of Livingston.

Copán, one of the most exciting archaeological sites in the Americas, is located off the beaten path, down a long dirt road and across the Honduras border. Far fewer travelers go there than to Tikal, but the number is growing rapidly, and an ambitious new museum at the site is bound to make Copán an even more popular destination in the years to come. The exquisite stone sculptures of Copán are so striking—indeed, haunting—that visitors unanimously agree it's well worth the trip.

▼▼▼▼▼▼▼▼▼
Copán

You can still feel the magic that inspired American explorer John Lloyd Stephens to write in 1841, "The beauty of the sculpture, the solemn stillness of the woods, disturbed only by the scrambling of monkeys and the chattering of parrots, the desolation of the city, and the mystery that hung over it, all created an interest higher, if possible, than I had ever felt among the ruins of the Old World." Of course, Stephens was not an impartial observer. He had just bought the site—insofar as one could "buy" land during the Central American civil war of the 1830s—for $50.

SIGHTS   The modern village nearby is called Copán Ruinas. The ruins of ancient Copán are called Copán. As the number of visitors to Copán has multiplied, Copán Ruinas—a town that owes its very existence to the ancient site nearby—has become such a delightful place, with bargain hotels, restaurants that serve good coffee, and not a soldier in sight, that even without the ruins it would be a fun, funky destination. The walk between the village and the ruins visitors center, along a pretty forest trail that parallels the road, takes you past monumental statues of ancient kings en route to the main ceremonial center.

Set on the bank of the Río Copán (also called the Río Amarillo), ancient **Copán** (admission) dominated an extensive series of valleys upriver for more than three centuries. Though it is one of the most remote parts of Honduras today, the valleys and forests around Copán were a densely populated region in ancient times. The city itself had a population of about 10,000, and most of the jungle in the valley had been cleared for agriculture, as it is today. Surrounding the main archaeological site, the vegetation has grown back in a wild tangle of hardwoods and vines, from which archaeologists have reclaimed the ancient city's central plazas. Beautifully carved stelae, which may mark astronomical alignments, stand on several hilltops reached by one- to two-kilometer foot trails from the main center, and if you take time to walk or ride horseback up to one of them, particularly **Stela 12**, you will be rewarded with a stupendous view of the ruins and the river valley over which the lords of Copán reigned. Carved on Stela 12 is the most complete genealogy anywhere of a Maya royal family; but only a few dozen people in the world know how to read the inscription.

The first thing you see as you arrive at the ruins after a stroll down the road from town is the big **Copán Museum of Maya Sculpture** (included in ruins admission), a white-and-red two-level, 40,000-square-foot structure. The entrance to the museum is through a snake's-mouth doorway and a serpentine tunnel. At the other end is a full-size replica of the Rosalila Temple, painted in its original colors. The temple this is modeled on, which was found buried within the larger Temple 16, is not open to the public. The museum exhibits six other building facades among its 3000 pieces of sculpture from Copán, some of which are copies of the ones owned by other museums around the world.

The first part of the ruins that you enter is a group of low, broad-stepped pyramids and ceremonial platforms that surround two small plazas designated the **East Court** and the **West Court**, with several pieces of less-than-awesome sculpture set in the stairways. Then, dramatically, you enter the **Great Plaza** of ancient Copán. Also known as the Plaza of Red Plaster, this broad ceremonial courtyard now covered with lawn was entirely paved during Copán's days of glory. It contains the most remarkable sculptures found anywhere in the Maya world. Although the major features of Copán—the great statues and the hieroglyphic stairway—are right on the plaza, visitors who have walked from the village to the ruins already realize that the ancient city covered a large area and that impressive stelae and unexcavated temple mounds can be found along several trails through the forest, shown on a relief map in the visitors center.

Carved from massive blocks of a fine-textured stone called andesite, the stelae of Copán stand about ten feet tall. Unlike the relief stelae sculptures of human forms seen at other sites like Chichén Itzá, Palenque and Tikal, the stelae of Copán are carved almost completely in the round. There are a dozen stelae in the Great Plaza. All portray rulers of Copán, and each statue is decorated with hieroglyphs that record the lineage, birth, death and marriage dates, and major accomplishments of the lord it represents. The headdresses, too, bear amazingly detailed ornamentation of stylized human and animal forms with symbolic meanings.

The stelae were originally painted bright red. **Stela C**, the only one in the plaza with faces on both sides, had fallen over and lain with one side protected from the weather for centuries, and so still shows traces of the paint. Each of the stelae has a cross-shaped underground vault at its base. Some of the vaults have been excavated to reveal objects such as knife blades, pottery, animal bones and even, in the vault below **Stela H**, pieces of gold imported from South America. The vaults are unique to Copán, and their exact meaning remains a mystery.

In front of several stelae are strange "zoomorphic" altars carved in highly stylized animal shapes—frogs, jaguars, giant snakes and more fanciful forms—patterned with hieroglyphs and sacred signs. The altars were used for religious offerings, including animal sacrifices. They may also have been used as thrones for priests. Near Stela H are two altars in the shape of plumed serpents and a third showing men's faces peering from the open jaws of a two-headed snake. The two-headed snake, **Altar G**, bears the latest-date hieroglyph found at Copán—A.D. 800.

You can't miss the most spectacular structure in Copán, the **Hieroglyphic Stairway**. It's the one shaded by the huge tarp, erected too late to save much of the ancient Maya writing it contained from being erased by acid rain. Rising between two balustrades decorated with serpent motifs, the stairway is made from 2500 blocks of stone—each carved with hieroglyphs. The longest inscription found anywhere in the Maya world, it appears to be a comprehensive history of Copán up to the stairway's dedication date, A.D. 763. On this masterpiece, as John Lloyd Stephens mused a century and a half ago, the rulers of Copán "published a record of themselves, through which we might one day hold conference with a perished race." More than a few archaeologists have dedicated their whole lives to deciphering the message of the Hieroglyphic Stairway. Unfortunately, archaeologists reconstructed the stairway long before they knew how to read Maya hieroglyphs, so they had no way of putting them in correct sequence. Today, using computers to piece pictures of the stones together like a jigsaw puzzle, experts have translated roughly a third of it.

In 1989, members of the Copán Acropolis Archaeological Project tunneled 56 feet in from an entrance beside the Hieroglyphic Stairway to discover a large burial vault containing the remains of a noble personage believed to be a son of Copán's greatest king, Smoke-Imix, and brother of the next king, 18-Rabbit. Buried with him were some of the most exquisite jade carvings and jewelry that archaeologists have ever found at a Maya site.

Besides those in the new sculpture museum, other artifacts found during excavations of the ancient city are exhibited at the **Museo Regional de Arqueología**, facing the central plaza in the village of Ruinas Copán. In ancient times, the finest pottery in the Maya world—notably polychrome pieces decorated with elaborate ceremonial scenes—was made at Copán, and some of the best examples are on display in the museum along with tools, jade masks and jewelry. Some hieroglyph panels have been moved to the museums for protection from wear and erosion, while replicas have been installed at the ruins. Included among the exhibits are the complete contents of the tomb of a priest or sorcerer, found in a section of the archaeological zone now called Las Sepulturas ("The Tombs") and dated to about A.D. 450.

Las Sepulturas (included in ruins admission), a small site that was once a ruling-class suburb of Copán where a group of large stone houses has been restored, is located two kilometers past the main ruins on the same road.

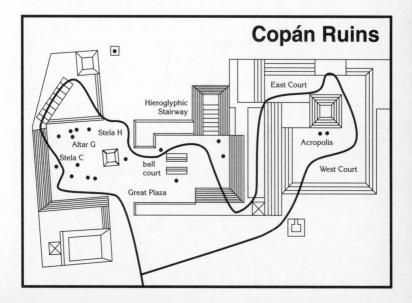

HIDDEN ►   Other points of interest around Copán Ruinas include **Agua Caliente**, a cluster of thermal pools along the banks of a jungle river. Minibuses go there and back from Copán Ruinas once or twice daily. Admission. ~ To get there, follow the road that turns off the ruins road by the walled-in soccer field as it climbs into the hills north of town. The hot springs are a 45-minute drive into the hills.

HIDDEN ►   At Santa Rita, a village nine kilometers along the road past Copán, you can hike up the river to the **Cascada El Rubí**, a lovely secluded waterfall.

At 20 kilometers past Copán is **Peña Quemada**, a private rainforest reserve teeming with birds and also inhabited by rare howler monkeys; you can visit only with a guide. Admission.

LODGING   Spending the night on the Honduras side of the border affords you the opportunity to visit the ruins in the cool, misty hours just after dawn, when you may find that you have the mystery-laden site all to yourself. There are several small hotels in the village of Copán Ruinas. Travelers arriving by early afternoon usually have no problem finding a room. Streets in Copán Ruinas have no names or addresses, but nothing is farther than two blocks from the central plaza. (The country code for phoning or faxing Copán Ruinas is 504.)

The best place in town is the 39-room **Hotel Marina Copán**. It has a restaurant, a swimming pool, a private courtyard with benches under flowering shade trees, and usually tour buses parked in front. The air-conditioned rooms are spacious and attractive, with large dark wood desks and armoires, and, most importantly, hot water; all have private baths and cable TV. ~ 8-983-070. DELUXE.

Another clean, modern hotel, smaller and located just off the park, is the 12-room **Hotel Los Jaguares**. Surrounding a central

✔ **CHECK THESE OUT**

- Cross over the Honduras border for a glimpse of the ancient sculpture at **Copán**. *page 218*
- Relax at the water's edge in one of the **Hotel Catamaran**'s bungalows on an island in the Río Dulce. *page 229*
- Tantalize your senses with fresh seafood and exotic decor at **African Place** in the hidden fishing village of Livingston. *page 232*
- Search out a guide or fisherman at the Puerto Barrios docks to take you to **Punta de Manabique**, one of the most pristine birdwatching areas in the Caribbean. *page 232*

courtyard, the rooms have hot water, air conditioning, phones, cable TV and private baths; some have private terraces. ~ 8-983-451. MODERATE.

One good budget bet is the 14-room **Hotel Maya Copán**, on the town square. The hotel offers decent rooms with white walls and private baths separated from the main part of the room by low divider curtains. Rooms open onto a courtyard so overgrown with flora that guests feel like they are staying in the jungle, not in town. Some second-floor rooms also have views of the town plaza. ~ BUDGET.

The **Hotel Los Gemelos**, two blocks west of the plaza, offers simple rooms with shared bath and ceiling fans. There's a pleasant sitting area, stocked with information on Honduras, off a friendly little courtyard, and the low-budget price is right. ~ BUDGET.

Down the road past the ruins, near the town of Santa Rita, the **Hacienda El Jaral** has 16 clean modern rooms with private baths, ceiling fans and cable TV in a group of duplex cabins on the mountainside. The forested hillside setting makes an ideal base for exploring foot trails that run throughout the area. A lagoon on the resort property attracts birds—especially from October to May, when it is home to a flock of 3000 cattle egrets that migrate from the southern United States. ~ BUDGET.

There are more than a dozen restaurants and *comedores* in Copán Ruinas. The favorite of gringos in the know is the **Restaurante Bar Tunkul**, an open-air place two blocks west of the plaza that serves giant burritos, garlic chicken and excellent vegetarian plates as well as good coffee. ~ BUDGET.

DINING

Across the street from the Tunkul, the **Restaurant La Llama del Bosque** bills itself as "Copán's original tourist restaurant," and judging from the stock of postcards and curios in the front part of the establishment, the claim is most likely accurate. The food is a mix of traditional Honduran dishes like *baleadas*, a local specialty, and various meats *parrilladas* (grilled). ~ BUDGET.

Glifos, the restaurant inside the relatively fancy Hotel Marina, features a gringo-oriented menu featuring such selections as open-faced roast beef sandwiches as well as daily gourmet specials. The setting is so civilized you'll forget you're in the backcountry. ~ 8-983-070. MODERATE TO DELUXE.

A more unusual choice for fine dining is **Los Gauchos**, a suburban-looking home on the edge of town that has been converted to a Uruguayan-style steakhouse serving up thick slabs of beef grilled over an open fire and served with cooked vegetables and spicy South American sauces and condiments. Seating on the long, narrow outdoor terrace has a view of neighboring farm pastures, cornfields and the mountains beyond. ~ MODERATE.

▼▼▼▼▼▼▼▼▼▼
Chiquimula

About the only thing that is likely to bring you to the hot, dusty, loud and lively ladino town of Chiquimula (pop. 45,000) is the need to find a place to spend the night en route to Copán. Chiquimula is 35 kilometers south of the turnoff from the Atlantic Highway on Route 10, and nine kilometers north of the turnoff from Route 10 toward Copán. Buses run there regularly from Río Hondo on the Atlantic Highway.

LODGING

There are about a dozen hotels in Chiquimula. All of them are in the budget range, and few operate with international tourists in mind. The only one that has air conditioning is the **Hotel Colonial de Oriente**. The 39 rooms in this three-story hotel are very plain, with yellow walls so bare one is tempted to draw on them; all have private baths. The cable TV has a full selection of U.S. networks. In fact, you can spot the hotel by all the satellite dishes on the roof. The local cable TV company operates from the ground floor of the hotel. ~ 7 Avenida No. 1-41; 9-422-367. BUDGET.

The **Posada Don Adan** may not look like much from the outside: all you see is a big steel door. Inside, you'll find a pleasant courtyard—probably the quietest place in Chiquimula—and helpful hosts. Rooms are plain but clean and comfortable with private baths, and there is off-street parking. ~ 8 Avenida No. 4-30; 9-420-549. BUDGET.

Another overnight possibility en route to Copán is the **Hotel y Restaurante Katu Sukchij**, a modern, motel-quality tourist hotel in the Maya town of Jocotán (pop. 40,000), 23 kilometers off the main highway on the road to Copán. ~ Jocotán; phone/fax 9-420-139. BUDGET.

DINING

Chiquimula cuisine is inexpensive and international. On the north side of the *parque central*, the **Restaurant El Tesoro** is a Chinese restaurant whose owners are actually Chinese. The food is mainly variations of "chao mein," "chap suey" and curries. The atmosphere is that of a disco, which this place turns into late in the evening, with loud dance music to dine by, formica tabletops, plastic flowers and waitresses in short skirts—something rarely seen in Guatemala. ~ BUDGET.

The **Restaurante Guayacan** not only doubles as a restaurant by day and a disco by night; it's also entirely purple. Purple walls, purple tabletops, even purple plastic plants. The purple menu promises pasta, shrimp and sandwiches plus a long list of novelty cocktails. ~ 3 Calle No. 8-11. BUDGET.

The **Las Vegas Pizzaria/Restaurante**, just south of the Parque Central, has copper-colored flowery wallpaper with murals intended to look like windows on a garden. Pizza, pasta and beef are the specialties of the house. ~ BUDGET TO MODERATE.

Crossing
the Border

If you are driving—the only easy, reliable way to get to the Honduras border unless you take one of the frequent package tours that are organized through travel agencies in Guatemala City and Antigua—you will need a document from the car rental agency giving you permission to take the vehicle into Honduras. If you don't have one, the next-best plan is to leave your vehicle on the Guatemala side of the border and take public transportation to the ruins. Crossing the border as a pedestrian is easy. You must clear both Guatemalan and Honduran authorities each direction. Telling the border guards of both countries that you are only visiting the ruins saves time and trouble. The Guatemalans will do a paper shuffle to dodge the immigration technicality that would otherwise bar travelers without multiple-entry visas from reentering Guatemala for 72 hours. The Honduran authorities will issue a frontier pass that eliminates the need to apply for a visa in advance. The cost of this convenience, payable when you cross from Guatemala to Honduras, is 10 quetzales (Q10) for Guatemalan immigration, Q5 for Guatemalan customs, Q20 for taking a vehicle out of Guatemala, 20 lempira (L20) for Honduran immigration, L10 for Honduran customs and L10 to bring a vehicle into Honduras—a total of about US$10.50. There are no charges for the return crossing into Guatemala.

The exchange rate is about L9 to US$1, or L1 to Q1.5. The buying power of one lempira in Honduras is about the same as that of one quetzal in Guatemala, making Honduras one of the best travel bargains to be found anywhere. Don't change more money than you expect to spend, though; you lose a few percent when you change U.S. or Guatemalan currency into lempira and a few more when you change it back to quetzales. Even if you changed U.S. dollars when crossing into Honduras, you probably will not be able to change lempira into U.S. dollars when returning to Guatemala.

▼▼▼▼▼▼▼▼▼▼

Quiriguá

The straight-line distance from Copán to Quiriguá is a mere 48 kilometers. Traveling as the macaw flies between the region's two great ancient city sites would carry you above a formidable mountain ridge, skimming the canopy of luxuriant, impenetrable rainforest as you glided over the international border. By road, however, the distance is more like 170 kilometers, and the trip, including the wait for shuttle buses to and from the border and the formalities of reentering Guatemala, takes half a day.

Quiriguá is situated in the middle of a vast banana plantation formerly owned by the United Fruit Company, which controlled Guatemala through the first half of the 20th century. Although Quiriguá was a small city, it covered a much larger area than the restored site would suggest today. Most of the city's temple mounds were razed and obliterated to plant banana trees. But the Great Plaza, with its huge, unique stelae and zoomorphic altars, was so remarkable that United Fruit hired a team of archaeologists in 1934 to restore it and set aside a tiny parcel of the once-magnificent jungle surrounding it. Quiriguá is about three kilometers off Route 9 where the highway descends along the Río Motagua from its steep-flanked valley into the broad, hot, moist delta that is Guatemala's major banana-growing region. It is 200 kilometers east of Guatemala City and 90 kilometers from the Caribbean coast. Buses will let you off on request, though you will have to return to the village of Los Amates, several kilometers up the highway, to catch an onward bus. Fleets of huge trucks on the wide unpaved road carry away unimaginable quantities of still-green bananas in a virtually nonstop tropical harvest. A quick look at a working plantation may change the way you look at bananas in the supermarket back home.

SIGHTS

Quiriguá (admission) was Copán's main rival for several centuries, from about A.D. 600 to 900. Archaeologists have devoted much energy to unraveling the true relationship between the two cities. Hieroglyphic records seem to suggest that the royal families of Quiriguá and Copán were related by marriage. An inscription at Copán reveals that one of its greatest rulers, Lord 18-Rabbit, was captured by soldiers from Quiriguá and later beheaded. Some experts also think that Copán captured Quiriguá earlier in 18-Rabbit's reign. Although most of the stelae at Quiriguá were done in a style much different from that of Copán, the first stele erected there—**Monument 8**, which bears an inscription dating it to A.D. 751—is so similar in style to those at Copán that many archaeologists believe the lords of Quiriguá hired artists from Copán to create it.

The original layout of Quiriguá, much of it now concealed by a thousand-year overgrowth of rainforest, was a lot like that of

Copán. The only structures that have been cleared and excavated at Quiriguá, however, are the small, plain temples surrounding the **Acropolis**, a sunken ceremonial plaza flanked all around by stone steps like the antithesis of a pyramid. Even more than Copán, Quiriguá is architecturally unimpressive but redeemed by its artwork. Towering stelae statues, the tallest in the Maya world by far, line the **Great Plaza**. The zoomorphic altars are also the largest found anywhere. The free-flowing, abstracted features, symbols and hieroglyphs of these imaginative giant frog and cockroach figures create a counterpoint to the rigid, formal statues.

Each of the statues and altars was carved from a single large slab or boulder of a peculiar reddish sandstone. It came out of the quarry soft, damp and easy to carve, but dried harder than concrete, so tough that statues made from it have survived a thousand years of abandonment and neglect in surprisingly good condition. Bringing the massive stones from the quarry five kilometers away was a remarkable feat. No one knows for sure how it was done. The tallest of the sculptures, **Monument 5**, stands 35 feet high and was carved from a single 43-foot stone monolith that weighed 65 tons.

All of the Quiriguá stelae were erected during the 64-year period from A.D. 746 to 810. For half of that period, Quiriguá was ruled by a single leader, Cauac Sky. Hieroglyphs on one stele record that earlier in his reign, in 737, Lord Cauac Sky waged war against Copán and put its leader to death. Although little is known of the history of Quiriguá before Cauac Sky ascended the throne, most experts believe that Quiriguá's independence from Copán was won in this war, and that the giant stelae were erected at Quiriguá after independence in order to establish that the city was every bit as magnificent as its rival to the south. Fully half of the stelae in Quiriguá's Great Plaza portray Lord Cauac Sky at different times during his reign. They include, in chronological order, **Monuments 8, 10, 6, 4, 5, 1** and **3**. (The stelae and zoomorphs are numbered according to their positions around the plaza, not the order in which they were made.) Hieroglyphs on **Monument 11** record his death. After his death, the statues of subsequent rulers were smaller and more modest, and most of the creative energy of Quiriguá's sculptors went into fantastic zoomorphic altars instead. At Quiriguá, as at Copán, many of the statues have beards. Lord Cauac Sky apparently introduced the fashion around A.D. 761, when Monument 6 was erected, and the style continued for 12 years after his death. The long goatee-style beards look remarkably like the ornamental chinpieces of ancient Egyptian pharaohs, and we can only speculate whether the lords of Quiriguá and Copán grew real beards or donned artificial ones.

It is best to visit Quiriguá late in the afternoon or on days when the weather is overcast, since in bright sunlight the thatched roofs that protect the huge stelae and zoomorphic altars cast shadows that make photographing them almost impossible.

LODGING   There is so little in the way of lodging around Quiriguá that travelers unwilling to settle for rock-bottom accommodations should plan to spend the night farther down the highway in the Río Dulce area. If you're stuck, the best place in the Quiriguá area is **Hotel Santa Monica**, which has off-street parking and private baths but little else to recommend it. ~ Los Amates; 9-478-536. BUDGET.

DINING   Aside from a few small food stands along the highway, the only restaurant in the vicinity of Quiriguá is the dining room at the **Hotel Santa Monica** in Los Amates. Boys often hang around the parking lot at the ruins selling big bunches of small, sweet bananas to visitors for a few pennies. ~ 9-478-536. BUDGET.

▼▼▼▼▼▼▼▼▼▼▼
Lago de Izabal
and Río Dulce

From the Quiriguá turnoff, continuing east along Route 9 for 41 kilometers will bring you to a road junction where Route 13 heads north to Castillo San Felipe, a distance of 34 kilometers. You can catch a launch at Puerto Barrios to Livingston and Río Dulce National Park, but a better plan is to take a launch from Castillo San Felipe *down* the river to Livingston.

SIGHTS   **Castillo San Felipe** (admission), a small stone fort complete with lookout towers, a drawbridge and cannons on the ramparts, was built in 1686 to guard the mouth of Lago de Izabal from British privateers like Sir Francis Drake. The fort, which is reached via a four-kilometer unpaved road from the north side of the toll bridge, has a shady picnic area and a beach for swimming. Car travelers who plan to catch a boat to Livingston and perhaps spend a night or two there will find guarded parking lots under the Castillo San Felipe bridge (also referred to as the Río Dulce bridge or the Frontera bridge; there's only one bridge, and this is it).

Lago de Izabal, the largest lake in Guatemala, is about 12.5 miles wide and 28 miles long. Its waters reach a depth of 60 feet. The lake's shoreline, dotted with more than a dozen fishing villages, is virtually inaccessible by land. The largest village, El Estor, can be reached by a grueling 140-kilometer (84-mile) unpaved road down the Polochíc Valley and takes all day to drive (see Chapter Nine). The other villages can only be reached by boat. Fishing is the main pastime on the lake, and motor launches piloted can be hired at the Castillo San Felipe bridge or any of the resort hotels located nearby.

Downriver from the Castillo San Felipe bridge, **Río Dulce National Park** is truly one of Guatemala's most magical spots. Less than 25 miles long, the river flows from the mouth of Lago de Izabal to Livingston with just enough force to keep the salt water of the Gulf of Honduras from encroaching upstream. A boat trip down the Río Dulce takes you first past a scattering of expensive vacation homes and several marinas full of mostly American yachts and sailboats, then across a broad expanse of open water called **El Golfete**, where local fishermen cast their nets from hand-hewn dugout canoes called *cayucas*.

Much of the north shore of El Golfete is protected as the **Chacón Machaca Preserve**, a wildlife sanctuary for the endangered West Indian manatee. Guides claim that jaguars and tapirs also still roam the deep forest along the north shore. Downriver, El Golfete narrows abruptly into a steep canyon whose walls, dripping with lush jungle vegetation, reach hundreds of feet above the water. Egrets peer from every tree, pelicans glide by just inches above the water, turtles sun themselves along the riverbank. Here and there a cluster of thatch-roofed huts nestles between the cliffs and the water. People who live along the Río Dulce—mothers with infant children and bundles of groceries from Livingston, even unaccompanied young children—paddle their *cayucas* up and down the river in the kind of uncomplicated purity that daydreams are made of.

The remote tropical paradise feel of the Río Dulce is in part illusory, for the boundary of the national park is defined by the top rim of the gorge. Just beyond it are endless banana fields and the shacks and villages of some of the poorest country people in Guatemala. Yet within the park, you can experience one of the last fragments of primeval America, much of it practically unchanged since the days of Columbus.

◄ HIDDEN

LODGING

Among the several waterfront resorts located around the upper end of the Río Dulce near the Castillo San Felipe bridge, my favorite is the **Hotel Catamaran**, a complex of bungalows set on an island downriver from the bridge. There is an inexpensive guarded parking lot under the bridge, and motor launches—often the same ones that go downriver to Livingston in the morning—wait nearby to take you across to the hotel. Guest accommodations, set along the shore and around grounds bursting with colorful flowers with a cage of parrots and a swimming pool in the middle, are rustic and simply furnished but quite large and airy, with screens to keep the mosquitoes out and balconies overlooking the water. The river gently lapping outside the window assures guests a sound night's sleep. ~ 9-478-361. MODERATE.

Another resort complex in the best sense of the word, the **Hotel Izabal Tropical** is situated on the shore of Lago de Izabal about four kilometers down a dirt road from Castillo San Felipe. Fourteen thatch-roofed bamboo-and-stucco guest cabañas with ceiling fans are scattered across a hillside overlooking the lake. The hotel has both a children's and an adults' swimming pool amid beautiful gardens that bloom year-round. It also has its own boat dock, and you can usually find boats for hire there with or without a pilot. ~ 9-478-401. MODERATE.

Campers will find their dream spot at **El Tortugal Resort**, a backpackers' retreat in a jungle setting one kilometer upriver from the San Felipe bridge. It offers swimming, kayak and canoe rentals and windsurfing. Sites are available for tent and hammock camping. A boat takes passengers there for Q5 each, leaving on request between 8 a.m. and 5 p.m. from the Cafetería Emy near the bridge. ~ Phone/fax 9-478-352. BUDGET.

DINING

In the Río Dulce resort area around the bridge at Castillo San Felipe, the best meals are served in restaurants at the various hotels along the river. The **Hotel Catamaran** has a thatch-roofed open-air restaurant built out over the water. The menu includes most of the standard Guatemalan restaurant items—fruit salads, *desayuno chapín* (black beans and corn tortillas), roast chicken, spaghetti, local fish—and you can watch big luxury sailboats with American names glide past as you eat. The hours of service are limited. ~ 9-478-361. MODERATE.

Accessible by dirt road instead of by boat, the **Hotel Izabal Tropical** also has a restaurant built over the water, with a range of menu choices and prices similar to those at the Catamaran. ~ 9-478-401. MODERATE.

Food stands clustered around the Castillo San Felipe bridge sell fish—most likely perch or tarpon—freshly caught from the lake, grilled with spices and served with tortillas and rice on the side. Try **Mary's**, a tiny place at the end of a dock just east of the bridge. ~ BUDGET.

SHOPPING

Souvenir and gift shoppers will want to save their money for another time as they relax along the Río Dulce. A few roadside stalls near the Castillo San Felipe bridge offer limited selections of the same kind of *típica* clothing found all over Guatemala, at prices considerably higher than you'd pay in the western highlands where it is made. A hut near the pool at the **Hotel Catamaran** houses a small gallery where members of a cooperative of American artists—who live on boats nearby—show their work.

▼▼▼▼▼▼▼▼▼▼
Livingston

At the mouth of the Río Dulce, where the gorge spills into the Gulf of Honduras, the southwesternmost corner of the Caribbean Sea, lies one of Guatemala's most unusual little towns. Isolated by unbridged river, roadless forest and the Belizean border just a short way up the coast, Livingston (pop. 3000) is Guatemala's only Garifuna community. The "Black Carib" residents claim descent from the fierce "Red Carib" Indians who made their home on the Caribbean island of St. Vincent and accepted into their tribe Africans who had escaped from slavery. They were deported from their island by the British after an uprising in 1795 and now live up and down the Mosquito Coast from southern Belize to Honduras. Most people in Livingston are multilingual, speaking Spanish and English as well as the African-based Garifuna patois.

It is not possible to reach Livingston by road. Motor launches run back and forth frequently to Livingston from Río Dulce, Puerto Barrios and Punta Gorda, Belize.

SIGHTS

Livingston's brightly painted wooden houses and storefronts run uphill from the docks along a single main street, which is paved although there is not a single motor vehicle in town—a fact to which the town owes its timeless tropical charm. In a few hours, you can stroll every street in town, visit the simple Catholic church with its ebony-skinned Jesus and Virgin of Guadalupe, then walk over the hill and up the narrow, hard, brown beach where Livingston's dreadlocked youth can usually be found savoring reggae and ganja, to the far end, where a trail leads up to **Siete Altares**, a series of waterfalls and pools just right for bathing. Hire a local to guide you there; please note that a few tourists have been robbed at the falls.

◄ HIDDEN

Beyond that, there's not much for either visitors or locals to do in Livingston. For both, people watching is a major pastime, and the most rewarding time to do it is on weekends, when settlers paddle to town from fishing camps up the coast and emerge from the jungle via foot trails to attend church services. No cars, no televisions, no soldiers or armed guards, and nothing at all to do. If you spend a night or two, you may find in Livingston one of the most relaxed and relaxing places on the continent, a welcome respite from some of the more nerve-jangling aspects of travel in Guatemala.

LODGING

An anomalous 45-room resort hotel tucked off the main street about a block above the docks in Livingston, the **Hotel Tucán Dugú** offers bright, modern rooms and suites in a huge thatch-roofed building with a swimming pool. There are standard rooms in the main building and pricier, more private bungalows along the walkway that leads down to the hotel's private beach. ~ 4-481-512. MODERATE TO DELUXE.

Practically across the street from the Tucán Dugú, you'll find a completely different kind of Caribbean charm at the **Hotel Río Dulce**, a plain but picture-perfect little blue two-story inn with a white picket fence, flower gardens and a big front porch perfectly situated for main-street people watching. Rooms share baths. Youthful backpackers find their way here from all over the world. ~ 4-481-059. BUDGET.

The waterfront **Hotel La Casa Rosada** has ten thatch-roofed bungalows with handpainted Guatemalan furniture and shared baths. Canoes are available to guests. The hotel serves a hearty breakfast, including the only fresh-ground coffee in town. ~ U.S. reservation number: 510-525-4470, fax 510-525-5427. BUDGET.

DINING

Livingston has several modest restaurants that cater to the low-key lunchtime tourist trade, since the locals generally catch their own meals. The **Restaurante Tiburongato**, a clean place with checkered plastic tablecloths and an open-air latticework facade that looks out on the town's main street, is typical. Menu items include *ceviche* and a local seafood stew called *tapado,* which is made with coconut and plantains. ~ BUDGET.

HIDDEN ►

If you're spending the night in Livingston, your best dinner bet is the amazing **African Place**. Designed and built by an immigrant from Spain, it is an authentic Moorish-style stone castle in miniature, patterned after those of southern Spain, with archways, ornate tilework and wrought-iron grillworks accenting windows that peer out into the jungle. The wonderfully imaginative seafood dishes include shrimp in garlic sauce and curried fish. ~ MODERATE.

SHOPPING

Many of the storefronts that line the main street of Livingston offer various handcrafted goods. Prices are very high for clothing brought in from other parts of Guatemala, but occasional locally made gift items such as coconut carvings and Afro-Caribbean paintings may bring a smile to your face as they tug at your wallet.

▼▼▼▼▼▼▼▼▼▼▼▼▼▼
Puerto Barrios and Punta de Manabique

From the turnoff to the San Felipe bridge between Lago de Izabal and Río Dulce, Route 9 continues east to Puerto Barrios, 51 kilometers away. **Puerto Barrios** (pop. 25,000), a hot,

SIGHTS

charmless town full of railroad tracks, used to be the United Fruit Company's shipping port. Today, bananas still travel by boat, but most set sail from the giant new dock complex at Santo Tomás de Castilla on the southern tip of the bay. Puerto Barrios has an evil reputation as a town of tough waterfront dives, drugs and prostitutes. Except for those seeking cheap and potentially dangerous thrills, there is really not much to attract visitors.

The remote wetland peninsula across the Bay from Puerto Barrios is only accessible by privately hired boat. It is usually possible to find a sightseeing boat going there on a Saturday or Sunday. During the week, you'll have to hire a fisherman to take you there from the Puerto Barrios docks.

HIDDEN ►

Punta de Manabique is beginning to gain a reputation among serious birders because of its large populations of seabirds and wading birds, including flamingos, which nest on the peninsula in mid-to-late spring. The Guatemalan government has set aside Punta de Manabique as a *biotopo*, or nature reserve—on paper, at least. Whether the reserve will be a lasting reality is questionable, however, since no organization has come forward with funding for it, while several resort chains have announced that they are exploring possibilities for building hotels on the peninsula's remote beaches. At the present time, at least, Punta de Manabique is as pristine as any place on Central America's Caribbean coast. One of the best options for wildlife viewing by boat is the **Canal de los Ingleses,** a manmade waterway through the heart of the peninsula that was dug by the British in the early 1900s to simplify boat travel to and from Punta Gorda, Belize.

LODGING

If you choose to stay in Puerto Barrios (as you might if you plan to catch a bus to Tikal or a boat to Punta Gorda, Belize), one of the town's better lodgings is the **Hotel Puerto Libre,** an American-style motel with air conditioning, TVs and a pool. Located out of town at the junction with the road to Santo Tomás de Castilla, the Puerto Libre can present a problem for those who are traveling by public transportation. ~ Carretera Atlántica Kilometer 292; 9-483-065. MODERATE.

In town, the **Hotel Del Norte** is a partly renovated, Caribbean-style wooden inn on the waterfront. Shuttered doorways open out onto private balconies with views of the bay. Only two of the bright, simply furnished rooms have private baths. ~ 7 Calle at 1 Avenida; 9-480-087. BUDGET.

The only hotel located on Punta de Manabique is the German-run **Pirate's Point Lodge,** a group of *palapa* huts with private bath at the very tip of the peninsula. There is a good beach at Pirate's Point, and there is an offshore shipwreck for diving. Boats can be hired for fishing or wildlife watching. Three meals a day are served, moderately priced and not included in the room rate. ~ 5-946-950 in Guatemala City. MODERATE.

DINING

Puerto Barrios has no restaurants special enough to search out. The restaurant at the **Hotel Del Norte** with its no-nonsense ambience and predictable menu of fish and chicken dishes is reputed to be the best in town. ~ 7 Calle at 1 Avenida; 48-00-87. MODERATE.

▼▼▼▼▼▼▼▼▼▼▼▼▼▼
Outdoor Adventures

FISHING

Resort hotels on Lago de Izabal and Río Dulce, as well as innkeepers in Livingston on the Caribbean coast, can usually arrange a fishing trip with a guide in an open motor launch. There is no fishing tackle for rent, though. Local people here fish with nets. The catch in the Caribbean off Livingston includes snook, tarpon and barracuda.

BIRD-
WATCHING
Near the archaeological site of Copán in Honduras, from October through May, the lake at Hacienda el Jaral resort is home to as many as 3000 snow-white cattle egrets. Birding tours are offered by **Xupki Tours**. ~ Copán Ruinas; 504-8-98-3435.

RIDING
STABLES
Horseback rides in the Petén rainforest, including pack trips to the newly discovered Maya ruins at Yaxha, are organized by **Campamiento El Sombrero**. ~ 2-050-5229 in Guatemala City. Near the ruins of Copán, children approach visitors and offer rental horses to travel to distant parts of the valley, where rarely seen Maya statues can be found.

SAILING
Three-day yacht tours around Lago de Izabal and down the Río Dulce to Livingston on a 46-foot catamaran are available for a price in the same range as a river raft trip, visiting waterfalls, hot springs, steam caves and the Chacón Machaca Preserve along the way. **Aventuras Vacacionales, S.A.** organizes these tours and also arranges private Río Dulce charters on 33-foot to 55-foot yachts. ~ 1a Avenida Sur No. 11-B, Antigua; 8-323-352; in the U.S., fax 502-255-3641.

RIVER
RAFTING
Near Copán, Honduras, Go Native Adventure Tours takes whitewater raft trips down the Río Copán to Santa Rita, navigating several Class III rapids and one Class IV. ~ Copán Ruinas, Honduras; 8-980-004.

▼▼▼▼▼▼▼▼▼▼▼▼
Transportation

AIR
Copán Ruinas has a small airstrip but no commercial airline service. Charter flights go there from Guatemala City and Santa Elena (Tikal). To arrange a charter, contact Jungle Flying Tours, 3-604-920, fax 3-314-995; e-mail jungle flying@guate.net.

Puerto Barrios also has a general aviation airport, but no commercial airline or charter service goes there on a regular basis.

CAR
To reach Copán, leave Route 9 (*The Carratera Atlantica*) at the Río Hondo crossroads, 130 kilometers east of Guatemala City, and proceed south on Route 10 for 44 kilometers, past the towns of Zacapa and Chiquimula, to the Vado Hondo intersection, where a sign points the way to Copán. Turn left there onto an unpaved road and continue for a slow 48 kilometers that takes about two hours. When the road winds its way through the streets of a Maya town called Jocotán, you'll know you're halfway there. You will arrive at a tiny border crossing called El Florido. (There's no town.) The border is open from 7 a.m. to 6 p.m. Copán is just 11 kilometers on the other side.

All other destinations in this chapter are near Route 9. Chiquimula is 35 kilometers south of the turnoff from the Atlantic Highway on Route 10. Quirigua is three kilometers off Route 9 on a wide unpaved road through a banana plantation. The San Felipe bridge, where Lago de Izabal drains into the Río Dulce, is 34 kilometers north of Route 9 on **Route 13**. Puerto Barrios is at the end of Route 9, a total distance of 287 kilometers from Guatemala City. Livingston cannot be reached by car.

BUS

Guatemalan second-class buses run from Chiquimula to the border but no farther. Honduran second-class buses meet travelers crossing the border and take them to the village and ruins.

Buses run frequently between Guatemala City (15 Calle No. 10-30, Zona 1) and Puerto Barrios. Second-class buses wait at the junction of Route 9 and Route 13 to meet passengers arriving on Guatemala City–Puerto Barrios buses and take them north to the San Felipe bridge, where Lago de Izabal empties into the Rio Dulce. These buses continue northward to Santa Elena, the nearest town to Tikal National Park (Chapter 11).

BOAT

There are two regularly scheduled passenger boats daily to and from Livingston, and two per week to and from Punta Gorda, Belize. (You will need to obtain an exit stamp from the Guatemalan immigration office at the end of 9 Calle, Livingston before purchasing a ticket to Belize.)

▼▼▼▼▼▼▼▼▼▼▼▼▼▼▼▼▼▼▼▼▼▼▼▼
Addresses & Phone Numbers

Police ~ Copán Ruinas; 8-984-060
Police ~ 6 Avenida and 5 Calle, Puerto Barrios; dial 120
Police ~ Main Street near the dock, Livingston; no phone.
Medical services (Copán Ruinas) ~ Dr. Luis Castro, 8-984-504; or Farmacia Jandal, 8-984-051
Fire department and ambulance ~ 5 Avenida between 5 and 6 Calles, Puerto Barrios; dial 122
Post office ~ Copán Ruinas; 8-984-447
Post office ~ 6 Avenida at 6 Calle, Puerto Barrios; 9-480-748

ELEVEN

Tikal and El Petén

A mist as thick as ocean fog shrouds Tikal in the hours before dawn. As the sun rises, the mist glows first pink and then golden. For a moment, you can glimpse the glory of Tikal in ancient times. Then the ancient temples, shadows at first, turn to stone as the mist burns away. The forest comes alive suddenly with the cries of monkeys and birds and the throbbing drone of insects, and the heat of the day begins in one of the world's most magical places.

Despite its size, Tikal National Park protects less than 2 percent of El Petén, the largest contiguous expanse of rainforest on the North American continent. The northern third of the Petén rainforest—all the land north of Tikal to the northern, eastern and western borders of Guatemala, has been designated as the Maya Biosphere Reserve, a unit of the UNESCO Man and Biosphere Program that protects inhabited wilderness areas, allowing some economic use of the forest in a buffer zone around a protected core area. The Maya Biosphere Reserve, encompassing an area of 5400 square miles, is one of the most ambitious efforts to save the rainforest anywhere in the world. La Ruta Maya Conservation Foundation, armed with a large grant from the MacArthur Foundation, hopes to go one step further, merging Guatemala's Maya Biosphere Reserve with Mexico's Calakmul Biosphere Reserve and Belize's Río Bravo Conservation Area to form the Maya Peace Park, a huge international park that would span the three nations' often-troubled borders and allow cooperative ecotourism development in the region.

The biggest problem facing visitors who would like to explore more remote areas of the Petén is lack of transportation. Very few travelers come to Tikal in their own vehicles, and public transportation is quite limited. A few enterprising guides, who don't advertise but can be found by word of mouth through any hotel or restaurant operator or shuttle van driver, run tours from Flores and Tikal to other Maya ruins in the Petén. Improved roads and improved public transportation are now opening the Sayaxché area, on the Río de la Pasión 50 kilometers southeast of Lago Petén Itzá, to expanded ecotourism.

Passenger planes land at the airport near Santa Elena on the south shore of Lago Petén Itzá, about an hour's trip by shuttle bus from Tikal National Park. One aspect of Tikal's magic is that it is so hard to reach. What was once the wealthy and populous centerpiece of the ancient Maya world is now a remote frontier backwater surrounded by millions of acres of almost impenetrable rainforest.

There is no easy way to get there overland. A notoriously bad road runs 205 kilometers north from the Castillo San Felipe bridge on the Río Dulce to Flores, capital of the vast, wild department of Petén and gateway to Tikal. The last 167 kilometers are unpaved and very rough. The distance may not sound daunting, but the grueling trip takes about 12 hours by second-class bus or private high-clearance vehicle. Another unpaved road runs from the border with Belize.

A decade ago, Guatemala's military government of the time received international aid to widen and pave the road to the Petén, but the funds were diverted by corrupt leaders and the road never got built. More recently, in connection with the Guatemalan government's agreement to set aside a large part of the Petén rainforest as a UNESCO Man and Biosphere Reserve, the World Bank pledged new funding to improve the road and stimulate tourism in the Petén—but the money will not be released until Guatemala convinces the bank that it will take all necessary measures to protect the Petén rainforest from pioneers flocking there to build new settlements and destroy the forest. In the meantime, the trip to the Tikal area is a battering, bruising, bone-jarring, muscle-wracking test of endurance.

The bus trip to Tikal from Belmopan, Belize, is shorter—52 kilometers by paved highway from the Belizean capital to the border and another 65 kilometers on an unpaved road from there to the intersection with the isolated stretch of highway that connects Flores and Tikal National Park. However, the hassle and delay of crossing the border and changing buses, along with persistent reports of bandit activity along this road, make it a trip that's not for the faint-hearted.

SIGHTS

Most of the population of El Petén today lives in **Santa Elena** (pop. 10,000) and the contiguous town of **San Benito** (pop. 15,000). Together, the two towns form a frontier boomtown sprawl laced with open sewers and rattling with gas-powered electrical generators. Though a modest tourist trade provides income for some area residents, more of the people here harvest renewable forest products such as chicle gum and pepsin leaves or join crews for oil exploration, the newest threat to the rainforest.

The capital of El Petén, **Flores** (pop. 1500) is built on a small island in the lake and is reached by a long earthen causeway from Santa Elena. A quintessentially quaint little town with an Old World feel to its tangled, claustrophobic streets, Flores is built on the site of Tayasal, the last ancient Maya stronghold to fall to the Spanish Empire. Tayasal was visited by Hernán Cortés, conqueror of Mexico, in 1525, but endured unmolested for nearly two centuries before a military expedition captured and razed it in 1697. You can walk all over town in less than an hour. The Ruta Maya Conservation Foundation and George Washington University's Institute of Urban Development Research have developed plans that would encourage the cultivation of Flores as a tourist center complete with houseboat accommodations on Lago Petén Itzá, a regional museum in the abandoned prison building facing the hilltop town square, and even a sewage treatment plant. All this is years in the future, though. For now, Flores is one of Central America's more low-key and isolated frontier towns.

Ask at any restaurant or hotel in the Flores–Santa Elena area and they can probably put you in touch with a guide who will take you on an inexpensive three-hour boat tour of the islands near Flores. Stops on the tour include a group of small temple mounds—all that remains of the old Maya fortress city of **Tayasal**—as well as a spot called **La Garrucha**, where you can climb a tall tower, hang from a cable and zip above the water to land on another island nearby, then climb another tower there and zip back.

The final stop on most boat tours is **Petencito**, a zoo occupied exclusively by animals native to the Petén rainforest, including many rare or elusive species—jaguars, cougars, marmosets, tepescuintles—that visitors are unlikely to spot in the wild. If you thought the cable slide at La Garrucha was fun, give the very scary 300-foot concrete water slide at Petencito a try! Admission.

Located just past the outskirts of Santa Elena, a little less than four kilometers from the causeway to Flores, **Gruta Actun Kan** (admission) is a pretty cave—better than Lanquín—with rock formations (though not many stalactites) and a small subterranean waterfall. There is electric lighting, but visitors are allowed inside only with a guide, and there are usually several boys outside the entrance awaiting their turn to lead a tour. The other end of the same cave, about two kilometers away on the other side of a hill, is marked as **Gruta Jobitinaj** (admission). A guide is not required here, but there are no electric lights, so each person in your party will want to bring a flashlight.

LODGING

In Santa Elena, one of the better hotels is the **Hotel Maya Internacional**. This compound of 20 rustic rooms with private baths in duplex bungalows on stilts over Lago Petén Itzá used to be the top of the line in the Petén region, but has lost most of its for-

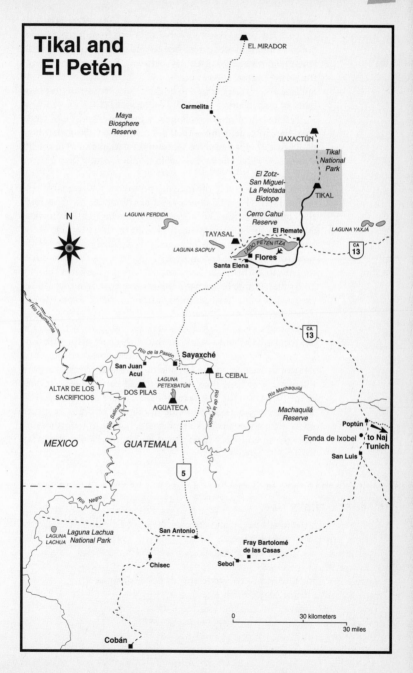

Tikal and El Petén

merly landscaped grounds to the rising water level of the lake over the past few years. Nature lovers can watch from the bungalow porch as multitudes of egrets, herons and other wading birds fish among the water lilies just a few feet away. Be careful of the electric water–heating shower heads, common in hotels around Santa Elena and Flores, but said to be dangerous because of the possibility of electrocution. ~ 9-261-276. MODERATE.

Perhaps the nicest of the hotels in the Flores and Santa Elena area, the **Hotel del Patio—Tikal** offers 22 air-conditioned rooms with private baths and cable TV around a parklike courtyard with a fountain. ~ 2 Calle at 8 Avenida, Santa Elena; 9-261-229, or from the U.S., 800-327-3573. DELUXE.

At the other end of the lodging spectrum is the venerable **Hotel San Juan**. The hotel doubles as a bus terminal, where second-class buses from Río Dulce, Poptún, Sayaxché and Cobán come and go day and night, making the rooms on the street side of the hotel very noisy. This is a long-established gathering place for adventurous travelers, and most local guides organize their tours from the lobby here. The 55 rooms (37 with private baths but only a very limited supply of solar-heated water) are as plain as can be, except that some have satellite television. ~ Santa Elena; 9-260-726. BUDGET.

Of numerous small lodgings in the island town of Flores, the modern **Hotel Sabana** is a favorite simply because of the view. Unlike most of the other hotels, which are located near the causeway, this one is located on the far side of the island overlooking the full expanse of Lago Petén Itzá. Of the 28 guest rooms, the ones at the back have the best lake views; there are no private baths. The four-story hotel has nothing in the way of decor to spruce up its plain concrete block architecture, but the grand panorama from the second-story patio makes up for it. ~ Flores; phone/fax 9-261-248. MODERATE.

◆◆

✔ **CHECK THESE OUT**

- Cruise through the jungle to the mysterious ruins of **El Ceibal**, hidden deep in pristine rainforest. *page 251*
- Slumber near the magnificent archaeological site of Tikal at **Tikal Inn**. *page 250*
- Sample authentic lowland Maya wild-game dishes at the unpretentious **La Mesa de los Maya** in Flores. *page 241*
- Trek the **Guacamaya Trail**, a rainforest route designed specifically for organized wildlife viewing expeditions. *page 253*

La Casona de la Isla has small, plain rooms with ceiling fans, private baths and central hot water. The best thing about this hotel is its swimming pool, where you can cool off in a pretty garden setting. ~ Flores; 9-260-662, fax 9-260-163. MODERATE.

The best budget bargain in Flores is the Posada El Tucán, a tiny four-room place. Rooms, though plain, are fairly large and share baths. There is a pier on the lake here. ~ Flores; phone/fax 9-260-577. BUDGET.

Flores has a number of rustic-but-nice restaurants that offer entrées of local game from the Petén rainforest, typically including alligator, venison, tepescuintle, armadillo, wild turkey, pheasant and rabbit. This is the traditional food of the region, and travelers who feel queasy about dining on freshly killed jungle animals may have to subsist on fruit salads. More conventional meats such as chicken and pork are found only in the dining rooms of better hotels. The town's best restaurants are in a cluster along Calle Centroamérica, the main street one block north of the island end of the causeway.

DINING

A favorite restaurant in Flores is La Mesa de los Maya. The servings are generous and the cuisine is out of this world. Hand-woven tablecloths and wall hangings brighten the two cozy, plain-but-honest little dining rooms, as does the friendly pet toucan. There is a full bar on the premises, though a drink costs much more than a dinner does. ~ Calle Centroamérica. MODERATE.

A block down the street, Restaurant La Jungla is overgrown with jungle plants—like a fern bar run amok. Inside, the decor features boa constrictor skins, jaguar heads, stuffed birds and other trophies. The food and service are okay, but all that taxidermy is enough to make you feel as if the rest of your dinner entrée were watching over your shoulder. ~ Calle Centroamérica. BUDGET.

Facing the waterfront about a block west of the causeway, El Faisan is another small restaurant and bar serving a similar selection of grilled wild animal meats. Rough wood paneling decorated from floor to ceiling with photos, drawings and maps of Tikal create an archaeology ambience that sets it apart from the other restaurants nearby. It is open later in the evening than most of the others, too. ~ Flores. BUDGET.

Midway along the highway between Tikal and Flores–Santa Elena, at the eastern tip of Lago Petén Itzá near the intersection with the road

Cerro Cahui Reserve

from Belize, a dirt road turns off and follows the north shore of the lake all the way back to San Benito. Cerro Cahui Reserve is located a few kilometers west of the turnoff, where the small crossroads village is known as El Remate, 33 kilometers from Santa Elena and Flores and 30 kilometers from Tikal.

SIGHTS

HIDDEN ▶

Cerro Cahui Reserve is a 1600-acre reserve set aside to protect a last fragment of natural habitat for several endangered wetland species—the Petén turkey, the Petén crocodile and the tapir. A six-kilometer loop trail leads through the verdant forest with scattered interpretive signs identifying plants. For visitors with less time, there's a shortcut midway that shortens the hike to three kilometers; but the pristine part of the forest, where you'll spot bright tropical birds and maybe javelinas, armadillos and spider monkeys, lies at the far end of the longer loop. Admission.

LODGING

The most luxurious accommodations in the Petén are at the **Westin Camino Real Tikal**, outside the national park near where the road from Belize intersects the highway between Santa Elena and Tikal. All 72 air-conditioned rooms have private baths and satellite TV complete with remote control—shamelessly indulgent in a region where most of the local people live without running water or indoor plumbing. Amenities include a swimming pool, a lakefront beach, tennis courts, restaurants, a bar and a disco. ~ El Remate; 9-260-206, fax 9-260-222, for reservations from the U.S. call 800-373-3573. ULTRA-DELUXE.

El Remate's other comfortable lodging is **La Mansión del Pajaro Serpiente**, a place along the main highway that has the appearance of an American mom-and-pop motel from the exterior but inside is nicely decorated with Mayan textile wall hangings and quality furniture. ~ El Remate; no phone. DELUXE.

Also near Cerro Cahui, **El Gringo Perdido** is a primitive jungle lodge with 12 four-bed cabins that share a restroom and shower facilities with eight low-budget camping *palapas* designed for hammocks. ~ El Remate; 9-267-683. BUDGET.

The former location of El Gringo Perdido in El Remate, located a block or so from the present location, now goes by the name **La Casa de Don David**. It has been upgraded a little, and although the rooms are basic, they're completely enclosed (unlike many accommodations in the El Remate area). ~ El Remate; no phone. BUDGET.

DINING

At El Remate, **El Gringo Perdido** has an open-air dining *palapa* where budget-priced meals are served, usually featuring vegetarian dishes. ~ El Remate; 9-267-683. BUDGET.

▼▼▼▼▼▼▼▼▼▼▼▼▼▼
Tikal National Park

Tikal was the greatest capital of the ancient Maya world. Founded as early as 600 B.C., it reached a peak population of about 50,000 people a millennium later and was one of the two largest cities in the

The Legacy
of
Michael DeVine

The best way to do the drive or bus trip to the Tikal area as painlessly as possible is to break up the journey by spending at least a night and maybe more in **Poptún** (pop. 7000), about midway along the route,

The **Fonda de Ixobel**, a country inn three kilometers south of Poptún, has become a standard stop—practically a pilgrimage site—for backpackers and other ecotravelers. The inn, a converted plantation house with simple, hostel-style rooms, a campground and a dining room that serves vegetarian meals, was founded in 1971 by two couples from the United States, Michael and Carol DeVine and Dennis and Louise Wheeler. ~ Poptún; phone/fax 9-277-363. BUDGET.

The inn found its place on the map the hard way 20 years later, in June 1990, when Michael was beheaded by Guatemalan soldiers for reasons that remain unknown. An army captain was convicted of the murder but allowed to escape from prison soon after. The murder of Michael DeVine and his widow's testimony in front of a U.S. congressional committee helped touch off a 1995 scandal concerning the CIA's links with Guatemalan officials involved in "death squad" activities.

During his 20 years in Poptún, Michael DeVine worked for environmental preservation as he explored this remote area. His legacy includes the **Pinos de Poptún Biotope**, a pristine area of pine forest in the Maya Mountains, and **Naj Tunich**, an ancient Maya ceremonial cave with hieroglyphic inscriptions on the walls, which DeVine discovered and explored in the early 1980s. The cave is now closed to the public because of vandalism, but tours to the cave are sometimes organized at Fonda de Ixobel.

Poptún is located 99 kilometers (60 miles) north of the Castillo San Felipe bridge, 107 kilometers (64 miles) south of Santa Elena and Flores and just 25 kilometers (15 miles) from the Belize border in the foothills of the impenetrable Maya Mountains.

Western Hemisphere during the Classic Period, along with Teotí-huacan in central Mexico. Tikal was situated in the exact center of the Maya land, equidistant from Copán in the south, Uxmal in the north, and Palenque in the west, and had close cultural ties to all parts of the region. Many experts believe the knowledge and ideas that shaped the classic Maya civilization originated in Tikal around A.D. 250, and the abandonment of Tikal around A.D. 900 coincided with the collapse of the high Maya civilization everywhere.

A visit to Tikal makes the perfect climax to any tour of Guatemala. Tikal is one of the true wonders of the world, a must-see destination, even if you don't plan to venture into any other part of Guatemala. No other Maya ruin can compare with it for majestic architecture and a setting that captures the imagination and won't let go. And if you want to experience primeval rainforest close up, Tikal is one of the best places on earth to do it.

SIGHTS   **Tikal National Park** (admission) is a different kind of experience from other major Maya ruins like Chichén Itzá, Uxmal, Palenque or Copán, in part because the archaeological site is so big. Most visitors find that trying to see everything at Tikal in a single day is too exhausting and that three days is just about right to fully appreciate the park.

There are two museums near the entrance to the ruins area. The **Tikal Museum**, located near the Jungle Lodge, contains many of the best small artifacts that have been found among the ruins, including pottery painted with elaborate scenes of ancient Maya life and polished bones etched with pictures of gods, demons and warriors. The highlight of the museum is a replica of the tomb of Lord Ah Cacau, the greatest ruler of Tikal, containing his bones, eight pounds of jade jewelry, incense pots and other treasures positioned as archaeologists originally discovered them in a vault below the Temple of the Great Jaguar. On the other side of the parking lot, a new building houses the **Visitors Center and Stelae Museum**. Although the Petén rainforest seems far removed from the industrial world, within the past few decades acid rain has seriously damaged many stelae, making it necessary to move the best ones indoors for protection. Outside the visitors center is a huge model, about nine yards square, showing what Tikal looked like 1100 years ago.

From the parking lot near the hotels and museums, a rocky causeway, or pedestrians-only road built by the ancient Maya and restored by modern archaeologists, cuts through the dense forest for 1.5 kilometers to the central Plaza Mayor, the heart of ancient Tikal. From there, a triangular loop trail takes you through the Mundo Perdido complex, to lofty Templo IV, then to clusters of nondescript structures, called simply Complex M, Complex P, Group H and Complex Q, before returning to the Plaza Mayor.

A separate trail leads to the solitary Temple of the Inscriptions. Park rangers have placed small concrete water basins beside the causeways at several points to attract monkeys and birds. A full circuit of the main ruins involves a hot, fairly strenuous hike of some ten kilometers through the rainforest.

At the center of the Tikal ruins area is the meticulously restored group of buildings flanking the four sides of the two-acre **Plaza Mayor** (Great Plaza). Now covered with neatly mown grass, the whole square was paved with stucco in ancient times and resurfaced about once every century-and-a-half. The plaza was in use as early as 150 B.C. The first layer of pavement has been dated to about A.D. 100 and the final layer to A.D. 700—a generation before any of the temples that now surround the plaza were completed. All of the structures at Tikal were painted bright red, with colorful bas-relief murals on the huge roof combs.

Along the north side of the plaza stand two rows of tombstone-shaped **stelae** with round altars in front of them. Other, similar stelae are set near the stairways of the various structures around the plaza. Most of the stelae are carved with the images of Tikal's noblemen in ceremonial garb with elaborate plumed headdresses, and many have hieroglyphs carved along the sides. As you explore outlying parts of the ruins, you will see dozens of massive stone stelae like these scattered throughout the forest. On some, the relief carving has been obliterated by time; others were quarried but never carved or erected, or were smashed on purpose as the leaders they glorified fell into disrepute; and the best-preserved still invite us to wonder about the meanings of the messages so painstakingly inscribed and dispatched across the centuries to us, the people of the future. The oldest dated stele at Tikal was erected in A.D. 292, and the most recent in A.D. 771.

At the east and west ends of the plaza stand two of the extremely tall, stepped pyramids unique to Tikal. On the east end, **Temple I**, sometimes called the "Temple of the Great Jaguar," is the taller. It towers 170 feet high with its lofty, crumbling roof comb. It is the only pyramid we've seen anywhere in the Maya world that the public is not allowed to climb. A sign on a chain across the narrow stairway says that it is closed temporarily for restoration, but tour guides claim that it has been closed indefinitely since a tourist fell down the steep stairs to his death in the early 1980s. The tomb of Ah Cacau, the most important of ancient Tikal's leaders, was discovered at the foot of this pyramid. He reigned during the early part of the eighth century A.D., and his name translates as "Lord Chocolate." His remains, along with artifacts from his tomb including priceless jade jewelry, can be seen in a replica of the burial vault at the Tikal Museum. Just to the south of Temple I is the main **ball court**, surprisingly small for such an important ceremonial center as Tikal.

Directly across the plaza, on the west side, is **Temple II**, also known as the "Temple of the Masks." It is squat and wider than Temple I, with three levels to Temple I's nine. The top level's broad walkway around all sides of the temple offers good views of the Plaza Mayor, the acropolises and the surrounding forest canopy. Temples I and II were built at the same time and are thought to represent the male and female principles. Carvings on the lintels and walls of the temple chambers on top suggest to some archaeologists that Temple II was a burial pyramid for the wife of Ah Cacau, who was buried under Temple I. This is mere theory, however, as her tomb has not been found.

Although the **North Acropolis** may lack the dramatic architecture of the pyramids, it is by far the more interesting structure to explore. It is a broad mound with a number of separate temples, apparently dedicated to different gods, and a tricky labyrinth of stairways and passages to reach them. Eight temples made up the acropolis in the eighth century, when Tikal's great pyramids were built. Archaeological digs have revealed that the mound on which the temples stand contains older temples built upon the ruins of yet older ones, dating back to 400 B.C. One excavation of the facade of a buried temple contains a huge stucco mask, taller than a person, of a fierce-eyed rain god with a bulbous, warty nose, perfectly preserved by earth and rubble while the stucco sculptures on the exposed buildings of Tikal were being obliterated by the rainforest climate. To the right of the giant mask, a dark vaulted passageway leads into the pyramid. Feel your way through the darkness to the end, then strike a match and you'll find yourself face-to-face with another gargantuan god mask.

The **Central Acropolis** covers an area of four acres. It is believed to have been the royal palace of Tikal, a complex of spacious multistory residences built around six separate courtyards. Only the front part of the palace, facing the plaza, has been completely excavated; the back part merges gracefully into the forest. The majestic roof comb that breaks the skyline behind the Central Acropolis is the top of **Temple V**, the second-tallest pyramid at Tikal at 185 feet in height. Still unexcavated and shrouded by trees, it shows what all five of the great temple pyramids at Tikal must have looked like when early archaeologists came to explore and photograph the site at the end of the 19th century. A narrow foot trail from the east end of the Central Acropolis leads into the rainforest to Temple V, then returns to the main trail near Mundo Perdido.

The **Mundo Perdido** ("Lost World") complex, which is southwest of the Plaza Mayor, presents a sharp contrast to the central ruins area. The massive **Main Pyramid** at the center of a group of 38 structures was built at least 500 years before the pyramids of the Plaza Mayor, suggesting that this area may have been the main ceremonial center for much of Tikal's history. Unlike the main plaza with its formal, landscaped feel, the Mundo Perdido complex has been excavated with an eye toward minimizing the impact on the surrounding forest, so the lower structures lie nestled among the roots and trunks of forest giants. From the top of the great pyramid, you can see the summits of Temples I and II on the Plaza Mayor, just the roof combs rising face-to-face, sun-and-moon, he-and-she through the canopy of a rainforest that rolls unbroken, astonishing in its vastness, all the way to the distant horizon. East of the pyramid and north of a small plaza with seven temples is a **triple ball court** thought to be the only one of its kind in the Maya world.

At the westernmost end of the ruins area, **Temple IV**, known as the Temple of the Double-Headed Serpent, is the tallest man-made structure at Tikal. At 228 feet in height, this pyramid was also the second-tallest structure in the ancient Maya world. It was believed to be the tallest until one pyramid at El Mirador, 43 miles directly to the north across the roadless depths of the Petén rainforest and presently inaccessible to sightseers, was measured at about a yard taller. Temple IV has been cleared but not excavated, so instead of a very steep stairway to the top, there's a very steep foot trail. As you reach the summit, a metal ladder affixed

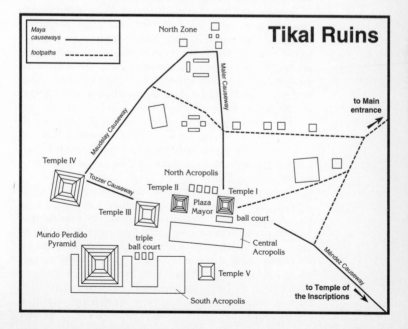

to the temple wall lets you climb all the way up to the roof comb. Near Temple IV are a parking lot, reached by a road that circles around the archaeological zone, and a group picnic area, so it is common to find busloads of schoolchildren swarming up and down the pyramid.

On the other side of the main ruins area, the Méndez Causeway branches away from the main trail and leads in a straight line through the forest for one kilometer to the **Temple of the Inscriptions**, a large, solitary temple on the outskirts of the ancient city. Covering the entire surface of the roof comb, you can still make out the only major hieroglyphic inscription found at Tikal. The temple is so far removed from the main ruins of Tikal that it was not discovered until 1951. Why this unusual and impressive temple should be set apart by both distance and architecture from the rest of the city is unknown. The stele that stands in front of the temple was intentionally smashed, probably by the people of ancient Tikal.

Visitors are not allowed to spend the night in the ruins area. Rangers check to see that everybody is out before dark. They explain that jaguars and other dangerous beasts roam the forest at night, and if pressed ("But I thought jaguars were almost extinct. . .") admit that it is other, supernatural beings that make the ruins a place to be avoided at night. Outsiders doubt it, they say, but everybody around there knows it is true.

So many visitors used to sneak into the ruins after midnight to experience them by moonlight that the entrance is now guarded all night. However, the opening hour in the morning has been moved back to 6:00 a.m. Dawn among the ruins at Tikal is an ultimate travel experience, absolutely worth the inconvenience of rising before first light. Early-to-bed, early-to-rise is less of a hardship here than it would be most places because the electricity shuts off at 9:30 p.m. in the national park hotels.

A dawn tour led by freelancing off-duty park rangers is well worth the small fee. The rangers, many of whom were born and raised on the edge of the Petén rainforest, are amazingly knowledgeable about the diversity of plant and animal species found in the park.

At any time of day you choose to walk among the various outlying ruins of Tikal, they quickly become a mere excuse for venturing deeper into the rainforest. At every turn, a smaller trail beckons you off into the deep jungle for a spontaneous visit to some half-buried temple or hidden forest glade. Monkeys create a din of excitement as you enter their territory. Colorful toucans scatter from the trees in front of you. The diversity of plant and animal life in the Petén jungle means that around every bend in the trail you discover something new—a tree full of orchids, a strange fruit, a kaleidoscopic butterfly swarm, a line of leafcutter ants marching in single file for as far as you can see. Jungle trails have a way of tempting people onward. Use good judgment. There is a risk of getting lost in this terrain.

Tikal National Park covers a forested area of 222 square miles. During Tikal's heyday, the whole area was cleared for small suburban farms where peasants grew maize, beans and tomatoes both for themselves and for the priests and rulers who lived in the great city center. Anywhere you go in the backcountry of Tikal National Park, you will find low mounds and tumbled-down stone walls that remain from these ancient homesteads—even in places that are almost inaccessible today. Archaeologists will never excavate all of the sites in the jungle of Tikal National Park, and visitors will always be able to wonder what undiscovered treasures may lie hidden there.

North of Tikal National Park in the Maya Biosphere Reserve is **Uaxactún**, located 20 kilometers north of the Tikal ruins on a newly improved road that is passable by passenger cars during the dry season. For centuries, Uaxactún was a rival city to Tikal. Nothing about these partially excavated but unrestored ruins suggests that this ceremonial site even came close to achieving the grandeur of Tikal, but inscriptions on Tikal's temples and stelae reveal that the two cities fought bloody wars and that, at least once, the army of Uaxactún conquered Tikal. Some backpackers hike from Tikal to Uaxactún. Camping equipment is a must, since even strong hikers find it impossible to walk there and back the same day. Or a local guide can take you there in a four-wheel-drive vehicle, a rough one-hour trip each way.

◄ HIDDEN

At least 25 other major ceremonial centers have been found in the Maya Biosphere Reserve. Most are accessible only by very primitive four-wheel-drive tracks that can be used only during the dry season, and several are located in terrain so impassable that archaeologists can reach them only by helicopter. Proponents of the Maya Peace Park plan hope that **El Mirador**, site of a large ceremonial center whose temples include the tallest-known Maya pyramid, will someday be opened to tourists by shuttle bus or even monorail. At present, however, the site can be reached only in the dry season by a week-long trek or horseback trip through difficult rainforest terrain from the village of Carmelita, a small chicle-tapping village 80 kilometers (48 miles) north of Santa Elena that is the farthest point accessible by public transportation—or by road. Don't forget to take camping gear and all the food you'll need. Experienced jungle trekkers can accomplish the trip unescorted, but even the most adventuresome travelers are well advised to hire a guide.

◄ HIDDEN

Staying at Tikal National Park is best because there is too much in the park to experience in a single day, and the shuttle trip be-

LODGING

tween Flores–Santa Elena and Tikal, an hour each way, costs more than a hotel room does. Staying in the park also lets you spend the night surrounded by the sounds of the jungle and visit the ruins in the eerie dawn mist.

There are three hotels in Tikal National Park, totaling 49 rooms among them. Because of development restrictions imposed by the Guatemalan government when the Maya Biosphere Reserve was created, no new hotels can be built. Thanks to this monopoly and rapid growth in tourism at Tikal, room rates at these hotels have skyrocketed in recent years. Sometimes tour groups fill them to capacity and other times they are almost empty. You don't know until you go there, because it's not easy to make advance reservations and none of the hotels has a telephone. The men who drive shuttle vans between the airport at Santa Elena and the national park may know about room availability. Otherwise, the best plan for travelers arriving on the morning plane is just to go to the park by noon and see whether you can find lodging. If you can't get a room, you'll have time to return to Flores by mid-afternoon and find one there.

My favorite hotel at the national park is the 15-room **Tikal Inn**, a classic jungle lodge that consists of an attractively rustic main building, where you'll find the dining room, lobby and four rather elegantly decorated guest rooms with four-poster beds, as well as a row of thatched-roof cabañas along one side of a broad expanse of lawn with a swimming pool in the center and dense rainforest around the perimeter of the grounds. The cabañas have complete modern conveniences, including electric light from 6 to 9:30 p.m. and private bathrooms with running water that is warm late in the day. Reservations can be made by sending a letter to "Tikal Inn, Tikal, Petén, Guatemala" telling what dates you want, then sending payment in full after you receive confirmation. A modified American plan is available. ~ Tikal National Park; reservations, fax: 5-946-944 in Guatemala City. MODERATE TO DELUXE.

The largest hotel at Tikal is the 32-room **Jungle Lodge**. It was originally built in the 1930s to house archaeological teams working at Tikal. A recent remodeling has converted the rustic old cabins into spacious, pleasant cabañas with tin roofs that are noisy in the rain and private baths with reliable hot water. ~ Tikal National Park; reservations, 29 Calle No. 18-01, Zona 12, Guatemala City, or call 4-768-775 in Guatemala City, fax 4-760-294.

The third option, the **Jaguar Inn**, next door to the Tikal Museum, has just two guest rooms (with private baths) in simple thatched-roof cottages. During the dry season, several large, furnished tents are also rented out as guest accommodations. The food here is not very good, so it is better to opt for a room only, without meals, and eat across the road at the campground. ~ Tikal National Park; reservations, 9-260-002 in Flores. MODERATE.

At Tikal, each of the hotels has its own small restaurant serving a set menu at set hours, with the price of breakfast and dinner included in the "modified American plan" room rate. The only alternatives are a series of *comedores* situated down the road from the campground, serving basic food at budget prices. The restaurant at the campground itself is the largest in the area and serves a budget-priced selection of soups, sandwiches and spaghetti.

The souvenir industry in the Flores and Tikal area is in its infancy. A cluster of four shops near the Tikal Museum and the entrance to the ruins area has a high-priced selection of *típica* clothing from other parts of Guatemala that is worth looking at only if you are not planning to visit the highlands on your trip. It also has lots and lots of Tikal T-shirts. Other makeshift shops along the narrow streets of Flores also stock limited selections of *típica*. The best souvenirs of Tikal I've come across are a videotape with aerial footage of the rainforest and the ruins and an audio tape of jungle sounds recorded at Tikal.

▼▼▼▼▼▼▼▼▼

Sayaxché

In the southern part of the Petén, the small river port town of Sayaxché (pop. 2000) on the Río de la Pasión has recently emerged as a new rainforest adventure travel headquarters, thanks to improved roads and expanded public transportation. The area has 32 known archaeological sites, countless caves and 14 lagoons that serve as key sanctuaries for turtles, alligators and many bird and fish species.

The principal Classic Maya site in the Sayaxché area is **El Ceibal** (admission), situated on several hilltops at the top of a 300-foot-high cliff above the west bank of the Río de la Pasión. The ruins can be reached by road, 17 kilometers from Sayaxché, or by hiring a boat there to take you 18 kilometers up the Río de la Pasión to the ruins. The jungle boat trip is more fun, providing a short sample of the long jungle river journey that is becoming one of the most popular backcountry expeditions in Guatemala.

El Ceibal's ceremonial center, made up of three plazas on separate hilltops separated by ravines, is noted by archaeologists as having the only circular temple in the entire Maya world. It also has 31 carved stone stelae, including one that certainly seems to depict a Maya warrior talking on the telephone! The stelae contain hieroglyphic inscriptions that are puzzlingly unlike those of Tikal, Copán and other lowland Maya sites. The stelae, altars and stone walls at El Ceibal are covered with a bright orange lichen, creating a dramatic contrast to the amazingly lush rainforest that constantly threatens to swallow the ancient city once more. Several trails lead from the ruins into the surrounding protected rainforest of Ceibal National Park, the most likely place for visitors to the Petén to see rare howler monkeys. The forest here is also known for its abundant bird life, including parrots, macaws and toucans. One bird unique to the forest along the Río Pasión is the snail hawk, a small raptor that preys on tree snails.

Sayaxché is 60 kilometers south of Flores and Santa Elena by car or bus on a good dirt road. There is also a new, direct route to Sayaxché from Cobán. The new road is a continuation of Route 5 that turns off the older, eastbound unpaved road through Fray Bartolomé de las Casas at Sebol Junction. It is 96 kilometers from Cobán to the road junction and another 112 kilometers to Sayaxché on a good, wide, mostly straight road that was built to accommodate heavy equipment for oil exploration.

HIDDEN ► Finally, travelers with a high tolerance for adventure can be among the first to explore the **Laguna Lachua National Park**. This park centers around a pristine lake in an old volcano crater in an otherwise flat area. The park was established in 1990 with assistance from the German and Dutch governments to protect the habitat of the largest population of macaws in Central America, but until recently it has been inaccessible for military reasons. The park is situated in the remote Ixcan region, the only area where guerrilla activity persisted as of early 1995. Now several adventure travel outfitters have begun organizing trips to the area using four-wheel-drive vehicles. If you have the use of such a vehicle—and plenty of nerve—you can get there on your own by turning off the Cobán-to-Sayaxché route (described above) at San Antonio, 22 kilometers (13 miles) northwest of Sebol Junction. From there, the 81-kilometer (48-mile) trip takes about seven hours. Bring food and camping gear—including a mosquito net.

Laguna Petexbatún, in the **Aguateca–Dos Pilas Reserve**, is accessible only by boat up the Río Petexbatún. The reserve also contains several Classic Maya sites, including three—**Dos Pilas, Punta de Chimino** and **Aguateca**—that are being restored by archaeological expeditions from U.S. universities. The sites can be reached by horseback or day hike on trails from either of the lodges on the lake. Several caves in the area contain Late Classic Maya ceremonial artifacts. One, which is closed to the public, is said to contain a mysterious subterranean lake filled with human skeletons.

Overnight motor-launch trips down the **Río de la Pasión** from Sayaxché take adventurous travelers past the **Laguna San Juan Acul**, another hidden rainforest location with abundant animal and bird life, and on to the Maya ruins known as **Altar de los Sacrificios**. It's the boat ride down the river more than the ruin itself that makes this trip fantastic.

LODGING The hotel scene in Sayaxché is limited. The best bet for travelers is the 11-room **Hotel Guayacán** on the riverbank in town. The rooms, all of which are on the second floor, have double beds, though not much else, and some have private baths with electric shower heaters. There is off-street parking. This hotel is a headquarters for arranging river trips and backcountry expeditions in this part of the Petén. ~ 9-266-111. BUDGET.

The **Posada de San Mateo**, a luxury jungle lodge with just six ◀ HIDDEN cabins, is one of the nicest small lodges in the Petén. Each naturalwood cabin is wrapped around by rainforest and has fine mesh mosquito screens instead of picture windows, providing a unique opportunity to experience the nocturnal jungle close-up yet in comfort. Each cabin is fully furnished and has modern plumbing. ~ Laguna Petexbatún; reservations, 2-324-483 in Guatemala City. ULTRA-DELUXE.

The modest little **Restaurant Yaxkin** in the village of Sayaxché **DINING** specializes in exotic local cuisine made with wild game from the rainforest, including deer, tepescuintle, armadillo and river turtles. ~ MODERATE.

▼▼▼▼▼▼▼▼▼▼▼▼▼▼
Outdoor Adventures

Tikal National Park is an outstanding area for birding not only because the protected status of wildlife there attracts birds in abundance but also because a good field guide, *Birds of Tikal*, is available in **BIRD-** most Guatemalan bookstores and an audiotape identifying var- **WATCHING** ious bird calls, *Sounds of Tikal*, is sold at the park. Birds and wild animals such as monkeys and coatimundis are becoming noticeably more abundant, or at least less shy of people, each year in Tikal National Park. Elsewhere in the Maya Biosphere Reserve, a major hiking trail for rainforest birdwatching called the Guacamaya Trail has recently been opened. Use is currently limited to organized groups. To make arrangements, contact **U and I Tours**, Hostel de Acuña, Cobán; 9-521-547.

Anglers make the long, slow trip to Laguna Petextabún south of **FISHING** Sayaxché in the Petén for a chance to catch a rare peacock bass.

Tikal National Park is a great place for rainforest hiking, with **HIKING** an extensive network of well-worn trails. The ultimate hike is to the ruins of **Uaxactún**, 20 kilometers north of the Tikal ruins and just beyond the north boundary of the national park. It is a fullday (one-way) hike along a rough jeep trail through the jungle.

Now considered the ultimate rainforest trek in the Petén, the hike to the Maya ruins at El Mirador (15 kilometers one-way) starts at the village of Carmelita. You can (and should) arrange guide services in either Flores or Carmelita.

▼▼▼▼▼▼▼▼▼▼▼▼
Transportation

AIR

The simple way to get to the Tikal area is by plane, a surprisingly short hop—less than an hour—from Guatemala City. There are daily flights to **Santa Elena Airport** from Guatemala City every morning on Aviateca, as well as flights several days a week from Belize City on Aerovías and from Cancún on Aeroquetzal or Aviateca. Additional flights are announced intermittently. Flying over the Petén during daylight hours, you can see vividly the deforestation that is currently taking place in this environmentally delicate region. Dense rainforest still blankets the ridgelines and hilltops, but each valley is cleared for crops and livestock grazing as fast as a narrow dirt jeep road can penetrate it.

Flights in and out of Santa Elena are routinely canceled whenever there are too few passengers. A flexible attitude is essential. If your flight is canceled and you can't get on another one the same day, the airline is required by international conventions to provide you with a hotel room and meals until the next available flight.

Aviateca operates intermittent (allegedly twice weekly) small plane flights from Santa Elena Airport.

Sayaxché has a small airstrip, and Aviones Comerciales (3-314-955) offers charter flights from Guatemala City and Santa Elena.

CAR

The 63-kilometer stretch of wide blacktop highway that runs between Santa Elena and Tikal National Park is the only pavement in the northern half of Guatemala. For much of the distance, the road runs past a huge but not very active army and air force base left over from Guatemala's long civil war, during which rebel guerrillas operated within the national park and throughout El Petén.

Sayaxché is 60 kilometers south of Flores and Santa Elena on a wide, graded dirt road. The road to Laguna Lachua National Park branches off this one; not as well-maintained, this road requires seven hours to cover the 81 kilometers to the park.

CAR RENTALS

Cars and four-wheel-drive vehicles can be rented at **San Juan Auto Rental**. ~ Hotel San Juan, Santa Elena; 9-260-042.

BUS

Buses run regularly to Santa Elena from Cobán and from Rio Dulce. Shuttle vans wait at the Santa Elena airport and the San Juan Hotel in Santa Elena to take passengers to Tikal National Park.

Daily second-class buses carry passengers to Sayaxché from Coban and Santa Elena.

▼▼▼▼▼▼▼▼▼▼▼▼▼▼▼▼▼▼▼▼▼▼
Addresses & Phone Numbers

INGUAT (tourist information) ~ Santa Elena Airport; 9-260-533
INGUAT (tourist information) ~ Parque Central, Flores; 9-260-022

Index

Lodging Index

Dining Index

HIDDEN GUIDES

Adventure travel or a relaxing vacation?—"Hidden" guidebooks are the only travel books in the business to provide detailed information on both. Aimed at environmentally aware travelers, our motto is "Adventure Travel Plus." These books combine details on unique hotels, restaurants and sightseeing with information on camping, sports and hiking for the outdoor enthusiast.

THE NEW KEY GUIDES

Based on the concept of ecotourism, The New Key Guides are dedicated to the preservation of Central America's rare and endangered species, architecture and archaeology. Filled with helpful tips, they give travelers everything they need to know about these exotic destinations.

Order Form

HIDDEN GUIDEBOOKS

____ Hidden Arizona, $14.95

____ Hidden Bahamas, $14.95

____ Hidden Baja, $14.95

____ Hidden Belize, $15.95

____ Hidden Boston and Cape Cod, $13.95

____ Hidden British Columbia, $17.95

____ Hidden Cancún & the Yucatán, $16.95

____ Hidden Carolinas, $17.95

____ Hidden Coast of California, $17.95

____ Hidden Colorado, $14.95

____ Hidden Disney World, $13.95

____ Hidden Disneyland, $13.95

____ Hidden Florida, $17.95

____ Hidden Florida Keys & Everglades, $12.95

____ Hidden Georgia, $14.95

____ Hidden Guatemala, $16.95

____ Hidden Hawaii, $17.95

____ Hidden Idaho, $13.95

____ Hidden Maui, $13.95

____ Hidden Montana, $14.95

____ Hidden New England, $17.95

____ Hidden New Mexico, $14.95

____ Hidden Oahu, $13.95

____ Hidden Oregon, $14.95

____ Hidden Pacific Northwest, $17.95

____ Hidden San Francisco & Northern California, $17.95

____ Hidden Southern California, $17.95

____ Hidden Southwest, $17.95

____ Hidden Tahiti, $17.95

____ Hidden Tennessee, $15.95

____ Hidden Washington, $14.95

____ Hidden Wyoming, $14.95

THE NEW KEY GUIDEBOOKS

____ The New Key to Costa Rica, $17.95

____ The New Key to Ecuador and the Galápagos, $17.95

Mark the book(s) you're ordering and enter the total cost here ➡ [_____]

California residents add 8% sales tax here ➡ [_____]

Shipping, check box for your preferred method and enter cost here ➡ [_____]

❏ BOOK RATE   **FREE! FREE! FREE!**

❏ PRIORITY MAIL $3.20 First book, $1.00/each additional book

❏ UPS 2-DAY AIR $7.00 First book, $1.00/each additional book

[_____]

Billing, enter total amount due here and check method of payment ➡ [_____]

❏ CHECK   ❏ MONEY ORDER

❏ VISA/MASTERCARD _____ EXP. DATE _____

NAME _____ PHONE _____

ADDRESS _____

_____

CITY _____ STATE _____ ZIP _____

MONEY-BACK GUARANTEE ON DIRECT ORDERS PLACED THROUGH ULYSSES PRESS.

ABOUT THE AUTHOR

RICHARD HARRIS has written or co-written 21 other guide-books including Ulysses' *Hidden Cancún and the Yucatán* and the bestselling *Hidden Southwest*. He has also served as contributing editor on guides to Mexico, New Mexico and other ports of call for John Muir Publications, Fodor's, Birnbaum and Access guides. He is a director and past-president of PEN New Mexico, as well as a director and officer of the New Mexico Book Association. When not traveling, Richard writes and lives in Santa Fe, New Mexico.

ABOUT THE ILLUSTRATOR

GLENN KIM is a freelance illustrator residing in San Francisco. His work appears in numerous Ulysses Press titles including *The New to Key Ecuador*, *Hidden Belize* and *Hidden Southwest*. He has also illustrated for the National Forest Service, several Bay Area magazines, book covers and greeting cards, as well as for advertising agencies that include Foote Cone and Belding, Hal Riney and Jacobs Fulton Design Group.